DEVELOPING AND VALIDATING MULTIPLE-CHOICE TEST ITEMS
2nd Edition

DEVELOPING AND VALIDATING MULTIPLE-CHOICE TEST ITEMS
2nd Edition

Thomas M. Haladyna
Arizona State University West

LAWRENCE ERLBAUM ASSOCIATES, PUBLISHERS

1999   Mahwah, New Jersey   London

Lawrence Erlbaum Associates, Inc., Publishers
10 Industrial Avenue
Mahwah, NJ 07430

Cover design by Kathryn Houghtaling Lacey

Library of Congress Cataloging-in-Publication Data

   Haladyna, Thomas, M.
Developing and validating multiple-choice test items / by Thomas M.
Haladyna. — 2nd ed.
         p.   cm.
   Includes bibliographical references and index.
   ISBN 0-8058-3147-9 (cloth : alk. paper).
   1. Multiple-choice examinations—Design and construction.
   2. Multiple-choice examinations—Validity. I. Title.
   1999
   371.26—dc21   98-54946
                                                               CIP

Books published by Lawrence Erlbaum Associates are printed on acid-free
paper, and their bindings are chosen for strength and durability.

The final camera copy for this work was prepared by the author, and therefore
the publisher takes no responsibility for consistency or correctness of typographical style. However, this arrangement helps to make publication of this
kind of scholarship possible.

Printed in the United States of America
10 9 8 7 6 5 4 3 2 1

CONTENTS

Introduction   **vii**

I   **A FOUNDATION FOR MULTIPLE-CHOICE TESTING**
1   Providing a Context for Multiple-Choice Testing   3
2   Constructed-Response and Multiple-Choice
      Item Formats   21
3   Multiple-Choice Formats   41

II **DEVELOPING MULTIPLE-CHOICE ITEMS**
4   Writing the Item   75
5   Measuring Higher Level Thinking   103
6   Item Shells   125

III **VALIDATING ITEM RESPONSES**
7   Validity Evidence Arising from Item Development
      Procedures   145
8   Analyzing Item Responses   163
9   Using Item Response Patterns to
      Study Specific Problems in Testing   183

IV **THE FUTURE OF ITEM DEVELOPMENT**
10   The Future of Item Development   205

References   221

Author Index   241

Subject Index   247

Introduction

This book is about writing effective multiple-choice (MC) test items and studying responses to items to evaluate and improve them. These two topics are two very important steps in the development of many cognitive tests. Two factors contributed to the writing of this book. The first is that although statistical theories of test scores are very well developed and understood, MC item writing and validating MC item responses are the least developed among the many activities in testing. Textbooks on testing provide information on MC item writing and item analysis, but typically these sections are brief and not linked to existing theory or research. Volumes devoted solely to MC item writing and validation are rare. Several writers have commented about the lack of research on item writing (e.g., Cronbach, 1971; Haladyna & Downing, 1989a, 1989b; Nitko, 1985). Thus, there is very little information to guide item writing practices. With item response validation, the study of item responses will very likely become more complex according to Wainer (1989), which will both increase and challenge us to better understand the dynamics of item responses for improving MC items.

Another reason for writing this book is the background provided by more than 25 years of experience in testing. I have been fortunate to have been involved in a variety of test development activities and research on testing in a variety of settings that included large-scale educational assessments in reading, writing, and mathematics, and also licensing or certification tests in accountancy, dietetics, emergency medicine, medical specialties (such as facial plastic surgery, hand surgery, cosmetic surgery, ophthalmology, otolaryngology), nursing, pharmacy, and dentistry. During this period, I also had the opportunity to help the U.S. Army in the evaluation of its Skill Qualification Tests used in their various training programs, including military police, military intelligence, aerial reconnaissance, chemical warfare, and rocket launch systems. To add to these experiences, teaching graduate students and undergraduates in teacher training has enriched my perspective about the need for more effective item writing and the validation of responses. This book draws from these experiences and the extant theory, research, and technology available.

Intended Audience

This book is intended for anyone seriously interested in cognitive testing. Students in graduate-level courses in educational measurement or testing may find this book helpful for better understanding these two critical phases of testing.

Those directly involved in developing tests may find this book useful as a source of new material to enhance their present understanding and their item development and item response validation practices.

Prior Work on MC Item Writing and Item Response Validation

Earlier treatments of MC item development and item response validation exist. It would be remiss not to mention and recognize these contributions. This earlier work contributed to the development of chapters in this volume.

With respect to item development, the chapter on testing in the first edition of *Educational Measurement* (Ebel, 1951) represented a major milestone in item writing. The chapter in the second edition of *Educational Measurement* by Wesman (1971) is another important contribution. Interestingly, both writers noted the paucity of theory and research on item writing, but their pleas for more serious study were largely ignored in the 1960s and 1970s. In Europe, books by Brown (1966) and MacIntosh and Morrison (1969) were followed by Woods (1977), whose monograph on testing was current to that date. Bormuth (1970) formulated a theory of item writing that attempted to make this process more objective and less under the idiosyncratic control of individuals. He attacked traditional ways of writing items as unscientific. His item-generating algorithms and the work of other theorists were chronicled in a book by Roid and Haladyna (1982). Millman and Greene (1989) provided a brief treatment of item development in the third edition of *Educational Measurement*. In that same volume, Nitko (1989) discussed the important idea of integrating teaching and testing. He offered us important emerging ideas about the many processes involved in pre-item writing activities in the realm of achievement testing. Nevertheless, his chapter did not provide precise advice about the actual writing of test items. Osterlind (1989) wrote the only other book devoted to item writing, and his second edition (Osterlind, 1997) takes a broader focus.

With respect to item response validation, we have witnessed an evolution in understanding that began with primitive ideas about item difficulty and discrimination in the 1930s. Item analysis has been a standard feature of virtually any type of testing program. Item response theory has expanded our understanding of the nature of the item responses. Chapters in successive editions of *Educational Measurement* by Henrysson (1971) and Millman and Greene (1989) have provided insights about this evolution, but many basic theoretical papers have provided a greater foundation for the concept of item response validation as presented in this volume.

Limitations of This Book

Although this book intends to provide a comprehensive treatment of item development and item response validation, it is limited in several ways.

Statistical theories for dealing with item responses and forming scales abound and are an active field of research. However, there is a lack of current theories of item writing such as described by Roid and Haladyna (1982).

Ideas about human intellect are constantly undergoing reexamination and change. Renewed interest in measuring higher level thinking has motivated us to consider new ways to measure the most desirable outcomes of schooling or training. Although the Bloom taxonomy has continued to be favored by many practitioners, scientific evidence supporting its use is lacking (Seddon, 1978). There is still no suitable taxonomy of higher level thinking on which to base item-writing practices. In this volume, a chapter is devoted to writing items to reflect higher level thinking, but, again, the advice is merely prescriptive and not grounded in theory. However, these prescriptions have proven helpful to item writers in phrasing items that putatively reflect higher level thinking.

The way we view human learning relates to how we teach and test. Two alternate views of learning are behavioral and cognitive psychology. Behavior learning theory has thrived with the widespread use of instructional objectives, mastery learning, and criterion-referenced testing. One current view involves a more encompassing idea, fluid abilities, that exist to be slowly developed over a lifetime. Cognitive psychologists and statistical test theorists are beginning to work in partnerships to link fluid abilities with ways to measure these processes. Fluid abilities provide a useful new paradigm for learning. Until greater clarity exists on fluid abilities, or the paradigm shifts to the cognitive viewpoint as it seems to be doing, there are still conflicts about how to best teach and test. The legacy of behavioral learning theory and behavioral instruction persists in sharp contrast to cognitive learning theories.

It is unlikely that any of these conditions affecting item writing will be resolved very soon. Item development and item response validation are still new, dynamic processes, greatly in need of more theorizing and validating research.

Attacks on and Reform in Testing

MC testing has experienced many attacks in the past, some justified and some not. In the 1960s, harsh criticism of the 'evils' of testing was leveled from such well known critics as Hoffman (1964), who wrote *Tyranny of Testing*. Owen (1985), in his book *None of the Above*, assailed MC testing. The object of his criticism was the MC *Scholastic Aptitude Test*, which is given to more than 1 million students annually. Even the well-known consumer activist, Ralph Nader, was quoted as saying that with standardized MC testing "sixty years of idiocy is enough" (*FairTest Examiner*, 1987, p. 1). Nader criticized the failure of the MC format to measure the more important outcomes of schooling and human enterprises such as determination, idealism, wisdom, strategic reasoning, judgment, experience, persistence, stamina, creativity, and writing ability. Although it is true that the MC format is not useful for measuring many highly prized human traits, responsible test makers have never claimed this ability for the MC format. The purpose of a MC item is to measure knowledge and some aspects of fluid abilities. Most test specialists still promote MC formats as the best tool among those available for measuring knowledge. With more complex cognitive ability, MC has a more limited but still a substantial role.

The attacks on MC testing have come more recently from other directions. For instance, Shepard (1993) contended that MC testing lends itself to MC teaching. Shepard further argued that such teaching and testing is harmful to learners. Her point may be that excessive attention to knowledge and testing for knowledge may cause us to overlook the teaching and testing of more important aspects of learning, involving the use of knowledge. Certainly, analyses of what teachers teach and test reinforce the idea that much of education occurs at the memory level, but this is not the fault of an item format.

Despite the attacks on the MC format, MC testing has actually thrived in recent years. The need to inform policymakers and evaluators is great enough to continue to support testing programs. Little doubt should exist that testing is a major enterprise that directly or indirectly affects virtually everyone in the United States. With more than 1,400 published tests and more than 400 test publishers, clearly testing is a big business (Osterlind, 1989). MC tests are used in many ways: placement, selection, awards, certification, licensure, course credit (proficiency), grades, diagnosis of what has and has not been learned, and even employment. According to Yeh, Herman, and Rudner (1981), more than 90% of schools and school districts use some form of standardized testing. State-mandated testing occurs in 42 of 50 states (*FairTest Examiner*, 1988). Of the approximately 40 million students in elementary and secondary schools, about 17 million take state-mandated tests annually (*FairTest Examiner*, 1988). More than 100 million people in the United States annually take some form of a standardized, MC test (*FairTest Examiner*, 1988).

Despite these attacks on MC testing, a major premise of this book is that there is, indeed, a place for MC testing for many legitimate purposes. Admittedly, many things are wrong with the way MC test results are presently interpreted and used. The public and many test developers and users need to be more aware of the

Standards for Educational and Psychological Testing (American Psychological Association [APA],1985). Once test users are clear about how test results should and should not be used, we can increase the quality of tests by sensible and effective item development and item response validation procedures as found in this book.

Organization of the Book

This second edition has undergone many changes that distinguish it from the first edition. For continuity, the book continues to be organized into four parts.

Part I provides a foundation for using MC items. Chapter 1 discusses the problems faced in measuring ability and achievement and the basis for using test items of various formats and tests in the framework of construct validation. Chapter 2 discusses the century-long debate over MC and constructed response formats for measuring cognitive behavior. Bearing on this important issue, recent research is reviewed and synthesized bearing on this important issue. Chapter 3 discusses strengths and weaknesses of various MC formats based on several current reviews of research. Many examples of different types of MC formats are provided in that chapter. Issues related to MC formats are also discussed.

Part II contains three chapters that provide advice on how to write various types of MC test items. Many examples are provided from various sources. Chapter 4 provides a recently revised typology of item writing rules and many examples of correctly and poorly written items in various formats. This typology is based on two sources: the collective wisdom of various textbook writers, and extant research. Chapter 5 provides a structure for writing and organizing items into various categories of higher level thinking. Chapter 6 describes the role of item shells in the creation of test items. Item shells are an item writer's aid to unblock "writer's block."

Part III addresses the complex idea of item response validation. Chapter 7 reports on the rationale and procedures involved in a coordinated series of activities intended to improve each test item. Chapter 8 deals with the statistical analysis of items to study and improve test items. A theoretical perspective is offered that accommodates working within the frameworks of both classical and item response theories. Chapter 9 offers information about how the study of item responses can be used to study specific problems encountered in testing. This chapter is very technically oriented.

Part IV contains chapter 10, which deals with the trends in item writing and validation. Unlike what we experience today, cognitive theorists are working on better defining what we teach and measure, and test theorists are developing item response models that are more appropriate to measuring some forms of complex behavior. This chapter reviews these emerging theories and the existing context in which they must be nurtured. The fruition of many of these theories will change the face of education and testing in very profound ways.

In closing, development of test items and validation of test item responses still remain as two critical steps in test development. This book intends to help readers understand the concepts, principles, and procedures available to construct better MC test items that will lead to better cognitive tests.

Tom Haladyna

I

A Foundation for
Multiple-Choice Testing

These three chapters provide an appropriate preparation and background for writing multiple-choice test items. The first chapter introduces basic terms and discusses validity and its importance in item development and the evaluation of item responses. The second chapter focuses on the long lasting debate over the merits and limitations of multiple-choice and constructed-response formats for measuring knowledge, skills, and abilities. The third chapter presents a wide variety of multiple-choice formats that can be used.

1

PROVIDING A CONTEXT FOR MULTIPLE-CHOICE TESTING

OVERVIEW

This chapter describes the place for the multiple-choice (MC) item format in cognitive testing. First the term *test* is defined because it is a commonly used device for measuring many cognitive traits.

A prevailing theme in this book is that fluid abilities are a worthwhile objective of testing in U.S. education, for certification and licensing testing and other cognitive tests. Fluid abilities are complex organizations of knowledge, skills, and application of knowledge and skill to complex encounters. Reading and writing are well-known fluid abilities. The measurement of fluid abilities is difficult and complex. MC has a prominent role in this measurement.

Another important prevailing theme is validity. Anyone using test scores for any purpose ought to be concerned about validity, because validity deals with the reasonableness of a specific interpretation or use of a test score.

Once we have an idea of what is being tested and how to validate test score interpretations and uses, the characteristics of test items used to measure these fluid abilities should be examined and evaluated. Three distinctly different item formats are described in this chapter.

Finally, the role of validity in test item development and item response validation is examined. An ideal process for item development and item response validation is presented. The chapter concludes with a table containing brief descriptions of subsequent chapters that provide a comprehensive treatment of MC test item development and item response validation.

Defining a Test

A test is a measuring instrument intended to numerically describe a characteristic under uniform, standardized conditions. In educational or psychological testing, most tests contain a single item or set of test items intended to measure cognitive traits. Responses to test items are scorable. The use of scoring rules helps to create a test score based on a test taker's responses to the test items.

The most central concern for a test score is how valid it is to interpret or use a test score. Therefore, any interpretation or use of a test score is subject to evaluation for validity. Once the kind of interpretation or use we wanted from a test score is stated, evidence is collected attesting to validity of interpreting or using that test score. Later in this chapter, the validity of test score interpretations and uses is closely examined and the idea of validity is applied to developing test items and interpreting item responses.

Although being the most basic element of any test, a test item can seldom stand by itself as a test. Responses to a single test item are often too fallible. Also, most human traits measured by a test are too complex to be adequately represented by a single item. That is why we score and aggregate item responses, which we call *test scores*.

What Do Tests Measures?

In defining any human cognitive characteristic that we would like to measure, a prevailing dilemma is whether we all agree on a definition of the characteristic and its measure, or whether the characteristic is sufficiently abstract to prevent such a consensus. The technical terms are *operational definition* and *construct*. The approach to measuring a characteristic does not answer the question about what tests measure, but it points us down a path. The operational definition makes our measurement job somewhat easy, whereas the construct involves a longer and more involved set of procedures.

Operational Definitions

Operational definitions are commonly agreed on by those responsible for measuring the characteristics. Traits defined by operational definitions are objectively and directly measured. We have good examples of operational definitions for time, volume, distance, height, and weight. In other words, the definitions are precise enough to enable precise measurement without the difficulties encountered with constructs. Operational definitions abound in education, but the human cognitive characteristics directly measured via operational definition are typically very simple. These behaviors are found mainly in curricula for special education and early childhood education. Operational definitions abound in mathematics and science and in professional and industrial training, where concrete, observable procedures are heavily emphasized. This book is not concerned with measuring operational definitions because the technology for this type of measurement is well established and easy to apply in virtually any setting (see Haladyna, 1997; chapter 6.) Most operationally defined traits can be directly observed or observed using a measuring instrument, such as a clock, ruler, or scale.

Constructs

Constructs defy operational definition. Constructs include such highly prized traits as reading, writing, speaking, listening, creative thinking, critical thinking, and problem solving. Constructs are by their nature complex, abstract entities. The process of defining and measuring a construct and then validating the interpretation or use of a measure of a construct is the concern in construct validation.

Although this book is concerned with MC testing, oddly enough, the most important constructs are not measured with MC item formats. Nevertheless, MC tests play a vital role in measuring aspects of most constructs. Next, fluid abilities, an emerging construct that is a focus of modern measurement is discussed. Then, we examine constituent parts of constructs.

Fluid Abilities

According to Lohman (1993), a worthwhile goal in education is the development of fluid abilities. Fluid abilities are well known to us and comprise most of the school curriculum. Some common fluid abilities are reading, writing, speaking, and listening. Problem solving, critical thinking, and creative thinking are also very highly prized fluid abilities. Any fluid ability is likely to consist of knowledge and skills. Another aspect of fluid abilities that Snow and Lohman (1989) believe to be very important is conative, the emotional aspect of human cognitive behavior. This emotional aspect is also becoming more formalized as an important aspect of human ability, termed *emotional intelligence* (Goleman, 1995). Thus, any fluid ability consists of knowledge, skills, and emotional predispositions used to perform some complex behavior. The crux of fluid ability, however, is not knowledge, skills, or emotional dispositions, but the complex combination of these areas toward some desired end, such as writing a book.

Fluid abilities grow slowly over a lifetime, influenced by maturation, learning, practice, and other experiences. Schooling represents a primary source of influence in the development of many fluid abilities, according to Lohman (1993). Graduate and professional schools reflect advanced education where fluid abilities are extended. Special academies are formed to concentrate on fluid abilities. Talented individuals spend lifetimes perfecting their fluid abilities, and fluid abilities influence one another. The fluid abilities of problem solving, critical thinking, and creative thinking seem universally important to the development of other fluid abilities, and are often mentioned in this book.

A familiar fluid ability is writing. Aspects of writing ability include different writing modes, such as narrative, expository, persuasive, and creative. Writing is evaluated based on various analytic traits, such as conventions, organization, word choice, and style. The development of writing ability begins with simple behaviors mostly involving knowledge and skills. Writing ability grows slowly over a lifetime.

Fluid abilities are very useful for all of us to apply to our occupations, and in other roles we play as citizen, homemaker, parent, and worker. Fluid abilities are also useful in many life interests and activities. Softball playing is a fluid ability. In fact, all sports and recreation represent forms of fluid ability. All visual and performing arts are fluid abilities, including poetry, play writing, performing on stage, sculpting, and architecture. Naturally, all fluid abilities are heavily influenced by other fluid abilities. A great novelist, like John Irving, must have great writing ability but must also have great creative thinking ability. An outstanding athlete, like Michael Jordan, must have considerable basketball ability but also must have problem-solving and critical thinking ability to perform at the highest level. The emotional element needed in fluid abilities is always evident with respect to motivation, attitude, perseverance, self-confidence, and self-esteem.

Fluid abilities also dominate certification and licensing testing. The underlying constructs of medical competence, or competence in any profession is much more than simply knowledge and skills. Professions require the use of knowledge, skills, and emotional elements in complex performance, that usually involve critical thinking, creative thinking, or problem solving.

All fluid abilities are teachable. The development of our fluid abilities is our most important lifelong occupation. In this book, and, I hope in your process of developing tests for educational achievement, you might consider fluid abilities in this way. Test items are important ingredients in the development of measures of fluid abilities as tests provide the test score scales to measure the growth of fluid abilities.

Chapter 5 provides many examples of MC items intended to reflect constituent aspects of fluid abilities. However, MC formats have limitations with respect to testing fluid abilities. Not all fluid abilities lend themselves well to the MC format. Usually, the most appropriate measure of a fluid ability involves performance of a complex nature. MC items cannot provide that kind of test score interpretation. Fig. 1.1 illustrates how a fluid ability rests on a foundation of knowledge and skills.

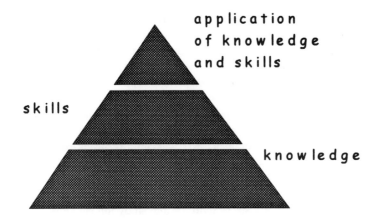

FIG. 1.1. Structure of a fluid ability.

Knowledge is always fundamental to developing a skill or a fluid ability. Sometimes, MC can be used to measure application of knowledge and skills in the performance of a fluid ability, but these uses are rare.

The Role of Intelligence in the Development of Fluid Abilities

Intelligence is another important construct. Intelligence has served for most of this century to describe a principal factor of human cognitive behavior. Other terms used synonymously for intelligence are *scholastic aptitude* and *mental ability*. No differentiation among these terms is intended throughout this book. The term *intelligence* has fallen into disfavor due to unfortunate historical misuses of intelligence test scores. Arthur Jensen's (1980) controversial research provoked significant reactions for and against his ideas about determinants of intelligence that may have contributed to the further unpopularity of this term. More recently, Herrnstein and Murray (1995) published their controversial book that has further fueled discussion about the origins of intelligence.

For most of this century, theory and research have favored a one-factor view of mental ability. The Spearman one-factor theory of intelligence has been well supported by research, including the famous Terman longitudinal studies of giftedness (Terman & Oden, 1959). However, the one-factor view of intelligence has been periodically challenged. In the 1930s, Thurstone (1938) formulated his primary mental abilities, and his test was widely used. In the 1960s and 1970s, Guilford's (1967) Structure of the Intellect model was supported by research but interest in this model waned considerably after his death. Gardner (1986) posited a theory of multiple intelligences, and Sternberg (1977) introduced a componential theory of human abilities. Both theories have received considerable attention. Although enthusiasm for multiple intelligence ideas has been renewed by these scholars, this century-long history of the study of human intelligence in the United States has shown that scientific revolutions of this kind are hard to sustain. The cumulative body of evidence continues to support a one-factor theory of intelligence.

One-factor intelligence is not an important theme in this book, simply because item writing in this book is focused on the development of human abilities that are amenable to teaching and development. However, intelligence is a measurable construct of humans that varies considerably. There is little doubt that intelligence can be measured and that it has some influence on the development fluid abilities. Knowing about intelligence helps us understand the rate and quality of development of human abilities. But as more people study human behavior are understanding, intelligence interacts with other human abilities. Higher levels of intelligence can ease the development of fluid abilities. But the challenge remaining is that all students need to develop fluid abilities to the extent that intelligence and emotional qualities will carry them. We recognize that intelligence predicts the rate and degree to which each fluid ability develops. Nevertheless, we should not overrate intelligence. The world is full of stories of people with highly developed fluid abilities who overcame obstacles through high motivation, perseverance, and persistence. Goleman (1995) provided a compelling, popular description of emotional intelligence, which he and many scientists believe account for successes and failures that intelligence fails to explain.

The Role of Knowledge in a Fluid Ability

One of the most fundamental aspects of fluid abilities and one that is most recognizable to us is knowledge. Educational psychologists call this *declarative knowledge*. As discussed in subsequent chapters, all tested knowledge falls into one of these categories: facts, concepts, principles, or procedures. The general assumption behind testing for knowledge is that it is foundational to performing skills or more complex forms of behaviors. In the analysis of any complex behavior, it is easy to see that we always need knowledge. The most efficient way to test for knowledge is with the MC format. Thus, MC formats have a decided advantage over constructed response (CR) formats for testing knowledge. Chapter 2 discusses the rationale for this more completely.

The Role of Skills in a Fluid Ability

Skills are also fundamental to a fluid ability. A skill's nature reflects performance. Skills are often thought of as singular acts. Punctuation, spelling, capitalization, and abbreviation are writing skills. Skills are critical aspects of complex performances, such as found in critical thinking, creative thinking, and problem solving. Although MC may seem like a worthwhile approach to measuring skill, MC simply measures knowledge of a skill. The actual performance of a skill is a different act. In some circumstances, the proximity of a test of spelling knowledge to a test of spelling skill may suggest to us that MC is better, but we need to keep in mind the fundamental differences in interpretation. In a high-stakes situation in life, such as life-threatening surgery, knowledge of a surgical procedure is not a substitute for surgical skill. And both knowledge and skills tests are not adequate measures of surgical ability. In low-stakes settings, we might be willing to substitute the more efficient MC test of knowledge for the less efficient performance test of skill because we know the two are highly correlated. The risk of doing this is clear: Someone may know how to do something, but is unable to perform.

VALIDITY

"Validity is an overall evaluative judgment of the degree to which empirical evidence and theoretical rationales support the adequacy and appropriateness of interpretations and actions based on test scores or other modes of assessment." (Messick, 1995, p. 741)

Kane (1992) stated that validity is not a property of tests but of test score interpretations and uses. The evidence that we assemble supports each specific interpretation and use. Strong evidence suggests more valid interpretation and use.

Messick (1989) also pointed out that specific interpretations and uses of test results are subject to a context made up of value implications and social consequences. Thus, thinking of construct validation as merely the systematic collection of evidence to support a specific test score interpretation or use is insufficient. We must also think of the context that may underlie and influence this interpretation or use.

A good example of consequences comes from well-documented practices in schools where publishers' standardized achievement test scores are used as a criterion for educational accountability. Because of external pressure to raise test scores to show educational improvement, some school personnel will take extreme measures to increase test scores. Nolen, Haladyna, and Haas (1992) showed that a variety of questionable tactics are used to raise scores that may not increase student learning. These techniques include excessive motivation, providing more time for the test, excusing students who are expected to score low, or erasing wrong answers and supplying right answers. Haladyna, Nolen, and Haas (1991) and Mehrens and Kaminski (1989) questioned the ethics of these practices that are undermining education. McGill-Franzen and Allington (1993) further questioned whether the issue is one of validity at all or more importantly a child advocacy issue. Paris, Lawton, Turner, and Roth (1991) reported on the pejorative effects of this pressure for accountability on children, and Smith (1991) described the demeaning of the profession of teaching due to this quest for accountability. Thus, the value of Messick's idea about context of social values and consequences is vividly illustrated by this collective national craze for raising test scores without considering the actual learning of students who are being manipulated to produce these scores. Indeed the context is part of construct validation.

In this book, the focus of validity is on both with test scores and item responses, simply because we interpret and use item responses just as we interpret and use test scores. Because items and item responses are subunits of test and test scores, validity at the item level is very important.

THREE STEPS IN THE PROCESS OF CONSTRUCT VALIDATION

According to Cronbach (1971), three essential, sequential steps in construct validation are formulation, explication, and validation. The first two steps are part of the process of theorizing leading to creation of a test. The third step is the validation process that involves collecting the evidence supporting the interpretation and use of test scores.

In formulation, theoretical constructs are named and defined, and their interrelationships are described in a causal network. According to Anderson (1972) and Cole (1990), the failure to adequately define such terms as problem solving, reasoning, abstract thinking, critical thinking, and the like may be one of the primary reasons why we have so much difficulty measuring higher level thinking. Writing is a well-developed construct in American education. Writing is well defined in school curricula, and its connection to other aspects of schooling and life is obvious and commonly accepted without argument.

Through this process of formulation, the definition and connectedness of constructs must be clear enough for researchers to construct variables that behave according to the lawfulness of our hypothetical constructs, as Fig. 1.2 illustrates. Two constructs are defined. The first is the quality of instruction and the second is the growth of the fluid ability that the quality is supposed to affect. In the first phase, both quality of instruction and the fluid ability to be developed are abstractly defined.

In explication, measures of each construct are created or identified. Generally, multiple measures are used to more adequately tap all the aspects of each construct. The process of explication encompasses all of those activities we know as *test development*, including development of content specifications and test specifications, item writing, test design, test construction, test production, and test administration. If our fluid ability in Fig. 1.2 is writing, the most direct

Construct Definition	Quality of teaching is defined and hypothesized to affect the development of a fluid ability, such as writing.	Writing ability is defined and is hypothesized to be affected by the quality of teaching.
Construct Explication	Measure of quality of teaching is developed to reflect the construct of *quality of teaching*.	Measure of writing ability is developed to reflect the construct of writing ability.
Construct Validation	The two measures are correlated. The size of this correlation can be used as evidence, along with other evidence, showing that the quality of teaching affects the development of ability.	

FIG. 1.2. The logic of construct validity.

measure would be a performance-based writing sample. MC items might measure knowledge of writing or knowledge of writing skills, but it would not provide a direct measure.

In validation, evidence is collected to confirm our hopes that a test can be interpreted and used validly. Some of the important specific studies involved in construct validation include (a) reliability of test scores, (b) group differences, trends over time, and (c) relationships. In each of these studies, implicit standards or objectives exist, and empirical verification is a desirable quality if an interpretation or use of a test score is construct valid. Not all this evidence comes in empirical forms. Evidence is also procedural, showing that certain steps in test development were completed. Chapter 7 in this book presents some critical item review procedures used as evidence in construct validation.

In Fig. 1.2, it is hypothesized that quality of instruction is highly related to the outcome, that is, performance in the fluid ability. The correlation tells us to what extent our prediction is borne out by the data. One could conduct formal experiments to establish the same causal relations.

Messick (1995) provided a structure for thinking about this validity evidence.

This structure includes:

- The content of the test, including its relevance to the construct and the representativeness of the sampling.
- The connection of test behavior to the theoretical rationale behind test behavior. Claims about what a test measures should be supported by evidence of cognitive processes underlying performance (Martinez, 1998).
- The structural aspect of test data involves an assessment of fidelity of item formats and scoring to the construct interpretation (Haladyna, 1998). Messick refers to this as "structural fidelity." Therefore, a crucial concern is the logical connection between item formats and desired interpretations. For instance, a MC test of writing skills would have low fidelity to actual writing. A writing sample would have higher fidelity.
- The generalizability aspect relates to how test scores remain consistent across different samples. One aspect of this is differential item functioning and bias, a topic treated in chapter 9. This aspect of validity evidence also refers to development of an ability over time.
- The external aspect relates to patterns of relationships among item responses, such as convergent and discriminant validity. The patterns among items responses should clearly support our interpretations. Evidence to the contrary works against valid interpretation.
- Finally, the consequences of test score interpretations and uses must be considered, as we discussed with misuses and misinterpretations of standardized achievement test scores.

Validity is an integrative summary (Messick, 1995). We take this evidence collectively as supporting or not supporting interpretations or uses to some degree. Cronbach (1988) and Kane (1992) described this process as the building of an argument supporting interpretation of test scores.

The interpretation or use of a measure of a familiar construct, such as writing, can be undermined by any of three types of problems:

1. Failure to define constructs adequately (inadequate formulation), a problem that has troubled education for quite some time;
2. Failure to identify or create measures of the aspects of each construct (an inadequate explication), which Messick (1989) referred to as *construct under representation*;
3. Failure to assemble adequate evidence supporting predictions made from our theorizing (inadequate validation).

Importance of Intended Interpretations and Uses

At the heart of validity is the concept of interpretations and uses of test results. For any formal test of any consequence to test-takers, policymakers, and the public, the validity of intended interpretations and uses is crucial. In fact, the *Standards for Educational and Psychological Testing* (APA, 1985) makes very clear the importance of validity evidence in Standard 1.1:

> *Evidence of validity should be presented for the major types of inferences for which the use of a test is recommended. A rationale should be provided to support the particular mix of evidence presented for the intended uses. (p. 13)*

The Role of Evidence

Central to the validation process is the idea of evidence. Validity evidence can come in many forms, including statistical, empirical, and even procedural. For instance, Downing and Haladyna (1997) provided an outline of the kinds of validity evidence one might assemble in support of a licensing or certification test. The responsibility for validation legally rests on the user of test results, but the users may depend on a testing service or company, or a publisher of tests.

Construct Validity Applied to Item Development

The reason that construct validity is one of the two prevailing themes in this book is that the process of validating test score interpretations and uses applies to item responses used to create test scores. This theme is consistent throughout this book. Chapters 8 and 9 reflect the attention paid to item responses as an integral aspect of construct validation. In other words, not only are we concerned with the appropriate development of test items, as we observe in the processes discussed in chapter 7, but we are also concerned about responses to items that mimic our test scores.

DEFINING THE TEST ITEM

A *test item* is the basic unit in any test. It consists of a command or question, a set of conditions for responding to the command or question, a manner in which examinees respond, and a set of rules for scoring the response.

Thorndike (1967) wrote that the more effort we put into building better test items, the better the test is likely to be. Toward that end, one can design test items to represent many different types of content and cognitive behaviors. A total score represents some aggregate of performance across all test items for a specific trait.

As defined in this book, the test item is intended to measure some aspect of human ability generally related to school learning or training. However, this definition of a test item is not limited necessarily to human ability.

At least three distinctly different types of test items exist. Chapter 2 discusses the research on these differences and how validity affects the choice of the item format. The three formats are MC, high-inference CR and low-inference CR.

MC Format

This type of format traditionally has a stem in the form of a question or partial sentence and choices in the form of an answer to the question or completions of the partial sentence. The anatomy of MC therefore is:

- Stem: Command or question
- Key: Correct choice
- Distractors: Incorrect but plausible choices

Chapter 2 addresses the issue of what MC and CR formats measure. Chapter 3 presents a variety of MC formats, two are which are not recommended.

High-Inference CR (Performance) Formats

Although this type of item is not the focus of this book, it is important to delineate how it is different from MC. High-inference human characteristics are abstract: organization, creativity, style, pace, expressiveness, and the like. All require professional, expert judgment using a scoring device. Performance testing is characterized by this structure. The anatomy of high inference CR items therefore is:

- Command or question
- Conditions for responding
- Scoring guides, often referred to as *rubrics* or more technically as *descriptive rating scales*.

Without doubt, many higher level abilities are well measured by this format, but this format has serious limitations, not the least of which are lack of objectivity in scoring, judge bias, and inconsistency, and the high cost of scoring. Haladyna (1997) provided more detailed discussion on how to develop this kind of test item.

Low-Inference CR

This type of test item is also not the focus of this book, but its mention provides a context for MC testing. Low-inference items are concrete in nature, intended for characteristics that we all agree are directly measured. Some common low-inference traits are time, weight, distance, and height. In educational testing, there are a variety of applications of low-inference CR items, including many simple behaviors observed in training in early childhood and special education. Four distinctly different low-inference formats exist.

Low-inference essay. One of these is the essay with a known or desired answer that is essentially right or wrong. For example, a short-answer essay may deal with economic trends in the country of Utopia?

> What are three prevailing trends leading to economic prosperity in Utopia?

This question has three right answers that we objectively determine from the student's response. Mathematics problems usually have a right answer that fits this item format.

Low-inference observation. A low-inference test item might call for a simple observation. For instance, a teacher might record if homework was completed: Yes or No. In special education for severely mentally handicapped, a life-long curriculum might have simple observations dealing with eating.

Low-inference observation using a measuring instrument. This type of low-inference item calls for simple, objective observation using a measuring instrument, such as a ruler, scale, or clock. Science experiments or activities might be good examples of this application.

Low-inference observation using a checklist. A checklist is a correlated set of objectively scored observations.

These low-inference formats are very useful. They are used in a variety of settings that include regular and special education, early childhood education, professional training, and industrial training. Low-inference formats are usually limited to low-level outcomes, simple developmental behaviors in early learning, and most psychomotor outcomes.

Table 1.1 displays the distinctions drawn in this section among three fundamental types of test item formats.

TABLE 1.1
Three Types of Test Item Formats

High-Inference Constructed Response (CR)	Multiple-choice (MC)	Low-Inference Constructed Response (CR)
Stimulus: Command or question	Stimulus: Command or question	Stimulus: Command or question
Conditions for performance	Student selection of choices	Conditions for performance
Student performance	Objective scoring	Student performance
Judge-mediated scoring using a descriptive rating scale		Objective scoring

DEVELOPING THE TEST ITEM

Toward the end of construct validation of test scores and interpretations, test item development is viewed as a critical step in test development. Downing and Haladyna (1997) provided a more complete discussion of the important steps in this process. This section summarizes these steps and provides an overview of the book and how other chapters contribute to the idea of construct validation as applied to test items and item responses.

The Rationale for MC

Before any type of item format is chosen as the preferred item format, a reasoning process needs to be completed that concludes that the construct being measured essentially involves knowledge. Chapter 2 provides a comprehensive discussion of the issues that need to be addressed. These issues revolve around validity. For instance, if you are developing a test to be used for placement or selection, prediction is the key issue in item format selection. The resulting test will maximize a correlation with a criterion. If one were developing a test of a fluid ability, such as the playing of a violin, the nature of the performance suggests a

CR format not a MC format.

In some circumstances, a MC item might serve as an effective substitute for a CR item because of its statistical proximity to the CR item or a higher fidelity to a criterion. Haladyna (1998) provided a discussion of this dilemma and of when and why MC might make a good choice. With some complex cognitive behaviors such as problem solving and critical thinking, MC might be very appropriate, particularly the item set format discussed in chapter 3.

Test Specifications

Test specifications (test blueprint or table of specifications) tell the test developers how many items are to be selected for the test, the content being tested, and the types of mental behaviors required of test-takers when responding to each item. Items are selected based on these specifications and other technical considerations, such as item difficulty and discrimination. Chapter 5 provides a discussion of ways in which items can be classified by content and by cognitive behavior.

Qualifications for Item Writers

Item writers should first and foremost be content experts who know their subject matter in an expert way. The use of persons training in item writing is not a good substitute for content experts. Content experts should be trained in item writing. At a minimum, they should know the anatomy of item formats, the formats used in the test for which items are being written (see chap. 3), and the rules for writing test items (see chap. 4). These item writers should also know how items are classified by content and cognitive behavior.

Content as the Basis for Writing the Test Item

Many ways exist to define content for constructing test items. A more traditional method was to work from instructional objectives. Item-writing algorithms have been suggested. Roid and Haladyna (1982) provided a comprehensive treatment of theoretical approaches to item writing, but little progress can be reported since the appearance of this book. In schools and states, curriculum standards form a basis for developing test items. The process can be very simple or very involved. The idea is to create items that reflect curriculum standards for the content that experts agree is suitable. The review process provides a method for validating this effort. No single method is recommended here, but the validation process suggested in the next section is crucial.

Drafting the Item

The first draft of a test item should contain the essential elements of the item, according to the format chosen. The variety of formats is shown in chapter 3. Sometimes, item writers who have inexperience in writing test items need some help. Chapter 6 provides item shells, which are syntactic structures of test items devoid of content. Item shells were developed to help new item writers get started. However, one should never over-rely on item shells because resulting tests would have a very limited scope. Item shells are simply a device to get item writers started.

Item Reviews

A number of reviews are recommended after each item is drafted. Chapter 7 provides descriptions of these reviews. Some of these reviews are key verification, bias sensitivity, and editorial. These reviews satisfy the need to polish items before the items are field tested.

VALIDATING ITEM RESPONSES

As suggested earlier, construct validity applies to items responses as well as test scores, because items are the building blocks of tests. The process of validating item responses is well known to test developers under the rubric *item analysis*. Chapter 8 provides information on item analysis, but emphasizes graphical methods of item analysis. Chapter 9 contains advanced topics on item response validation that are more appropriate for formal and larger scale testing programs.

Because the test score and the item response have a logical connection, the process that is defined for validating test score interpretations and uses also applies to item responses. We can define what an item is supposed to measure and the type of cognitive behavior it elicits. We can write the item (explication) and then we can study the responses to the item to determine if it behaves the way we think it behaves.

SUMMARY

In this chapter, two major themes have been introduced that pervade all chapters in this book: the need to develop fluid abilities and construct validity. Test and test items have been defined, and it has been shown that item formats come in various forms. Table 1.3 summarizes the chapters of this book.

Table 1.3
Summaries of Chapters in This Book

Part I	A Foundation for MC Testing
1	Fluid abilities and construct validity are prevailing themes in this book. Validity centers on how test scores are interpreted and used. Tests and test items are defined, and an ideal process for item development is described.
2	The debate about the roles of MC and CR item formats is discussed in light of recent reviews. A place exists in educational testing for all types of item formats.
3	A wide variety of MC item formats are shown and evaluated, and some are not recommended.
Part II	Developing MC Items
4	Basic information is presented about writing test items.
5	A long-existing need has been to test for student learning that is more complex than simple recall. Suggestions are provided for how to do this.
6	New item writers often suffer from "writer's block." A method is presented for helping item writers so afflicted.
Part III	Validating Test Item Responses
7	When an item is written, a set of activities improves the overall quality of these items.
8	Conventional item analysis is important in validating test item responses.
9	Advanced topics in item analysis are presented for more formal testing programs where stakes are higher and more resources are available for validity studies.
Part IV	The Future of Item Writing and Item-Response Validation
10	A glimpse of the future is offered that suggests that item writing will still be difficult, but we can expect computers to play a central role in this process.

2

CONSTRUCTED-RESPONSE AND MULTIPLE-CHOICE ITEM FORMATS

OVERVIEW

As stated in chapter 1, we can choose between constructed-response (CR) and multiple-choice (MC) item formats when developing a test to measure a body of knowledge, a set of skills, or an ability. Does it matter whether the test item requires the test-taker to choose an answer instead of writing out the answer? In other words, does the use of CR or MC change the interpretation of what we are measuring. The answer to this question is not a simple, declarative "yes" or "no." In some circumstances it does matter which format we use, and in other circumstances the choice of an item format may be immaterial. This chapter examines this issue in the framework of validity. In this framework, the intended use of the test affects the answer to the question about item format. Five validity arguments are identified that organize the evidence for answering this question. First, a brief history of MC testing is presented to provide some background into this problem. Then the validity framework is reviewed. Next, the five validity contexts are presented and discussed. These discussions are grounded in extensive research. The purpose in presenting these validity contexts is to help item writers evaluate the issues and decide which format to use. Also, this chapter faces current criticism of the use of MC items. At the end of the chapter, recommendations are made for the appropriate use of item formats. The determination of appropriateness leads to consideration of (a) the kind of content to be tested, and (b) the cognitive behavior intend to be elicited when answering the question or responding to the item's command.

KNOWLEDGE, SKILLS AND FLUID ABILITIES

This section provides a foundation for understanding the nature of educational constructs and the tests used to measure these constructs. The three elements (knowledge, skills, and abilities) were briefly introduced in chapter 1. This section elaborates these ideas and sets the stage for studying the problem of what item format to use in a specific circumstance.

Knowledge involves facts, concepts, principles, or procedures. Possession of knowledge is a private, personal event. We infer or attribute knowledge to someone by interpreting their responses to test items. A term commonly used for the CR test item is *essay*. However, many other CR formats exist and are identified later in this chapter.

Skill refers to the actual performance or the result of a performance, namely a product. If a student learning outcome or instructional objective involves hitting a baseball, this action is clearly performance. If the student learning outcome is baseball hitting effectiveness, computing the batting average measures it. The batting average is the result of performance, so in a sense it is a product. Skill involves many products, for example, a skilled surgeon repairs a facial injury or an accomplished artist completes a painting. We can distinguish mental skills from physical skills. The latter are obviously performance-oriented. Mental skills are performance-oriented, but test developers tend to use MC instead of performance because of the economy of MC testing. For instance, spelling, punctuation, and grammar usage can be tested with MC, but these are writing skills. Many mathematics computations involve skills of adding, subtracting, multiplying, and dividing, and conversions to fractions and decimals. These are performance-oriented skills of a mental nature. MC is not a direct measure of skills, but test developers like to use MC as an indirect measure of skills. However, the use of MC to indirectly measure a skill is deceiving. Knowing how to perform a skill is not quite the same as actual performance.

We introduced fluid abilities in chapter 1 as complex human characteristics that grow slowly over a lifetime and consist of knowledge and skills, emotional characteristics, and the tendency to integrate these in some complex behavior toward some desired end. Schools develop fluid abilities, but other experiences outside school also contribute to the development of fluid abilities. Fluid abilities are often interrelated. For example, good writers need creative thinking and critical thinking abilities to complement their outstanding writing ability. Fluid abilities can be taught and learned, but there is a poor history of testing them (Anderson, 1972; Cole, 1990; Lohman, 1993). Fluid abilities are highly prized in any society. Those societies with advanced technology seem to value fluid abilities more than do less advanced societies. In other words, the development of fluid abilities is very worthwhile.

One seemingly valid criticism of education and professional training is heavy emphasis on teaching and testing knowledge and skills at the expense of fluid abilities. One can be a fountain of knowledge and have many skills, but if he or she is unable to apply that knowledge or those skills to complex problems in daily life, the acquisition of knowledge and skills seems pointless.

A TAXONOMY OF ITEM FORMATS

A variety of MC and CR item formats exist. Haladyna (1997) presented a variety of item formats that follow basic distinctions provided in chapter 1. Table 2.1 is based on this taxonomy. Chapter 3 provides a very detailed treatment of various MC formats. Many examples appear in that chapter. Chapter 3 also discusses many issues related to using MC items, such as the use of calculators and guessing.

The list of item formats serves to illustrate that CR testing is quite varied and elicits many cognitive and psychomotor behaviors. This point is made more strongly later in the chapter. Interestingly, MC also has many formats that make it attractive for measuring various types of knowledge while also promising something for some types of skills and fluid abilities.

DISTINCTIONS AMONG ITEM FORMATS

As shown in chapter 1, CR item formats come in two main varieties: high inference and low inference.

High-Inference Formats

The high-inference format requires expert judgment about the trait being observed, so that one or a set of descriptive rating scales are used, sometimes called *rubrics* or *scoring guides*. Many abstract qualities are evaluated this way. For instance in measuring writing ability, organization, style, and word choice are measured using rating scales, because these writing traits have an abstract nature.

Low-Inference Formats

The low-inference format simply involves observation because there is some behavior or answer in mind that is either present or absent. Writing conventions can be measured by noting misspelled words, capitalization, and punctuation errors, and poor grammar. These writing skills are directly observable in student writing.

TABLE 2.1
Item Formats

Constructed-Response	Multiple-Choice
Anecdotal	Conventional
Critique or Review	Alternate-Choice
Demonstration	Matching
Discussion	Complex Multiple-Choice*
Essay	True-False*
Exhibition	Multiple True-False
Experiment	Comprehension Item Set
Fill-In-The-Blank/Short Answer	Pictorial Item Set
Writing Sample	Problem-Solving Item Set
Interview-Observation	Interlinear Item Set
Instrument-aided Observation	Experimental/Innovative
Oral Report	
Performance	*Not recommended for use
Portfolio	
Project	
Research Paper	
Visual Observation	

We have only four CR item formats for this type of behavior:

1. Essay or short-answer completion, where a right answer is known,
2. Simple observation (present or absent),

3. Simple observation involving a measuring instrument (clock, scale, ruler), and
4. Checklist, a series of simple observations.

Table 2.2 presents characteristics of each CR format. However, one should not compare high-inference and low-inference item formats in terms of each's strengths or limitations, because the only salient issue is the interpretation of test scores resulting from a choice of an item format. Generally speaking, the high-inference format is good for some types of cognitive behaviors for which an operational definition does not exist, and the low-inference format is good for other types of cognitive behaviors for which there is an operational definition. Table 2.2 serves to provide information that is useful in planning to use one of these types of CR formats.

Testing specialists prefer MC testing for the same reasons offered in current textbooks, namely that it is more efficient to construct, administer, and score, and it leads to the measurement of seemingly the same constructs so inefficiently and unreliably measured by the old-type CR format (Eurich, 1931; Godshalk, Swineford, & Coffman, 1966; Hurd, 1932; O'Dell, 1928; Patterson (1926), Ruch, 1929; Tiegs, 1931; Traub & Fisher, 1977).

In the unified approach to validity, Messick (1989) called bias construct irrelevant variance, something that pollutes test score interpretations. The bias extant when judges interpret student responses with the use of one type of CR items could be avoided by using MC items. These biases include handwriting, word processing, reading ability, verbal skills, and writing style (Coffman, 1971). The efficiency issue also strongly influenced the switch over from CR to MC. So the rationale for rejecting CR items in test design was well grounded in theory and research during these early days of standardized testing.

In the current era of debate over item format differences, many new perspectives have emerged that enrich the debate and provide guidance. Traub (1993) provided periodic appraisals of research and surrounding issues. He identified flaws in earlier research that made these studies less useful. He also pointed to methods of study that would overcome the flaws of earlier studies and help in the next generation of studies. His brief review of nine exemplary studies was inconclusive, leading him to argue that a better approach to the study of this problem is a theory of format effects. This emerging theory suggests that the choice of format influences the measurement of the construct of interest.

Snow (1993) considered the problem of item format differences not from a purely psychometric perspective but from a psychological perspective that includes cognitive processing demands on the examinee. Snow also stated that the study of performance on contrasting item formats should include noncognitive aspects as well. This psychological perspective is often missing from studies of item format differences. Snow suggested a multifaceted approach that includes a

TABLE 2.2
Attributes of High-Inference and Low-Inference Item Formats

Attribute	High-Inference Formats	Low-Inference Formats
Type of Behavior Measured	Usually abstract, most valued in education	Usually concrete, may seem trivial
Ease of Construction	Design of items is very complex, involving command or question, conditions for performance, and a set of descriptive rating scales	Design of items is not as involved as high inference, involving command or question, conditions for performance, and a simple scoring mechanism
Cost of Administration	Can be group administered and therefore inexpensive, but if individually administered can be very time consuming.	Because behavior has to be observed with each test-taker, administration can be very costly.
Cost of Scoring	Scoring involves training judges and observing student work. This is very expensive.	Scoring is very simple, so this cost is not very great.
Reliability	Reliability is a problem with this kind of testing due to problems with rater consistency and lack of variation in scores.	Results can be very reliable, because observation is so direct.
Objectivity	Scoring is subjective.	Scoring is objective.
Bias: Systematic Error	Many threats to validity exist, including overrating or underrating and halo	Seldom yields biased observations.

variety of conditions and a set of working hypotheses to be tested in this framework. Of the eight offered, three are noncognitive (attitudes, anxiety, and motivation) and only the eighth is psychometric in nature. Later in this chapter, a section is devoted to this perspective, drawing from a recent research review by Martinez (1998).

Bennett (1993), like Snow (1993) and many others, believe that the adoption of the unified approach to validity has salience for the study of this problem. Bennett emphasized values and consequences of test score interpretations and use. We have seldom applied these criteria on past studies of item format differences.

In summary, the study of item format differences has continued over most of this century. The earliest studies were focused on format differences using simple correlation methods. As the debate evolved, cognitive psychology entered and our notion of validity sharpened to consider context, values, consequences, and the noncognitive aspects of test behavior. Improvements in methodology and the coming of the computer made research more sophisticated. Nevertheless, the basic issue seems to remain the same.

EVALUATING THE ITEM FORMAT ISSUE USING VALIDITY AS A BASIS

For most of the 20th century, the debate about item formats has been sustained with cycles of increased interest followed by quieter times. The next five sections of this chapter focus on research that sheds light on the viability of MC formats in various validity contexts. The term *argument* is used here because in validation, evidence is used to build an argument that a specific test score use or interpretation is valid. The validity of the MC item format is examined in five contexts, building an argument that results in a supportable conclusion about the role of MC in a test for a specific test use.

Validity Argument 1: Prediction

The prediction of a criterion is one of the most time-honored traditions in American testing. Generally, student grades in college or graduate school are predicted from earlier achievement indicators such as grades or test scores. Indeed, the well-known ACT (American College Test) and SAT (Scholastic Assessment Test) are given to millions of high school students as part of the ritual for college admissions, and the Graduate Record Examination is widely administered to add information to graduate school admission decisions. The predictive argument is the simplest to conceptualize. We have a criterion (designated Y) and predictors (designated as Xs). The extent to which a single X or a set of Xs correlates with Y determines the predictive validity coefficient. Unlike other validity arguments, prediction is the most objective. If one item format leads to tests that provide better prediction, then we resolve the answer to the question of which item format is preferable.

Downing and Norcini (1998) reviewed studies involving the predictive validity coefficients of CR and MC items for various criteria. Instead of using an exhaustive approach, they selected research that exemplified this kind of research. All studies reviewed favor MC over CR, except one in which the CR test consisted of high fidelity simulations of clinical problem solving in medicine. The authors concluded that adding CR measures do little or nothing for improving prediction, even when a CR criterion resembles the CR predictor. These authors concluded that although there may be many good reasons for using CR items in testing, there is no good reason to use CR items in situations where prediction of a criterion is desired.

Validity Argument 2: Content Equivalence

This validity argument concerns the interpretableness of test scores when either CR or MC formats are used. In other words, a certain interpretation is desired based on some definition of a construct, such as writing or reading comprehension. This section draws mainly from a comprehensive, integrative review and meta-analysis by Rodriguez (1998) on this problem. Simply stated the issue is:

If a body of knowledge, set of skills, or a cognitive ability is being measured, does it matter if we use a CR or MC format?

If it does not matter, then the MC format is desirable because it has many advantages, some of which are efficient administration, objective scoring, automated scoring, and higher reliability. With knowledge and skills, MC items usually give more content coverage of a body of knowledge or a range of skills, when compared with short-answer items, essays, or other types of CR items.

The answer to the question about when to use MC is complicated by the fact expressed in Table 2.2 that a variety of CR item formats exist. Martinez (1998) pointed out that CR formats probably elicit a greater range of cognitive behaviors than the MC, an assertion that most of us would not challenge. Rodriguez mentioned another complicating factor, which is that the MC and CR scales underlying an assumed common construct may be curvilinearly related due to difficulty and reliability differences. The nature of differences in CR and MC scores of the assumed same construct are not easy to ascertain. Martinez provided a useful analysis of the cognition underlying test performance and its implications for valid interpretations. Rodriguez's meta-analysis addressed many methodological issues in studying this problem. He presented a continuum of design features that bear on the answer to this question.

Dimensionality is a major issue with these studies. Whereas Martinez (1998) warned us not to be seduced by strictly psychometric evidence, studies reviewed by Thissen, Wainer, and Wang (1994) and Lukhele, Thissen, and Wainer (1994) provided convincing evidence that in many circumstances CR and MC items lead to virtually identical interpretations due to unidimensional findings following factor analysis. Some of Martinez's earlier studies (e.g., 1990, 1993) offer

TABLE 2.3
General Findings About MC and CR Item Formats
in Construct Equivalence Settings

Type of Test Design	General Findings
Stem-equivalent MC and CR	Very high correlations
Content-equivalent MC and CR	Very high correlations, slightly below stem-equivalent findings
Not content-equivalent MC and CR	High correlations, but distinctly below content-equivalent MC and CR
Essay type items	Moderate correlations

evidence that different formats may lead to different dimensions, but when content is intended to be similar, MC and CR item scores tend to be highly related, as Rodriguez's review shows.

A final point was made by Wainer and Thissen (1993) in their review of this problem, from their study of Advanced Placement Tests where CR and MC items were used: Measuring a construct not as accurately but more reliably is much better than measuring the construct more accurately but less reliably. In other words, a MC test might serve as a reliable proxy for the fundamentally better but less reliable CR test. Their advice applies to the third finding by Rodriguez in Table 2.3, where content is not equivalent, but MC may be a better choice simply because it approximates the higher fidelity CR that may have a lower reliability.

Several conclusions are justified:

- If a construct is known to be knowledge-based, the use of either a CR or MC format will result in highly correlated scores, and the MC format is superior in these settings.
- If a construct is known to be skill-based, CR items have a greater fidelity. However, MC items might serve better because they correlate highly with the truer fidelity measure and have greater efficiency. With physical skills, MC does not seem worthwhile.
- If a construct is a fluid ability, CR items of a more complex nature seem appropriate. MC items typically cannot reflect a fluid ability, however, one format, the item set, comes closest to modeling aspects of some fluid abilities.

Validity Argument 3: Proximity to Criterion

This section examines the issue of CR and MC with respect to some well-understood criterion that we wish to measure. This criterion may be tangible and observable, such as writing, or it can seem remote, intangible, and difficult to observe directly, such as professional competence in alchemy. Two ideas are presented here to form the basis of the argument, and then research is reviewed and synthesized leading up to some conclusions about criterion measurement.

Mislevy (1996a) characterizes a criterion as:

> ... *any assessment task stimulates a unique constellation of knowledge, skills, strategies, and motivation within each examinee.* (p. 392)

The complexity of any criterion, particularly a fluid ability, challenges us to design tests that tap the essence of the criterion. At the same time, we need some efficiency as we maintain high reliability of the test scores. To facilitate the study of the problem of criterion measurement, two ideas are introduced and defined.

Fidelity

Fidelity is concerned with the logical, judged relationship between a criterion measure and the criterion. The judges are experts in the content being measured. Given that a criterion is unobtainable, some measures have more in common with the criterion than others. We can construct a hypothetical continuum of fidelity for a set of measures of any ability. In doing so, we can argue that some tests have greater fidelity to a hypothetical construct than others. The continuum begins with the actual criterion as an abstraction and then a series of measures that have varying fidelity to the criterion. Tests of highest fidelity come closest to the criterion for cognitive and affective characteristics believed to be defined in that fluid ability.

Writing prompts are used to infer the extent to which a student has the fluid ability of writing. Breland and Gaynor (1979) stated that the first formal writing assessment program was started by the College Board in 1901. However, it was later that we experimented with MC measures of knowledge of writing skills. A common reference to writing elicited from prompts is *direct assessment*, whereas MC items used to measure knowledge of writing skills is referred to as *indirect assessment*. In this book, direct assessments are viewed as having high fidelity for measuring writing. However, writing prompts are contrived experiences used to elicit writing samples. We should not argue that the use of prompts elicits criterion measures of writing, because real writing is natural and not elicited by the types of prompts seen in typical writing assessments. In fact, there is some evidence that the type of prompt affects the measurement of the ability (Wainer & Thissen, 1994). In some assessment programs, choices of prompts are offered to give students a better chance of showing their writing ability. Knowledge of writing and writing skills provides a foundation for the fluid ability of writing. But it would be difficult to make the logical argument that a MC test of writing knowledge is a high fidelity measure of writing ability. However, an issue of practical importance that arises for test policymakers and test designers is the fidelity that exists between different types of measures and their ultimate criterion measure. Fidelity can be addressed through analysis of the cognitive processes involved in criterion behavior. Recent efforts at the Educational Testing Service have shed light on the process of cognitive task analysis with a measurement system that attempts to tap criterion behavior (Mislevy, 1996a). Other methods rely on judgment of surface features of each test to the mythical criterion. Table 2.4 presents a continuum of fidelity for medical competence.

Supervised patient practice has high fidelity to actual patient practice, but falls short of being exactly like actual practice. As noted previously in this chapter and by many others (Linn, Baker, & Dunbar, 1991), this high fidelity measure may suffer from many technical and logistical limitations. Such measurement can be incredibly expensive and rest almost totally on the expertise of trained judges. An alternative to live patient examination is an interactive CD or video where the candidate for certification or licensure encounters a high fidelity simulation that

TABLE 2.4
A Continuum of Indirect Measures of a Criterion
for Medical Competence

Fidelity to Criterion	Criterion: Medical Competence
Very high fidelity	Supervised and evaluated patient treatment
High fidelity	Interactive CD or video
Moderate fidelity	Patient-management problem
Lower fidelity	MC context-dependent item set based on a patient scenario
Lowest fidelity	MC tests of knowledge that are thought to be part of the competence needed to treat patients safely

approximates supervised or actual patient treatment. The cognitive aspects of patient treatment are simulated, but actual patient treatment is not done. Scoring of such complex behavior is only experimental and is in development at this time. Thus, this is not a viable testing format, but, according to Mislevy (1996a, 1996b), recent work at the Educational Testing Service promises to provide workable models in the near future.

An alternative with less fidelity is the patient management problem (PMP). These paper-and-pencil problems have been computerized, but success with these has been disappointing, and active projects promoting their use have all but disappeared. The promise of PMPs has been replaced with the higher fidelity simulations identified in Table 2.5. Scenario-based MC item sets are very popular (Haladyna, 1992a). Although item sets provide less fidelity than others just described, they have major advantages. Scoring can be simple and highly efficient. But some problems exist with item sets that warrant caution. Namely, responses are locally dependent. Thus, coefficients of reliability are likely to be inflated. The attractive aspect of this item format is efficiency over the other higher fidelity options. The testing approach that has the least fidelity involves conventional MC items that reflect knowledge related to the definition of competence. The test specifications may require recall, interpretation, and problem solving, but essentially candidates must choose an answer from the list, and usually, the choice reflects nothing more than knowledge in the profession. This option has the lowest fidelity although currently it dominates certification and licensing testing.

Proximity

Proximity is simply a measure of the relation among measures of varying fidelity. These correlations are flawed by the fact that their reliabilities attenuate our estimation of the true relation. Disattenuated correlations answer the question: Do two measures of a construct seem to tap the same underlying hypothetical construct? The amount of common variance provides an estimate of proximity of two measures to one another. Proximity does not replace content analysis or cognitive task analysis where the constituent knowledge, skills, and other fluid abilities required in criterion performance are identified. The implication is that when two measures of a criterion have good proximity, the more efficient one may be a reasonable choice. But when two measures of varying fidelity have low proximity, the one with higher fidelity may be the most justifiable.

Haladyna (1998) reported the results of a review of studies of criterion measurement involving CR and MC items. Conclusions from that study are presented in Table 2.5.

TABLE 2.5
Conclusions About Criterion Measurement

Criterion	Conclusion About MC and CR
Declarative knowledge	Most MC formats provide the same information as essay, short answer, or completion formats. Given the obvious benefits of MC, use MC formats.
Critical thinking ability	MC formats involving vignettes or scenarios (item sets) provide a good basis for many forms of critical thinking. In many respects this MC format has good fidelity to the more realistic open-ended behavior elicited by some CR formats.
Problem solving ability	MC item sets provide a good basis for testing problem solving. However, research is lacking on the benefits or deficits of using MC problem solving item sets.
Creative thinking ability	It is hard to imagine a MC format for this. Many have spoken of this limitation (see Martinez, 1998).
School abilities (e.g., writing, reading, mathematics)	Performance has the highest fidelity to criterion for these school abilities. MC is good for measuring foundational aspects of fluid abilities, such as declarative knowledge or knowledge of skills.
Professional abilities (e.g., in professions such as physician, dentist, lawyer, teacher)	Certain high-fidelity CR items seem best suited for this purpose. Some MC formats can tap more basic aspects of these abilities such as knowledge and the elements of professional practice including critical thinking and problem solving.

Validity Argument 4: Gender and Item Format Bias

Part of the argument against MC has been a body of research pointing to possible interaction effects of CR/MC formats with test performance for boys and girls and men and women. Ryan and Franz (1998) recently integrated and evaluated this research, and this section draws from their observations and conclusions, as well as from other excellent studies contributed by Wightman (1998) and DeMars (1998).

A suspicion is that MC formats work against women and girls, providing lower estimates of their knowledge, skills, or abilities than deserved. If CR items were used, more accurate estimates might be obtained. The opposite argument is that verbal abilities interplay in more complex types of CR where writing is expected. Because girls have higher verbal ability (Ryan, Franz, Haladyna, & Hammond, 1998), performance on CR items with a heavy demand for verbal ability produces systematic error and biases test score interpretations. Both arguments involve bias, so the issue is a serious one.

Ryan and Franz (1998) approached the problem using meta-analysis of 14 studies and 178 effects. They reached the following conclusion:

> *Females generally perform better than males on the language measures, regardless of assessment format; and males generally perform better than females on the mathematics measures, also regardless of format. All of the differences, however, are quite small in an absolute sense. These results suggest that there is little or no format effect and no format-by-subject interaction.* (p. 14)

Although the authors urged caution in using these results because more studies are still being added to the analysis to complete their review and because of some methodological limitations, the results speak clearly about the existence of small differences between boys and girls that may be real and not a function of item formats.

Ryan and Franz (1998) offered a validity framework for future studies of item format that should be useful in parsing the results of past and future studies on CR and MC item formats. Table 2.6 captures four categories of research that they believe can be used to classify all research of this type. The first category is justified for abilities where the use of CR formats is obvious. In writing, for example, the use of MC to measure writing ability seems nonsensical, even though MC tests scores might predict writing ability performance.

The second category is a subtle one, where writing ability is interwoven with ability being measured. This situation may be very widespread and include many fields and disciplines where writing is used to advance arguments, state propositions, review or critique issues or performances, or develop plans for solutions to problems. This second category supports CR testing in a complex way that supports verbal expression.

The third category is a source of bias in testing. This category argues that verbal ability should not get in the way of measuring something else. One area of the school curriculum that seems likely to fall into this trap is the measurement of mathematics ability where CR items are used that rely on verbal ability. This tends to bias results. Constructs falling into this third category seem to favor using MC formats, while constructs falling into the first or second categories seem to favor CR formats.

The fourth category includes no reliance on verbal ability. In this instance, the result may be so objectively oriented that a simple performance test with a right and wrong answer may suffice. In these circumstances, MC makes a good proxy for CR, because MC is easily scorable.

A study of advanced placement history by Breland, Danos, Kahn, Kubota, and Bonner (1994) nicely expressed two of the important findings of the Ryan and Franz review. They found gender differences in MC and CR scores of men and women, but attributed the higher scoring by men to more knowledge of history, whereas the scores for men and women on CR are about the same. Quite a bit of

TABLE 2.5

A Taxonomy of Types of Research on Gender By Item Format

Type	Description
Criterion-related CR	A CR format is intended for measuring something that is appropriate, that is, high fidelity, such as a writing prompt for writing ability.
Verbal ability is part of the ability being measured.	In these CR tests, verbal ability is required in performance and is considered vital to the ability being measured. An example is advanced placement history, where students read a historical document and write about it.
Verbal ability is correlated to the construct but not part of it.	CR tests of knowledge might call for recall or recognition of facts, concepts, principles, or procedures, and writing ability might influence this measurement. This is to be avoided.
Verbal ability is uncorrelated to the construct being measured.	In many types of test performance in mathematics and in science, verbal ability may not play an important role in CR test performance.

attention in this study was drawn to potential biases in scoring CR writing. Modern high-quality research such as this study reveals a deeper understanding of the problem and the types of inferences drawn from test data involving gender differences. In another recent study, Wightman (1998) examined the consequential aspects of differences in test scores. She found no bias due to format effects on a law school admission test. A study by Demars (1998) of students in a statewide assessment revealed very little difference in performance despite format type. Although format-by-gender interactions were statistically significant, the practical significance of the differences was very small. Demars also presented evidence suggesting the MC and CR items measured the same or nearly the same constructs. The research review by Ryan and Franz (1998) does not put to rest the suspicion about the influence of item format on performances by gender. But if effects do exist, they seem to be very small. Research should continue to uncover sources of bias, if they exist. The most important outcome of this study is the evolution of the taxonomy of types of studies. Knowing more about the construct being measured has everything to do with choosing the correct item format.

Validity Argument 5: Cognition

As noted in the history of the issue of item format, a recent, emerging interest is in the mental state of examinees when they take a test. Do CR and MC items elicit different mental behaviors? At the lowest level, is recall really different from recognition? With higher level behaviors, does format really makes a difference in interpretation, or can we feel comfortable with the more efficient MC?

Martinez' studies (1990, 1993 ; Martinez & Katz, 1996) and his recent review (Martinez, 1998) provided greater understanding about the nature and role of cognition in test performance. To be sure, other studies are contributing to this growing understanding. Martinez offered 10 propositions that seem worthy to review. Paraphrases of his propositions are provided in italics with commentary following.

1. *Considerable variety exists among CR formats in terms of the kinds of behavior elicited.* This is certainly true. Consider for example, the range of item formats shown in Table 2.1 on page 24.
2. *MC items elicit lower levels of cognitive behavior.* Two studies are cited showing a tendency for MC to elicit recognition and similar forms of lower level behaviors, but this criticism has been aimed at item writers not the test format. MC is certainly capable of better things. Also, MC items eliciting complex behavior are difficult to write, but again, this is not the fault of the format but of item writers in general. For the most part, most

tests suffer from the malady of testing recall or recognition. This is not a function of item format but limited ability to elicit higher levels of thinking in both teaching and testing. Few would argue with the idea that the range of CR item formats for testing higher levels of cognition is greater than the range of MC formats.

3. *MC item formats can elicit complex behavior, but the range of complex behavior elicited by CR item formats is greater.* This point should not be arguable. Table 2.1 provides a comprehensive set of CR item formats that suggest a wide range of cognition available. MC item formats presented in the next chapter hardly represent such a wide range.

4. *CR and MC items may or may not have similar psychometric properties, depending on the conditions evoked.* This issue is the object of the review by Rodriguez (1998), and is the most complex problem of all. Martinez (1998) argued that the development of options in MC testing relates to the cognitive demands on examinees. The problem stated in the item stem also has an important role. Limiting evaluation to psychometric criteria, Martinez believes, is a mistake. A theoretical analysis should precede the choice of an item format. Others agree with this point (e.g., van den Bergh, 1990). In his interesting study, van den Bergh argued from his testing of the reading comprehension of third graders that format made little difference in test score interpretation. His theoretical orientation provided a stronger rationale for findings than prior studies. Earlier in chapter 1, the discussion centered on construct definition and the need to theorize about the relation of test behavior to the abstract construct definition. Indeed, if we can give more thought to the nature of cognition in testing, test items might improve.

5. *Response elimination strategies may contribute to construct-irrelevant variation in MC testing.* This criticism is aimed at faults in the item writing process. Good item writers follow guidelines, such as developed by Haladyna and Downing (1989a, 1989b). Most formal testing programs do not have flaws in items that allow examinees the opportunity to eliminate options and increase the chances of guessing the right answer. Ironically, recent research points to the fact that most MC items have only two or three working options (Downing & Haladyna, 1997). However, evidence that response elimination strategies provide a source of bias in MC testing has not been identified.

6. *Test anxiety can influence CR performance.* Test anxiety indeed can be a powerful influence in all forms of testing, especially when the stakes are high, such as in employment, certification, licensing, and graduation testing. Evidence is cited for higher anxiety in CR testing, but when the cognitive demand is great and students have not yet had enough experience with complex CR formats, greater anxiety is to be expected.

7. *CR formats have greater potential for diagnosis of student learning and program effects.* Evidence is growing to support this statement. For example, Mukerjee (1991) examined reading comprehension test results for children in a Cloze format which requires a constructed response and multiple-choice formats and found useful diagnostic information from both. His conclusion was that both formats had something to contribute to deepening understanding about reading comprehension. At the same time, recent work at the Educational Testing Service with inference networks and cognitive task analysis (Mislevy, 1996a) promises to increase our ability to diagnose learning problems in a MC format.

8. *CR might contribute to richer anticipatory learning.* This is a primary claim of test reformers like Wiggins (1989) among others. This also follows from the fact that most of educational testing concentrates on basic knowledge and skills of a very low cognitive level, often involving recall or recognition. As students prepare for CR or MC tests, differences in learning may appear, but much has to do with the design of the tests and what cognition they elicit. As most testing specialists point out, both formats can elicit higher levels of cognition.

9. *Policy decisions about CR and MC formats can be assisted by research but should not be prescribed.* Simplistic comparisons between CR and MC formats using psychometric criteria such as item difficulty, item discrimination, and reliability are helpful but often misleading. If construct interpretations differ, then such discussions are pointless. Researchers including Traub (1993) emphasize validity (test interpretation and use) rather than simplistic criteria. Of course, cost and efficiency are powerful factors in policy decision. Legislators, school boards, licensing and certification authorities and boards all need to be more sophisticated in their appraisal of test interpretations and uses as they pertain to item formats.

10. We need more research. Many more important questions remain to be answered via theoretical development and research. The area of cognition and testing is relatively new. As cognitive psychologists address these questions and testing specialists continue to be involved, the discussion of item formats may be less important as computerized scoring replaces judgment-based scoring. Several good examples exist of research on cognition in testing. Haynie (1994) examined delayed retention using short-answer CR and MC. He found MC to be superior in measuring delayed retention of knowledge.

CONCLUSIONS ABOUT CHOOSING AN ITEM FORMAT

Generally speaking, three principles emerge from this chapter:

11. The most efficient and reliable way to measure knowledge is with MC formats. CR formats offer a weak alternative and do not seem justified.

12. The most direct way to measure skill is via performance. But many mental skills can be tested via MC with a high degree of proximity (statistical relation between CR and MC items of an isolated skill). The idea that MC can serve as a proxy for CR in these settings is attractive, but has some limitations. If the skill is critical to the ultimate interpretation, such as in a profession like medicine, knowledge of a skill tested via MC is not preferable to performance of skill via CR.

13. When measuring a fluid ability or intelligence, the complexity of such human traits favors CR item formats of a complex nature. Simple completion or short-answer CR formats are not satisfactory, but many of the formats shown in Table 2.5 would serve well in measuring fluid abilities. In some circumstances, the item set may serve as a useful proxy for CR in the measurement of fluid abilities, particularly involving problem solving or critical thinking. Chapter 3 provides comprehensive treatment of this MC format.

3

MULTIPLE-CHOICE FORMATS

Overview

This chapter discusses the advantages of multiple-choice (MC) test items, illustrates a variety of MC formats and discusses issues in the use of MC formats. Most MC formats in this chapter are traditional, and a few are nontraditional. Some experimental formats are also presented.

Contexts for Using MC Formats

Two main contexts exist for using MC formats. The first is classroom testing, where the objective of a MC test is to obtain measures of student learning that are often efficient and easy to aggregate. This measure is helpful when a teacher assigns a grade at the end of the grading period. The second context is a large-scale testing program such as for a school district, a statewide assessment, or a certification or licensing test. Reference is made in this chapter for which context a specific item format is most useful.

Section One: Features of MC Items

In chapter 2, the discussion of constructed-response (CR) and MC formats centered on the issue of which format is preferable for certain purposes. This section briefly summarizes the arguments that favor MC over CR when it has been established that knowledge is the objective of testing. In chapter 2, it was stated that a MC format is not always considered the equivalent of a CR format, so when comparing MC and CR formats, we must be certain that the MC format is viable when making a comparison. To reiterate:

- When we are testing for knowledge, MC and CR may yield similar or identical interpretations.
- When we are testing for mental skills, MC and CR measures may correlate highly, but interpretations tend to differ. MC would not be a good choice for measuring these types of mental and physical behaviors.
- When we are testing for fluid abilities, CR seems to have more fidelity than MC, but certain aspects of a fluid ability might be well tested by MC.

The discussion of MC versus CR for testing knowledge or some mental skills centers on a 1-hour examination format where each format is being considered.

Science of Item Writing

Whereas critics including Cronbach (1971) and Nitko (1985) have stated that item writing is a neonatal science, the extensiveness study of the MC format as suggested from the many references to research in this book provides evidence that MC item writing is a growing science. Those references dated 1990 or later provide further evidence of recent increased scientific interest. We cannot say the same for CR item writing. Advice on CR item writing can be chronicled in textbooks and other sources and is very much based on common sense and experience (see Haladyna, 1997; Linn & Gronlund, 1995; Popham, 1997). Research on writing CR items is diffuse and asystematic. Research on essay testing is well chronicled in a classic chapter in *Educational Measurement* by Coffman (1971). Subsequent extensive treatment of CR item writing is not available.

Item Construction

Testing specialists generally regard MC items to be more difficult to prepare than essay items. The wording of the stem, the identification of a single correct answer, and the writing of several wrong but plausible choices is a challenging task. In a 1-hour test, you might administer 50 to 60 MC items or 1 to 3 CR items. Considering time to write items, CR is easier to prepare.

Item Review

Chapter 7 provides various types of item review for MC items. Reviewing CR items is easier because a 1-hour test only has several CR items whereas the MC test would have 50 to 60 items.

Test Design and Construction

Once the CR items are written, preparing a test is very easy. It is strongly recommended that model answers be prepared for CR items, particularly essays. Answer preparation can be a significant activity, as model answers are typically recommended in standard textbooks on this subject (e.g., Ebel & Frisbie, 1991; Linn & Gronlund, 1995).

With the coming of word processing, laser printers, and item banking systems, the storage and retrieval of MC items is routine. Preparing the key for a MC test is easy.

Overall, constructing the CR test is easier than the MC test. However, modern technology is making it easier to construct MC test items once they are stored in a computer. Indeed, some forms of automated item writing and item banking may make MC item writing even easier in the future. Chapter 10 addresses some trends for the future of MC testing.

Administration

Essay tests require more time because each test-taker has to write the response. A 1-hour essay test is a physically demanding exercise, whereas selecting answers in a 1-hour MC test is far less demanding.

Scoring

Essay tests are judgmentally scored, usually with a rating scale or a checklist. The ideal procedures for scoring are highly involved and laborious (Coffman, 1971). Many biases threaten the validity of essay test scores. Chase (1979) presented evidence for an expectation effect on essay test scores, and the influence of handwriting, a finding that Hughes, Keeling, and Tuck (1983) replicated. The relation between sentence length and test score and the influence of penmanship on the test score are well documented (Coffman, 1971). Chase (1986) cited several studies showing the existence of racial and gender bias in scoring essays. A MC test is objectively scored. One can use a key, a scoring template (overlay) that identifies the right answer on a MC answer sheet, or an optical scanner, which provides a total score for each test-taker. The optical scanner also provides an electronic file that can be used to analyze characteristics of the total test scores and the items.

Setting the Passing Score or Creating Standards for Grading

The science of standard setting is well established for MC test scores but this science is very new for CR testing. Combining MC and CR items to create test scores makes standard setting even more problematic. For classroom testing, the use of CR and MC item formats is greatly simplified when a teacher uses a system that simply sums points earned from CR and MC tests and also from other activities that go into a student's grade.

Equating

In classroom testing, equating is not a problem, but in larger testing programs, alternate forms of the test should be equivalent in terms of difficulty and content. This technical process is well described in Kolen and Brennan (1995) for MC tests, but is very immature for CR tests.

Analysis and Evaluation of Test Items

CR test items are not easily analyzed and evaluated. The ambiguous essay test item is difficult to detect; the difficulty of an essay test is hard to determine. What constitutes effective and ineffective essays is not clearly discernible. A curious oddity in educational measurement textbooks is the lack of attention paid to item analysis and evaluation of essay test items. With MC tests, many standard computerized item analysis programs provide complete summaries of item and test characteristics. Chapters 8 and 9 provide methods for using these item analysis results to improve future MC tests and understand the dynamics that may explain MC test results. Besides these statistical summaries, there are many activities that go into evaluating and improving MC test items that are described in chapter 7.

Guessing

With CR essay tests, there is less tendency for students to guess the right answer. However, students will often confess the temptation to bluff an essay answer. With MC tests, guessing is a nuisance because there is a chance that students will guess right answers. However, this is a very weak criticism of MC. First, we tend to overrate the effects of guessing. The probability of guessing a right answer is the ratio of one to the number of options in the MC item. For any 4-option item, the probability of guessing a right answer is 1/4 or 25%. The probability of guessing correctly 10 right answers is about .000000009! The risk of student guessing producing an artificially high score is very remote with tests of 50 items or more. If a student scored between 20% and 40%, we would likely interpret that result as due to random guessing and that the student does not possess the knowledge that the test is supposed to measure.

Cuing and Option Elimination Strategies

Related to guessing is the idea that a natural flaw of the MC format is the tendency for students to eliminate options and make educated guesses. Some researchers call this *cuing*. Fajardo & Chan (1993) studied an experimental MC format that has several hundred options. Their research showed promise for this uncued MC. With stem-equivalent items, the uncued MC were 6.7% harder. They attributed this difference to the cuing effect of conventional MC. Harvill and Davis (1997) studied reasons for answer changing behavior. A surprising yet consistent finding in answer changing research is that the student's first choice is usually not the right choice. If students review their choices, they are more likely to change from wrong to right than from wrong to wrong or from right to wrong. Reasons for answer changing include consideration of item content, clerical corrections, mismarking, finding clues to answers later in the test, rereading and reconsidering, and better understanding and better memory later in the test administration.

Reliability

Reliability is a necessary condition in test validation. Reliability relates to measurement error in a set of test scores. Measurement error associated with a test score can be large or small, positive or negative. Principles derived from the theory of reliability help us control and reduce measurement error. Although we never really know whether a measurement error is positive or negative, we can shrink the overall extent of error by increasing reliability. Two important ways to increase reliability are to make tests longer and improve the discriminating ability of the items appearing in the test.

For comparable administration times, the essay test yields a lower reliability than the comparable MC version (Lukhele, Thissen, & Wainer, 1993). This is due in part to the subjective system of scoring. In fact, Wainer (1992) briefly reviewed the history of subjective scoring of essays, showing that even as early as 1911, it was noted that variation among judges exceeded variability among grades. Indeed, this problem has persisted throughout this century. Because we administer fewer items with the essay, and although rating scales or checklists are used, the variability of scores is too limited to really differentiate among different levels of performance. However, we have made progress in the scoring of essay test results, and there is continued hope that this format might produce high reliability (Braun, 1988).

The MC format generally produces higher reliability than the essay format, particularly if the administration time is 1 hour or more. Generally, you can administer about one MC item per minute. A 50-item MC test can produce highly reliable scores. With an essay test, writing for 1 hour or more can be exhausting, and the quality of measurable information may be less dependable than wanted.

Diagnostic Value

In classroom testing, giving CR and MC tests of student knowledge may lead to similar or identical interpretations, but some have argued that CR items provide more information about student misconceptions (e.g., Badger, 1990; Martinez, 1990, 1998). This diagnostic advantage for CR items involves judgment from someone who is intimate with the instructional setting who also designs, administers, and scores the essay test. This may also explain why so many teachers use essay tests despite these well-known limitations. Martinez (1990) studied students taking tests with item stems that were identical but the response options were either MC or open-ended. He detected student misunderstandings of the items from the essay test, information that is not normally available from the MC format. Thus, it seems that some forms of essay testing provide insights into common student misunderstanding and failure to learn. This potential for essay testing is only at an experimental stage.

Recognition Versus Production

Critics of MC contend that the essay measures something different from what the MC measures (Fiske, 1990; Nickerson, 1989). In short, they believe that picking the right answer from a list of possible answers is different from writing the right answer in terms of cognition. The persistent use of the essay test is justified with this line of reasoning.

Cognitive psychologists have hypothesized that the recognition and recall test formats elicit different thought processes (Anderson & Bower, 1972; Kintsch, 1970). However, does this simple distinction deceive us? If both formats measure the underlying construct, the choice is simple: MC. As Rodriguez (1998) pointed out in his extensive review: Do results produced from an essay test of some specific knowledge differ from results produced from a comparable MC test? The answer to that question appears to be NO. Bennett, Rock, and Wang (1990) also concluded from their review that "the evidence presented offers little support for the stereotype of MC and free-response formats as measuring substantially different constructs (i.e., trivial factual recognition vs. higher-order processes" (p. 89).

Because the essay format can detect steps in multistage thinking that we find in critical thinking, problem solving, and creative thinking, it is preferable to MC. This line of reasoning would favor using essay formats when the construct requires complex, multistep behavior.

Summary

When measuring knowledge, whether the test is classroom-specific or part of a large-scale testing program, MC might be better suited for this purpose than any CR item format. The arguments presented in this section are well supported by research. When measuring a mental skill, the nature of skill is performance, so MC is not a good choice. When measuring aspects of fluid abilities, MC is seldom a good choice. Complex thinking may be modeled with MC, but some CR formats seem better suited to this task.

SECTION TWO: MC ITEM FORMATS

This section presents a variety of multiple-choice formats that can be classified as either traditional, innovative, or experimental. Two of these formats are not recommended. The experimental formats need further research and positive results before they can be recommended.

Conventional MC

The most common variety of MC is the *conventional* format, shown with three variations at the top of the next page. Conventional MC has three parts: a stem, the correct answer, and several wrong answers, called foils or distractors.

Stem

The stem is the stimulus for the response. The stem should provide a complete idea of the problem to be solved in selecting the right answer. The stem can also be phrased in a partial-sentence format, called the incomplete-sentence format. Whether the stem appears as a question or a partial sentence, it also can present a problem that has several right answers with one option clearly being the best of the right answers. This is the best answer format; for example: A list of options can all be correct in the sense that each is an advantage, but one of these is the best.

QUESTION FORMAT
Who is John Galt? ←――――――――stem
A. A rock star ←―――――― foil or distractor
B. A movie actor ←―――――― foil or distractor
C. A character in a book ←――――― correct choice

INCOMPLETE STEM (PARTIAL SENTENCE)
John Galt is a character is in Ayn Rand novel who is remembered for his
A. integrity.
B. romantic tendencies.
C. fighting ability.

BEST ANSWER
What is the best way to measure an exact amount of liquid?
A. To use a measuring cup and read from above the container.
B. To pour the liquid into a graduated cylinder and read from eye level.
C. To pour the liquid into a container for which you already know its
   volume.

Correct Answer

The correct answer is undeniably the one and only right answer. In the question format, the correct choice can be a word, phrase, or sentence. In some rare circumstances, it can be a paragraph or even a drawing or photograph (if the distractors are also paragraphs, drawings, or photographs).

Distractors

Distractors are the most difficult part of the test item to write. Distractors are unquestionably wrong answers. Each distractor must be plausible to test-takers who have not yet learned the knowledge that the test item is supposed to measure. To those who possess the knowledge asked for in the item, the distractors are clearly wrong choices. Distractors should resemble the correct choice in grammatical form, style, and length. Subtle or blatant clues that give away the correct choice should always be avoided.

The number of distractors required for the conventional MC item is a matter of recent study (Haladyna & Downing, 1993). When analyzing a variety of tests, these researchers found that most items had only one or two "working" distractors. They concluded that three options (a right answer and two distractors) was natural.

Few items had three "working" distractors. This issue is revisited in chapter 4 in greater detail. Chapter 8 discusses how to evaluate distractors.

The conventional MC is the most frequently used MC format. It is the standard of the testing industry, because of its familiarity to millions of test makers and test-takers and its many fine qualities. However, in this book, most of the examples contain three options because both theory and research suggest that MC works best with three options, including two distractors.

Variations of Conventional MC

Several creative innovations in conventional MC have added to the variety presented in this chapter. The first is a format that is easy to prepare and avoids the tendency for students to use supplied options in mathematics to decide the correct answer. In other words, some testing researchers suspect that the conventional MC provides too many clues in the options. Johnson (1991) suggested a standard set of numbers from low to high as options. The students code the option that is closest to their answer. That way guessing or elimination strategies do not work. The generation of numbers for distractors is easy, and because this is one of the hardest steps in writing MC items, this variation can be very effective for quantitative items.

Another variation is the uncued MC (Fajardo & Chan, 1993), which was briefly discussed earlier in this chapter as a deterrent to option elimination strategies. By providing a key word or key phrase list in the hundreds, we expect the student to read an item stem and search the list for the correct answer. Guessing is virtually eliminated. These items have good qualities, namely they provide diagnostic information about failure to learn (Fenderson, Damjanov, Robeson, Veloski, & Rubin, 1997).

Draw four samples randomly from a distribution with a mean of 50 and a standard deviation of 10. Find the standard deviation of your sample of four.

A	B	C	D	E	F	G	H	I
1.0	1.5	2.0	2.5	3.0	3.5	4.0	4.5	5.0

Test designers can study patterns of response and determine what wrong choices students are making and study why they are making these wrong choices.

The uncued MC also tends to be more discriminating at the lower end of the test score scale and yields higher reliability then conventional MC. Researchers argue that the writing of distractors for many items is eliminated once the key word list is generated. Of course, this format limits the kinds of testing to basic recall or understanding.

Matching

A popular variation of the conventional MC is the matching format. This format has two or more options presented first, followed by the item stems. The instructions that precede the options and stems tell the test-taker how to respond and where to mark answers. As shown here, we have five options and six statements. We could easily expand the list of six statements into a longer list, which makes the test more comprehensive in testing student learning.

An unusual example, adapted from Technical Staff (1937), is a complex matching item, and it appears in Fig. 3.1. The matching format should

SIMPLE MATCHING FORMAT
Mark your answer on the answer sheet. For each item select from options provided.

A. Minnesota
B. Illinois
C. Wisconsin
D. Nebraska
E. Iowa

1. Home state of the Hawkeyes
2. Known for its cheese heads
3. Land of many lakes
4. Cornhuskers country
5. The largest of these states
6. Contains Cook County

continue to be used. As a variation of the conventional MC, constructing a matching set of items is efficient and easy to administer. Matching items are well suited for testing understanding of concepts and principles.

The matching format has many advantages:

1.   The format lends itself nicely to testing associations, definitions, or characteristics or examples of concepts.
2.   Matching is efficient based on the amount of student testing time consumed and space taken by the set of test items. The example just provided could be expanded to produce as many as 30 items on a single page.

Choice	Personality Type	Type Characteristic
A. Kretschmer	___1. hypokinetic	___2. intellectual
B. Berman	___3. rationalistic	___4. indifferent, hedonistic
C. James	___5. extrovert	___6. pleasantly toned
D. Morgan	___7. knowing	___8. unpleasantly toned
E. Jung	___9. mercurial	___10. immature, docile
F. Thompson	___11. aesthetic	___12. objective, social
G. Warren	___13. sanguine	___14. short, obese

FIG. 3.1. Unconventional matching exercise. *Note.* From *Manual of examination methods* (2nd ed.); (p. 73) by the Technical Staff, 1937, Chicago: University of Chicago. Adapted with permission.

3.   The options do not have to be repeated. If we reformatted this into the conventional MC, then it would require the repeating of the five options for each stem.

Among the few limitations of the matching format are:

1.   A tendency exists to write as many items as there are options, so that the test-takers matches up five items to five options. Making the number of options unequal to the number of items can avoid this problem.
2.   A tendency exists to mix the options. For instance, one may use people and places as options. This tendency is the problem is "nonhomogeneous options." It can be solved by ensuring that the options are part of a set of things, like all people, or all places. In the example provided above, the options were all states.

Because this format is very similar to the conventional MC, there is no research to report on its unique features. The matching format is often recommended by textbook authors. Matching is useful in classroom testing but seldom seen in large-scale testing programs.

Alternate-Choice

This format is nothing more than a two-option MC:

> **ALTERNATE-CHOICE**
>   What is the most effective way to motivate a student?
>   A. Intermittent praise
>   B. Consistent praise

Ebel (1981, 1982) was a staunch advocate of this format. He argued that many items in educational achievement testing are "either/or," lending themselves nicely to the alternate-choice format. Downing (1992) reviewed the research on this format and also concluded that it is very viable. Haladyna and Downing (1993) examined more than 1,100 items from 4 standardized tests and found many items have a correct answer and only one working distractor. The others were nonfunctional. They concluded that many of these items were naturally alternate-choice.

Below is an example of an alternate-choice format for testing knowledge of a writing skill.

> 1.   (A-Providing, B-Provided) that all homework is done, you may go to the movie.
> 2.   It wasn't very long (A-before, B-until), Earl called Keisha.
> 3.   Knowledge of (A-preventative, B-preventive) medicine will lengthen your life.
> 4.   All instructions should be written, not (A-oral, B-verbal).
> 5.   She divided the pizza (A-between, B-among) the three boys.

Although the alternate-choice item may not exactly measure writing skills, it is congeneric with the construct of writing to provide good information about the writing skills of students using a MC format.

Although alternate-choice is a downsized version of conventional MC, it is NOT a true-false item. Alternate-choice offers a comparison between two choices, whereas the true-false format does not provide an explicit comparison among choices. With the true-false format, the test-taker must mentally create the counter example and choose accordingly.

The alternate-choice has several attractive characteristics and some limitations:

1. The most obvious advantage is that writing it is easy. One only has to think of a right answer and one plausible distractor.
2. The efficiency of the use of this format with respect to printing costs, ease of test construction, layout, and storage and retrieval is high.
3. Another advantage is that if the item has only two options, one can ask more questions per testing period than with conventional MC. Consequently, the alternate–choice format will provide better coverage of content.
4. Alternate–choice items are not limited to low-level thinking and can be written to measure higher level thinking (Ebel, 1982).
5. Ebel (1981, 1982) argued that alternate–choice is more reliable than MC because more alternate–choice items can be asked in a fixed time. Research on alternate–choice supports Ebel's contention (Burmester & Olson, 1966; Ebel, 1981, 1982; Ebel & Williams, 1957; Hancock, Thiede, & Sax, 1992; Maihoff & Mehrens, 1985; Sax & Reiter, n. d.). Also, alternate–choice items have a history of exhibiting satisfactory discrimination (Ruch & Stoddard, 1925; Ruch & Charles, 1928; Williams & Ebel, 1957).
6. Lord (1977) suggested another advantage: A two-option format is probably most effective for high-achieving students because of the tendency to eliminate other options as implausible distractors. Levine and Drasgow (1982) and Haladyna and Downing (1993) provided further support for such an idea. As reported earlier in this chapter, they found that most items contained only one or two plausible distractors. Many of these items could have been easily simplified to the alternate–choice format. If this is true, then two options should not only be sufficient in many testing situations but also a natural consequence when useless distractors are removed from an item containing four or five options.

The most obvious limitation of the alternate–choice format is that guessing is a factor—the test-takers may choose the correct answer even if they do not know the answer. The chance of randomly guessing the right answer is 50% for one item. By recognizing the floor and ceiling of a test score scale consisting of alternate–choice items, we overcome this limitation. For instance, the lowest probable score for a 30–item alternate–choice test is 50%, if random guessing happens. The ceiling of the test is, of course, 100%. A score of 55% on such a test is very low, whereas a score of 75% is in the middle of this scale. Given that guessing is a larger factor in alternate–choice items when compared with conventional MC, you one only has to make an interpretation in keeping with the idea that 50% is about as low a score as can be expected. Any passing standard or other evaluative criteria used should be consistent with the effective range of the alternate–choice test score scale, which is from 50% to 100%.

Fig. 3.2 contains a set of alternate–choice items designed to measure word meaning in sentences. Alternate–choice is useful for classroom testing. Downing

(1992) recommended it for formal testing programs, because alternate–choice has been found to be comparable to three- or four-option items, if properly constructed (Burmester & Olsen, 1966; Maihoff & Phillips, 1988). The added advantage for alternate–choice is that more items can be used per time period. Also, the construction of alternate–choice items is easy.

For each sentence, select the most appropriate (for formal English) of the two words given, and write its letter in the space provided.
____1. (A-Providing, B-Provided) that all is quiet, you may go up.
____2. The (A-exact, B-meticulous) calculation of votes...
____3. I make (A-less, B-fewer) mistakes now than previously.
____4. All orders should be written, not (A-verbal, B-oral).
____5. The climate of Arizona is said be very (A-healthful, B-healthy).

FIG. 3.2. Example of alternate-choice items for testing word meaning

---

True-False

This format has been well established for informal testing but seldom used in standardized testing programs. There has been significant, increasing evidence to warrant its use with caution or not at all (Downing, 1992; Haladyna, 1992b). Like other MC formats, it is subject to many abuses. The most common abuse may be a tendency to test trivial knowledge. The example shows a more effective use of this format:

Mark A on your answer sheet if true and B if false.
1. The first thing to do with an automatic transmission that does not work is to check the transmission fluid. (A)
2. The major cause of tire wear is poor wheel balance. (B)
3. The usual cause of clutch "chatter" is in the clutch pedal linkage. (A)
4. The distributor rotates at one half the speed of the engine crankshaft. (B)

Fig. 3.3 presents a very effective, although unconventional, use of this format. The items in Fig. 3.3 occupy a small space but provide a complete analysis of plant anatomy. There are more subtle and serious problems with the true–false format.

Place an "X" beneath each structure for which each statement is true?

		Root	Stem	Leaf
1	Growing point protected by a cap			
2	May possess a pithy center			
3	Epidermal cells hair-like			
4	Growing region at tip			

FIG. 3.3. Example of an Innovative True-False Format

For example, Peterson and Peterson (1976) investigated the error patterns of positively and negatively worded true–false questions that were either true or false. Errors were not evenly distributed among the four possible types of true–false   items. Although this research is not damning, it does warn item writers that the difficulty of the item can be controlled by its design.

Hsu (1980) pointed out a characteristic of true–false items when they are presented as a group using the generic stem:

> **Which of the following statements are true?**

Such a format is likely to interact with the ability of the group being tested in a complex way. Both the design of the item and the format for presentation are likely to cause differential results. Ebel (1978), a proponent of true–false items, was opposed to the grouping of items in this manner.

Grosse and Wright (1985) described a more serious threat to the usefulness of true–false. They argued that true–false has a large error component due to guessing, a finding that other research supports (Frisbie, 1973; Haladyna & Downing, 1989b; Oosterhof & Glasnapp, 1974). Grosse and Wright claimed that if a test-taker's response style favors true instead of false answers in the face of ignorance, the reliability of the test score may be seriously undermined. A study comparing conventional MC, alternate–choice, and true–false showed very poor performance for true–false in terms of reliability (Pinglia, 1994).

As with alternate–choice, Ebel (1970) advocated the use of true–false items. The chapter on true–false testing by Ebel and Frisbie (1991) remains an authoritative work. Ebel's (1970) arguments are simply that the command of useful knowledge is important. We can state all verbal knowledge in terms of propositions, and each proposition can be truly or falsely stated. We can measure student knowledge by determining the degree to which each student can judge the truth or falsity of knowledge. Frisbie and Becker (1991) synthesized the advice of 17 textbook sources on true–false testing. The advantages of true–false items can be summarized in the following way:

1. True–false items are easy to write.
2. True–false items can measure important content areas.
3. True–false items can measure higher thought processes.
4. More true–false items can be given per testing period than MC items.
5. True–false items are easy to score.
6. True–false items occupy less space on the page, therefore minimizing the cost of production.
7. The judgment of a proposition as true or false is realistic.
8. We can minimize reading time.
9. Reliability of test scores is adequate.

The disadvantages are as follows:

1. Items tend to reflect trivial information.
2. True–false items tend to promote rote learning.
3. Guessing is too influential.
4. The format is resistant to detecting degrees of truth or falsity.
5. True–false tests tend to be slightly less reliable than comparable MC tests.
6. There are differences between true true–false items and false true–false items, which have caused some concern.
7. True–false items are not as good as alternate–choice items (Hancock, Thiede, & Sax, 1992).

We can defend some of these criticisms. The reputation for testing trivial content is probably deserved, but only because item writers write trivial items. Trivial content can be tested with any format. The more important issue is: Can true–false items be written to measure nontrivial content? A reading of the chapter on true–false testing in the book by Ebel and Frisbie (1991) provided an unequivocal "yes" to this question. The issue of testing higher level thought processes is also answered by better item-writing techniques.

The criticism about rote learning is similar to the criticism about test content. Testing for recall is a chronic problem in American education, and is not limited solely to true–false testing. Again, Ebel and Frisbie (1991) provided examples of true–false items that measure higher level thinking.

As with alternate–choice, guessing is not much of a factor in true–false tests, for the same reasons offered in the previous section. If one keeps in mind that the floor of the scale for a true–false test is 50% and the ceiling is 100%, then our interpretations can be made in that light. It is very difficult for a random guesser to exceed 60% on these tests when the test length is substantial, say 50 to 100 items. This is the same argument that applies to alternate–choice.

Despite Ebel's persistent support of true–false, this format does not measure up very well to the alternate–choice or the conventional MC. This format is not recommended for standardized testing programs but may be useful for classroom testing, and is certainly open to experimentation.

Complex MC

The Educational Testing Service first introduced this format, and the National Board of Medical Examiners later adopted it for use in medical testing (Hubbard, 1978). Because many items used in medical and health professions testing programs had more than one right answer, complex MC permits the use of one or more correct options. Because items are scored either right or wrong, it seems sensible to set out combinations of right and wrong answers in a MC format where only one choice is correct:

Although this format is very popular in formal testing programs, Albanese (1993), Haladyna (1992b), and Haladyna and Downing (1989b) gave several reasons to recommend against its use:

> Which actors appeared in
> movie Lethal Weapon 10?
> 1. Mel Gibson
> 2. Dannie Glover
> 3. Minnie Driver
>
> A. 1 and 2
> B. 2 and 3
> C. 1 and 3
> D. 1, 2, and 3

1. Complex MC items may be more difficult than comparable single-best-answer MC.
2. Having partial knowledge, knowing that one option is absolutely correct or incorrect, helps the test-taker identify the correct option by eliminating distractors. Therefore test-taking skills have a greater influence on test performance than intended.
3. This format produces items with lower discrimination, which, in turn, lowers test score reliability.
4. The format is difficult to construct and edit.
5. The format takes up more space on the page, reducing the overall efficiency of the testing process.
6. The format requires more reading time, thus reducing the number of items of this type one might put in a test. Such a reduction negatively affects the

sampling of content, therefore reducing the validity of interpretations and uses of test scores.

Recent studies by Case and Downing (1989), Dawson-Saunders, Nungester, and Downing (1989), and Shahabi and Yang (1990) provided additional evidence of the inferiority of the complex MC. Subhiyah and Downing (1993) provided evidence that no difference exists, that complex MC items have about the same qualities as conventional MC. Further, this format fills a need when "list-type" questioning is needed. Fortunately, multiple true–false is a viable alternative to the complex, MC format.

Multiple True-False

This alternative to complex MC is the multiple true–false (MTF), sometimes known as *Type-X*. The example at the right shows a statement followed by a series of words or phrases, some of which are true and some of which are false. Generally, the number of true and false answers are balanced. The MTF format is really an item set, and the list of items can be quite lengthy, as much as thirty. This is a very attractive

> Below are references to creatures.
> Mark A if absurd and B if realistic
> 1. Aquatic mammal
> 2. Fish with a lung
> 3. Fern gemtophyte with spores
> 4. Algae with no nucleus
> 5. Chordate without a notochord
> 6. Single-celled metazoa
> 7. Featherless, flying mammal
> 8. Flatworm with a skeleton
> 9. Amoeba with a fixed mouth
> 10. Warm-blooded reptile

feature of the MTF, the ability to administer many items in a short period of time.

Frisbie (1992) reviewed research on the MTF format and supported its use. However, he stated that one detriment to its use is a lack of familiarity by item writers. Downing, Baranowski, Grosso, and Norcini (1995) compared MTF and conventional MC in a medical testing setting. They found that MTF items yielded more reliable scores, but they found conventional MC to be more highly correlated with complex measures of competence than MTF. They concluded that MTF in this study seemed to reflect more basic knowledge.

The advantages of the MTF format are as follows:

1. This format avoids the disadvantages of the complex MC format.
2. Recent research shows that the MTF item format is very effective in terms of reliability and validity (Frisbie, 1992). Several researchers have established that the MTF format produces higher reliability estimates when compared with the conventional MC items (Albanese, Kent, & Whitney, 1977; Downing et al., 1995; Frisbie & Druva, 1986; Frisbie & Sweeney, 1982; Hill & Woods, 1974).
3. Frisbie and Sweeney (1982) reported that students perceived the MTF items to be easier and preferred to conventional MC. Oddly enough, Hill and Woods (1974) reported that the MTF items seemed harder, but several students anecdotally reported that the MTF items were better tests of their understanding.
4. This format is very efficient from the standpoint of item development, examinee reading time, and the number of questions that can be asked in a fixed time. For instance placing nearly 30 MTF items on a page is possible and administering more than 100 questions per 50-minute testing period is feasible. Given that guessing can play a strong role in such items, the effective range of scores for such a test will range from 50% to 100%. As with alternate–choice and true false, guessing will not greatly influence scores if enough items are used.

There are some potential limitations to this format:

1. The MTF format appears limited to testing the understanding of concepts by listing examples and nonexamples, characteristics and noncharacteristics. Although MTF items are further illustrated in chapters 4 and 5, the variety of content seems limited.
2. One technical problem that might arise with the MTF format is that of estimating reliability. Generally, MC test items (including the MTF format) are assumed to be independent from one another with respect to responses. Dependence occurs when one item cues another item. The technical term for this is *local independence*. Dependency among items of a single MTF item set would make that set of items operate as one MC item. Frisbie and Druva (1986) and Albanese and Sabers (1988) established that no dependence existed with their test data. Nonetheless, local dependency will result in an overestimation of reliability and is a caution with this format.

The MTF format is an effective substitute for the complex MC. Because the MTF has inherently good characteristics for testing knowledge, it should be more widely used. Figures 3.2 and 3.3 present examples that illustrate the variety and scope of this format for testing achievement.

A MTF Variation: The Multiple Mark (Multiple-Multiple-Choice)

According to Pomplun and Omar (1997), this variation has a history (Cronbach, 1941; Dressel & Schmid, 1953) but has been neglected until recently. With this variation, students mark the choice if it is correct or true and do not mark it or leave it blank if it is not correct. With MTF, students mark each option. These researchers found that when students guess with this MTF variation, they tend to make an error of omission. With MTF, they tend to guess true. This research, along with the study by Grosse and Wright (1985) calls our attention to problems with the true-false format and guessing strategies that might introduce bias in to test scores. Both MTF and the multiple mark formats get good grades in terms of performance when compared with other MC formats. As research continues to explore the MTF and multiple mark, we will see this format more widely used both in classroom testing and in formal, standardized testing programs. The economy of presenting many items in a short period of time is the main attraction of this format.

Context-Dependent Item Sets

Although this format has a long history, it is becoming more popular, perhaps because methods of scoring are improving. Terms used to describe item sets include *interpretive exercises, scenarios, vignettes, item bundles, problem sets, super-items,* and *testlets*.

The item set lends itself nicely to testing a variety of types of complex thinking, such as problem solving or critical thinking. One can present an introductory stimulus and then ask between 2 to 10 questions of any MC format concerning the information presented. In fact, the items in an item set may even be in a CR format. The stimulus for any item set might be a work of art, photograph, chart, graph, table, written passage, poem, story, cartoon, problem, experiment, narrative, or reference to an event, person, or object. An item writer has tremendous opportunity for creativity in shaping the item set.

Haladyna (1992a, 1992b) reviewed the research and development of this format and found that there has been very little formal study of this format, although this format appears in many standardized achievement tests and some professional licensing and certification examinations. For example, the National Association of Boards of Pharmacy has adopted this format for its national licensing examination. The 1997 revision of the National Council on Architectural Registration Boards (NCARB) adopted vignettes for its Building Design test.

Wainer and Kiely (1987) and Thissen, Steinberg, and Mooney (1989) introduced and described testlets as bundles of items with a variety of scorable predetermined paths for responding. This is a more complex idea than presented here, but the technical issues addressed by these authors offer some guidance in future research on item sets. Like the MTF format, context effects or inter-item dependence is a threat. In fact, the MTF format is a type of item set. If items are interdependent, the discriminative ability of the items, and the reliability of scores, will be diminished (Sireci, Thissen, & Wainer, 1991). Wainer & Kiely (1987) explored methods for scoring these *item bundles*, as applied to computerized adaptive testing, but these methods can apply to conventional fixed-length testing. They further explored hierarchical testlets, but this is futuristic, and little if any technology presently exists for doing this. One theoretician suspects that the problem of dependence may not be very serious if we score item sets as minitests (testlets). For more information about this, see the discussion by Rosenbaum (1988).

There are several types of item sets, each intended for a certain type of cognitive activity: (a) reading comprehension, (b) problem solving, (c) interlinear, and (d) figural. Each type is briefly discussed to provide the essence of what type of content is being measured, and each is illustrated. Item sets are also illustrated in chapters 4, 5, and 6.

Comprehension

The item set shown in Fig. 3.4 presents a poem for elementary grades language arts students, and asks questions to measure student understanding of the poem. Typically, one can get six MC items to a page. So the two-page item set might contain as many as 10 to 12 items, allowing for a brief introductory passage on the first page. Reading comprehension item sets are common in standardized tests. One page is devoted to a narrative or descriptive passage or even a short story, and the opposing page is devoted to questions that test understanding of the passage. The items might take a generic form an item set structure is established. Some items might systematically ask for the meaning of words, phrases, or the entire passage. Some items might ask for prediction (e.g., what should happen next?). Other items might analyze characterizes or plot. Once the set of items is drafted and used, it can be re-applied to other passages making the testing of comprehension very easy.

Problem Solving

Fig. 3.5 contains an example of mathematical problem solving, a variation of the traditional story problem, except that the test items provide for a more thorough problem solving exercise. It is important to note that each item tests a different step in the solution process. Item 1 requires the test-taker to decide the total cost by multiplying, deducting a 10% discount and correctly adding the handling charge to arrive at the total cost. Distractors should represent common student errors in solving this very difficult and complex problem. Item 2 requires

"The radiance was that of full, setting, and blood-red moon, which now shone vividly through that once barely discernible fissure of which I have before spoken as extending from the roof of the building, in a zigzag direction, to the base. While I gazed this fissure rapidly widened—there came a fierce breath of the whirlwind—the entire orb of the satellite burst at once upon my sight—my brain reeled as I saw the mighty walls rushing asunder—there was a long, tumultuous shouting sound like the voice of a thousand waters—and the deep and dank tarn at my feet closed sullenly and silently over the fragments of the House of Usher."

1. What is Poe referring to when he speaks of "the entire orb of the satellite"?

    A.   The sun.
    B.   The moon.
    C.   His eye

2. What is a "tarn"?

    A.   A small pool
    B.   A bridge
    C.   A marsh

3. How did the house fall?

    A.   It cracked into two pieces.
    B.   It blew up.
    C.   It just crumpled.

4. How did the speaker feel as he witnessed the fall of the House of Usher?

    A.   Afraid
    B.   Awestruck
    C.   Pleased

5. What does the speaker mean when he said "his brain reeled?"

    A.   He collected his thoughts.
    B.   He felt dizzy.
    C.   He was astounded.

FIG. 3.4. Comprehension type item set.

A thermos bottle is filled with a mixture of yeast, sugar, and water at 15 degrees C and the contents are examined 24 hours later.

1. What happens to the temperature?
   A. Increases
   B. Stays the same
   C. Decreases

2. What is the reason for that result?
   A. Yeast plans respire
   B. Yeast plants do not respire.
   C. Yeast plans absorb heat in order to live
   D. Heat cannot be conducted into or out of the thermos bottle

3. What has happened to the number of yeast plants?
   A. Increased
   B. Decreased
   C. Remained about the same

4. What about the sugar?
   A. Increased
   B. Decreased
   C. Remained about the same

5. What has happened to the content?
   A. Increased in oxygen
   B. Deceased in oxygen
   C. Increased in carbon dioxide
   D. Decreased in carbon dioxide

FIG. 3.5. Problem-solving type item set.

careful reading and the adding of the ticket price and the handling charge. Item 3 requires the test-taker to compute the amount of the 10% discount for each ticket and multiply by four.

Problem solving also can be done abstractly, for instance in a nursing examination. Fig. 3.6 illustrates a patient problem with a slight variation in the problem solving; the stimulus presents the problem and several questions later, a change in the scenario introduces a new problem, with new questions asked. This format can simulate a complex patient problem, and the line of questions can

Ms. Maty Petel, 28-years-old, is seen by her physician for complaints of muscular weakness, fatigue, and a fine tremor of the hands. Hyperthyroidism is suspected and her prescriptions include a radioactive iodine uptake test.

The nurse should explain to Ms. Petel that the chief purpose of a radioactive iodine uptake test is to
A.   ascertain the ability of the thyroid gland to produce thyroxine.
B.   measure the activity of the thyroid gland.
C.   estimate the concentration of the thyrotropic hormone in the thyroid gland.
D.   determine the best method of treating the thyroid condition.

In preparing Ms. Petel for the radioactive iodine uptake test, the nurse should provide which of the following instructions?
A.   "You will have to rest quietly in bed from the time you receive the radioactive iodine until the procedure is completed."
B.   "You will have to save all your urine for 48 hours after the ingestion of the radioactive iodine."
C.   "You will have a series of x-rays taken immediately after the injection of the radioactive iodine."
D.   "You will have a thyroid scan done 24 hours after taking the radioactive iodine."

The results of the diagnostic tests confirm a diagnosis of hyperthyroidism. Ms. Petel consents to surgery on a future date. Her current prescriptions include propylthiouracil.

The nurse should explain to Ms. Petel that the propylthiouracil initially achieves its therapeutic effect by which of the following actions?
A.   Lowering the metabolic rate
B.   Inhibiting the formation of thyroxine
C.   Depressing the activity of stored thyroid hormone
D.   Reducing the iodide concentration in the thyroid gland

Two months later, Ms. Petel is admitted to the hospital and undergoes a subtotal thyroidectomy.

During the immediate postoperative period, the nurse should assess Ms. Petel for laryngeal nerve damage. Which of the following findings would indicate the presence of this problem?
A.   Facial twitching
B.   Wheezing
C.   Hoarseness
D.   Hemorrhage

FIG. 3.6. Problem-solving item set in professional testing.

approximate the steps in a problem solving process. Such a format has a chance of replacing a higher-costing, less-efficient CR format.

Interlinear

Fig. 3.7 presents an example of the interlinear item set. This format is very useful for measuring writing skills via a MC format. As noted previously in this book, the measurement of writing skills via MC is efficient but does not have high fidelity. Knowledge of a skill is not exactly equal to the ability to perform a skill. The example in Fig. 3.7 is effective in terms of using a viable substitute for the more costly performance test.

For each numbered pair of choices, choose the letter next to the correct spelling of the word and fill in your answer sheet with that letter next to the number of the item.

There (1. A. our or B. are) many ways to invest money. You can earn (2. A. intrest or B. interest) by buying savings bonds. Or you can (3. A. bye or B. buy or C. by) corporate bonds. Or you can become a (4. A. part-owner or B. partowner) of a company by owning stock in a company. As a shareholder in a company, you can share in company (5. A. profits or B. prophets).

FIG. 3.7. Interlinear item set.

Innovative Variations of the Item Set Format

The pictorial variation of the context-dependent item set offers considerable opportunity to ask questions in interesting and effective ways. Fig. 3.8 provides an example of a table showing number of participants and number of injuries for 20 sports. Test items can be written to test one's understanding of the data and inferences can be made from these data. The test items reflect reading the table and evaluating the data presented.

Summary

The context-dependent item set is one of several effective ways to measure complex thinking. CR questioning has been a traditional option for such testing, but historical efforts as reported by the Technical Staff (1933, 1937) and more current efforts clearly illustrate that writing such items may be more difficult than with other formats, but the results are more realistic of mental processes involved in problem solving and in other types of higher level thinking.

SPORT	INJURIES	PARTICIPANTS[1]
1. Basketball	646,678	26.2
2. Bicycle riding	600,649	54.0
3. Baseball, softball	459,542	36.1
4. Football	453,684	13.3
5. Soccer	150,449	10.0
6. Swimming	130,362	66.2
7. Volleyball	129,839	22.6
8. Roller skating	113,150	26.5
9. Weightlifting	86,398	39.2
10. Fishing	84,115	47.0

[1]In millions.

SOURCE: National Safety Council's Consumer Product Safety Commission, National Sporting Goods Association

1. Which sport has the greatest number of participants?
    A. Basketball
    B. Bicycle riding
    C. Soccer

2. Which sport in the list has the least number of injuries?
    A. Gymnastics
    B. Ice hockey
    C. Fishing

3. Which of the following sports has the highest injury rate, considering numbers of participants?
    A. Basketball
    B. Bicycle riding

FIG. 3.8. Sports and the emergency room.

Unusual, Experimental Formats

This section introduced MC item formats proposed by various writers for specific purposes. Although these formats may not be widely known or used, they offer readers some idea about the creativity possible in the design of MC formats and their potential for measuring different types of cognitive behavior.

Sore-Finger Items

Bauer (1991) experimented with items that put grammar and other rules of writing in context but retain a MC format. This format resembles the interlinear item set, but each item stands alone.

> Which one of the following verbs is passive?
>
>   A   B
>
> The car is **being repaired**. The mechanic **replaced** the thermafropple. It
>
>   C   D
>
> **malfunctioned** yesterday. The car **needs** new tires as well.

Bauer (1991) claimed that this item format contextualizes writing and brings MC closer to realistic editing. He offered several other examples of items dealing with text idioms and vocabulary. The main idea is to provide written text in student language that has errors one would expect the students to find. It should be pointed out that Bauer's sore-finger items could be reformatted as item sets or in MTF formats where all verbs are subjected to active/passive determination, for example.

SECTION 3: FORMAT ISSUES

Calculators and MC

The use of inexpensive, simple electronic calculators became part of the MC testing experience. Because the National Council of Teachers of Mathematics (1989) strongly encouraged the use of calculators in instruction, using calculators both during instruction and for testing seems natural. Prominent standardized testing programs have recently introduced calculators into the testing situation (e.g., the recently renamed Scholastic Assessment Test and the Uniform Certified Public Accountancy Examination). However, the use of calculators may affect test results or redefine what we are trying to measure via our test items. Calculators can be used in the testing process but with the understanding that the use of calculators may change the performance characteristics of items intended for use without calculators.

Loyd (1991) made some noteworthy observations about using calculators with these item formats. Although calculation errors will likely diminish with the use of calculators, time needed for administration of a test consisting of calculator items may actually increase because the nature of the task being tested becomes more complex. Actual performance changes under conditions of calculators and no calculators, depending on the type of material tested (e.g., concepts, computation, problem solving) and grade level is very complex (Lewis & Hoover, 1981). Some researchers reported that calculators have little or no effects on test performance because the construct tested is not affected by using calculators (Ansley, Spratt, & Forsyth, 1988). Loyd (1991) further reported that these studies show that in an item-by-item analysis of the use of calculators, some items requiring calculation have improved performance because of calculators, whereas other items are impervious to the use of calculators. A study by Cohen and Kim (1992) showed that the use of calculators for college-age students actually changed the objective that the item represented. These researchers recommended that even the type of calculator used can have an untoward effect on item performance. Poe, Johnson, and Barkanic (1992) reported a study using a nationally normed standardized achievement test where calculators had been experimentally introduced several times at different grade levels. Both age and ability were found to influence test performance when calculators were permitted. Bridgeman, Harvey, and Braswell (1995) reported a study of 275 students who took SAT mathematics questions, and the results favored the use of calculators. In fact, Bridgeman et al. (1995) reported that one national survey indicated that 98% of all students have family-owned calculators and 81% of 12th-grade students regularly use calculators. The universality of calculators coupled with the ecological validity of using calculators to naturally solve mathematics problems seems to weigh heavily in favor of calculator usage in mathematical problem solving. Bridgeman et al. (1995) concluded that the use of calculators may increase validity but test developers need to be very cautious about the nature of the problems where calculators are used.

Therefore, research shows that the use of calculators should be governed by the nature of the task at hand and the role that calculators are supposed to play in answering the question. Thus, the actual format of the item (e.g., MC or true–false) is not the issue in determining whether a calculator should be used. Instead, we need to study the mental task required by the item in conjunction with the decision to use a calculator.

Calculators should be used with test items if the intent is to facilitate computations as part of the response to the test items. With standardized tests, calculators should be used in such a way as to minimize the variability of experience in using calculators, and interpretations should be made cautiously in this light. This is analogous to giving a test in English to a non-English speaker and drawing the conclusion that the person cannot read. Calculators should not be used if the standardized test was normed under conditions where calculators were not used. Thus, using calculators may provide an advantage that will bias the reporting and use of test scores. If the test is classroom-specific, then the use of calculators can be integrated with instruction, and any novelty effect of calculator use can be avoided.

On the Value of Accompanying Graphs, Tables, Illustrations, and Photographs

Many standardized tests and credentialing tests use graphs, tables, illustrations, or photographs as part of the item. There is some research and many pros and cons to consider before choosing to use accompanying material like this, and some research.

Primary among the reasons for using material is that it completes the presentation of the problem to be solved. In many testing situations it is inconceivable that we would not find such material. Imagine certification tests in medicine for plastic surgery, ophthalmology, dermatology, orthopedic surgery, and otolaryngology that would not have items that present patient diseases, injuries, or congenital conditions in as lifelike a manner as possible. Tests in virtually any subject matter can be enhanced by visual material. But are such items better than items with no visual material? Washington and Godfrey (1974) reported a study on a single military test where the findings provided a scant margin of advantage for illustrated items. Lacking descriptive statistics, this study can hardly be taken as conclusive.

The arguments against using illustrated items is that they require more space and take more time to read. One would have to have a strong rationale for using these items. That is, the test specifications or testing policies would have to justify illustrated items. The main advantage would appear to be face validity.

Dictionaries

To the extent that students have additional aids in taking tests there may be an improvement or decrement in the validity of test score interpretations. Calculators are one of these aids, and dictionaries are another that may prove useful in tests where the language used is not native to the examinee. Nesi and Meara (1991) studied the effect of dictionary usage in a reading test, citing an earlier study where the use of dictionaries had no effect on test scores or administration time. In this study, they found similar results, but noted that dictionaries in both studies did not necessarily provide information useful to students. It would seem that the provision of any aid would have to be justified on the grounds that it increases the ecological validity of the items as well as intentionally has information that students can use to answer items. Like calculators, the issue is more complex than would seem on the surface. Two studies in nearly 20 years is hardly informative about this issue.

Grouping Items

Studies on textbook effectiveness and instruction favor grouping content. The extension of grouping to test items has been tried experimentally by Townsend, Moore, Tuck, and Wilton (1991). They found no difference between items grouped by content and items distributed throughout the test. The idea behind grouping is to help students organize knowledge and even give inter-item clues. Although their study failed to produce the expected differences, this topic is worthy of more research.

Dangerous Answers

The purpose of any licensing/certification test is to pass competent candidates and fail incompetent candidates, to protect the public from incompetent practitioners. In the health professions, one line of promising research has been the use of *dangerous answers*, distractors that if chosen would have seriously harmful effects on patients portrayed in the problem. The inference is that a physician who chooses a dangerous answer potentially endangers his or her patients. The use of dangerous distractors in such tests would assist in the identification of dangerously incompetent practitioners.

Skakun and Gartner (1990) provided a useful distinction. Dangerous answers are choices of actions that cause harm to patients, whereas deadly answers are fatal actions. Their research shows that items can be successfully written, and that the inclusion of such items was agreed as content relevant by appropriate content review committees of professional practitioners. The study by Slogoff and Hughes (1987), however, provided a more thorough analysis. First, they found that passing candidates chose 1.6 dangerous answers and failing candidates chose 3.4 dangerous answers. In a followup of 92 passing candidates who chose four or more dangerous answers, a review of their clinical practices failed to reveal any abnormalities that would raise concern over their competence. They concluded that the use of such answers was not warranted. Perhaps the best use of dangerous answers is in formative testing during medical education and training in other professions.

SUMMARY

This chapter presented and evaluated seven types of MC item formats. The conventional MC, the matching, the alternate–choice, and the MTF formats are clearly useful for testing many types of cognitive behavior. The complex MC and true–false formats are not recommended. The item set is the most problematic because of our lack of experience with it and lack of research on its effectiveness. Scoring item sets presents a challenge as well. However, with significant increased interest in testing fluid abilities, the item set may be the most valued member of the family of MC formats to be used in the future. Some experimental item types were briefly discussed, but these formats need more research before they are recommended for classroom or large-scale testing.

II

DEVELOPING MULTIPLE-CHOICE ITEMS

Overview

Thorndike (1967) noted that constructing good test items is probably the most demanding type of creative writing imaginable. Not only is item writing creative, but the process demands our understanding of content we hope to test, the type of mental behavior intended, the choice of an item format, and the skill in actually writing the item. Insight, originality, and clarity are key ingredients in writing the test item. The set of three chapters in Part II of this book is comprehensive with respect to writing MC items. Chapter 4 provides a validated list of guidelines to follow when writing items. These guidelines derive from past and current research (e.g., Haladyna & Downing, 1989a, 1989b; Haladyna, Downing, & Rodriguez, 1998). Chapter 4 contains many examples of MC items, most of which violate item-writing guidelines. Chapter 5 deals with the important topic of writing MC items to test for various types of higher level thinking ranging from understanding to more complex types. One admitted limitation of MC is its inability to capture the essence of many types of higher level thinking. This chapter stretches the limits of MC, using this more efficient format to capture several types of high level thinking. Chapter 6 shows how structurally hollow items known as *item shells* can be used to unlock item writers' block and help novice item writers write good MC items.

4

WRITING THE ITEM

OVERVIEW

The procedure for developing test items in any testing program is substantial. For instance, Adams (1992) described the steps involved in item development for the Multistate Bar Examination. These steps include: an inventory of current items, an evaluation of the item pool, assignment of new items to be developed to well-trained item writers, reviews by other item writers, rewrites of promising items, professional editing, key checks, content checks, cognitive behavior checks, and tryouts with candidates. It is easy to see why the survival rate of new items is not very high. Our best efforts to create test items might result in less than 50% of the items remaining. For the instructor or teacher trying to develop classroom test items, the ideal procedure for writing the test item is daunting. Over a period of many years, teachers can develop adequate item pools for their classroom testing purposes, but the road to establishing a collection of high quality items is very long.

To add to this problem, Bormuth (1970) noted that item writing is not a science but simply a collection of guidelines based on experience and the wisdom of mentors, often captured in textbooks. Indeed, for some time little scientific basis existed for advice on item writing, but slowly a science is emerging. This chapter contains a collection of item-writing guidelines. The basis for these guidelines originally drew from two studies. The first, by Haladyna and Downing (1989a), involved an analysis of 46 textbooks and other sources on how to write MC test items. The result was a list of 43 item-writing guidelines. Author consensus existed for many of these guidelines. Yet for other guidelines, a lack of a consensus was evident. A second study by Haladyna and Downing (1989b) involved an analysis of more than 90 research studies on the validity of these item-writing guidelines. Only a few guidelines received extensive study. Nearly one half these 43 guidelines received no study at all. Since the appearance of these two studies and the 43 guidelines, we reprised our study (Haladyna, Downing, & Rodriguez, 1999). We examined 23 new textbooks and more than 30 new studies of these guidelines. From this review, we revised the original 43-guideline list.

The guidelines in this chapter are still based on advice, not scientific principles or laws of item writing as Bormuth had so strongly desired. All advice should be taken with the proviso that MC item writing is still only an emerging science. In the long term, theories of item writing, like Bormuth's algorithmic approach, are desirable. An item-writing theory might lead us to develop items in a more standardized way. In the short term, before the development and maturation of item-writing theories, item writers need a set of working principles and procedures on which to base their item writing. Item writers should apply these guidelines judiciously but not rigidly, as the authenticity of some guidelines still appears to be in question.

Table 4.1 summarizes these guidelines. As seen in that table, the main categories for these guidelines are content, format, style, stem, and choices. The guidelines are discussed in greater detail in this chapter, and examples are presented to exemplify a use or misuse of the guideline. Some of these guidelines are still controversial, and reference is made to a recent meta-analysis by Rodriguez (1997) bearing on the controversies.

CONTENT CONCERNS

1. Base Each Item on Specific Content and a Type of Mental Behavior.

Every item has a purpose on the test, based on the *test specifications*, also known as a *test blueprint* or a *two-way grid*. Generally, each item has a specific content code and mental behavior code. The content code can come from a topic outline or a list of major topics. The mental behavior is usually recall, understanding, critical thinking, or problem solving, as discussed in chapters 1 and 2. Chapter 5 presents more information on types of mental behavior that MC formats test well, and many examples of tests items measuring types of mental behavior are provided.

Table 4.1
Guidelines for Writing MC Items

CONTENT CONCERNS
1. Base each item on specific content and a type of mental behavior.
2. Keep the specific content of items independent from one another.
3. Avoid overly specific and overly general knowledge.
4. Focus each item on a single behavior instead of a chain of behaviors.
5. Avoid opinion-based items.
6. Avoid trick items.

FORMATTING CONCERNS
7. Use formats recommended in chapter 3; avoid true–false and complex MC formats
8. Format the item vertically instead of horizontally.

STYLE CONCERNS
9. Edit and proof items.
10. Keep vocabulary simple for the group of students being tested.
11. Use correct grammar, correct punctuation, capitalization, and spelling.
12. Minimize the amount of reading in each item.

WRITING THE STEM
13. Use either a question stem or a partial sentence.
14. Ensure that the directions in the stem are very clear.
15. Include the central idea in the stem instead of the choices.
16. Avoid window dressing (excessive verbiage).
17. Word the stem positively, avoid negatives such as NOT or EXCEPT.

WRITING THE CHOICES
18. Use as many good choices as possible, but three seems to be a natural limit.
19. Make sure that only one of these choices is the right answer.
20. Vary the location of the right answer according to the number of choices.
21. Place choices in logical or numerical order.
22. Keep choices independent; choices should not be overlapping.
23. Keep choices homogeneous in content.
24. Keep the length of choices about equal.
25. Avoid using *none-of-the-above, all-of-the-above,* or *I don't know.*
26. Phrase choices positively; avoid negatives such as NOT.
27. Avoid giving clues to the right answer, such as
    a. Specific determiners including always, never, completely, and absolutely.
    b. Clang associations, choices identical to or resembling words in the stem.
    c. Grammatical inconsistencies that cue the test-taker to the correct choice.
    d. Conspicuous correct choice.
    e. Pairs or triplets of options that clue the test-taker to the correct choice.
    f. Blatantly absurd, ridiculous options.
28. Make all distractors plausible.
29. Use typical errors of students to write your distractors.
30. Avoid humorous choices.

2. Keep the Specific Content of Items Independent from One Another.

A tendency when writing sets of items is to provide information in one item that helps the test-taker answer another item. For example, consider a line of questioning focusing on main ideas of a novel, as shown to the right. Once a student correctly answers Item 1, this testwise student will look for clues in the next item. If Roxie is correct for Item 1, it must be incorrect for Item 2. Kate and Roxie were

The following questions come from the story "Stones from Ybarra."

1. Who was Lupe's best friend?
    A.   Kate
    B.   Dolores
    C.* Roxie

2. Who was quarreling with Lupe?
    A.   Kate
    B.* Sara
    C.   Roxie

mentioned in Items 1 and 2, whereas Sara was not mentioned in Item 1. Might Sara be the right answer? Yes.

Testwise students use these kinds of strategies to select answers to items they do not know. In writing sets of items from a common stimulus, care must be exercised to avoid this kind of cuing.

3. Avoid Overly Specific and Overly General Knowledge.

The concept of specificity of knowledge refers to a continuum that ranges from overly specific to overly general. Most items should probably be written with this continuum in mind. We should avoid the extremes of this continuum.

Overly specific knowledge tends to be so specific as to be trivial to the core of learning required to support the performance of skills or higher level fluid ability. In other words, having some high level of a fluid ability does not seem logically connected to possessing ultra specific knowledge.

Who wrote the *Icon of Seville?*
A. Lorca
B. Ibanez
C. Rodriguez

The problem with general knowledge is that sometimes the generality is not true or it has many exceptions, and the question becomes ambiguous. The two examples on the next page show items testing content that is overly general.

Which is the most serious problem in the world?
A. Hunger
B. Education
C. Disease

What is life?
A. The exchange of oxygen for carbon dioxide
B. The existence of a soul
C. Movement

The judgment of specificity is subjective. Each item writer must decide how specific or how general each item must be to reflect adequately the content topic and type of mental behavior desired. The danger in being too general is that no answer is truly satisfactory. The danger in being too specific is that the answer may seem trivial.

4. Focus Each Item on a Single Behavior Instead of a Chain of Behaviors.

Every test item should be based on a single idea. The principle is that for a single fact, concept, principle, or procedure, one item represents one type of content. If a test item represents a complex, multistage thinking process to reach the correct answer, when a student misses the item, the instructor does not know what step in the process was not learned. Look at the item below. To simplify the improper fraction requires two steps, simplifying the improper fraction to 5/2 and then changing it to a complex fraction 2 ½. Complex, multistage thinking can be measured, but with a battery of items, such as found in the context-dependent item set or through a performance test with a checklist linked to these essential steps.

Simplify the improper fraction: 10/4.
A. 2 2/4
B. 2 ½
C. 5/2

5. Avoid Opinion-Based Items.

UNQUALIFIED OPINION ITEM
What is the best comedy film ever made?
   A.   Abbott and Costello go to Mars
   B.   Young Frankenstein
   C.   A Day at the Races

QUALIFIED OPINION ITEM
According to *American Film Institute*, what is the greatest American film?
   A.   It Happened One Night
   B.   Citizen Kane
   C.   Gone With the Wind
   D.   Star Wars

This advice derives from the value that items should reflect well-known and publicly supported facts, concepts, principles, and procedures. To test a student on an opinion about any content seems unfair, unless the opinion is qualified by some logical analysis, evidence, or presentation cited in the instructional materials. The items above show an unqualified opinion and a qualified opinion. The former item seems indefensible for most testing purposes, whereas the second item is probably more defensible. In other words, the criteria for judging "best" are unclear. Items like these need qualifiers.

6. Avoid Trick Items.

Trick items are hard to define and illustrate. In a review and study, Roberts (1993) found just a few references in the measurement literature on this topic. Roberts clarified the topic by distinguishing between two types of trick items: those items deliberately intended by the item writer, and those items that accidentally trick test-takers. Roberts' students reported that in tests where more tricky items existed, these tests tended to be more difficult. Roberts' study revealed seven types of items that students perceived as tricky including items:

1. where the item writer's intention appeared to deceive, confuse, or mislead test-takers;
2. representing trivial content (which violates one of our item writing guidelines),
3. where the discrimination among options was too fine,
4. that had window dressing that was irrelevant to the problem,
5. with multiple correct answers,
6. that present principles in ways that were not learned, thus deceiving students, and
7. that were so highly ambiguous that even the best students had no idea about the right answer. This type of trick item may also reflect a violation of guideline 2.

> Is there a 4th July in England?
>
> Some months have 31 days. How many have 28?
>
> How many animals of each gender did Moses bring on his ship?
>
> A butcher in the meat market is 6 feet tall. What does he weigh?

The items in the side panel are trick questions. Yes, there is a 4th of July in England. All months have 28 days. It was Noah not Moses who loaded animals on the ark, and the butcher weighs meat. Items like these are meant to deceive you not to measure your knowledge. Trick items often violate one of the other guidelines stated in Table 4.1. Roberts encouraged more work on defining trick items. His research has made a much needed start on this topic.

A negative aspect of trick items is that such questioning strategies, if frequent enough, build an attitude by the test-taker characterized by distrust and potential lack of respect for the testing process. There are enough problems in testing without contributing more by using trick items. As Roberts pointed out, one of the best defenses against trick items is to allow students opportunities to challenge test items and also allow them to provide alternative interpretations. Such procedures are discussed in chapter 7.

7. Use Formats Recommended in Chapter 3; Avoid True-False and Complex MC Formats.

This guideline merely states that any of the recommended formats presented in chapter 3 might be used for classroom testing or large-scale, standardized testing programs, but one should avoid the complex MC and true–false formats.

8. Format the Item Vertically Instead of Horizontally.

Below is a vertically formatted item.

> You draw a card from a deck of 52 cards. What is the chance you will draw a card with an odd number on it?
> A. 36/52
> B. 32/52
> C. About one half

Here is the item reformatted horizontally:

> You draw a card from a deck of 52 cards. What is the chance you will draw a card with an odd number on it?
> A. 36/52   B. $\frac{1}{2}$ C. 1/3   D. Not given

The advantage to the latter format is that it occupies less space on a page and is therefore more efficient as to printing cost. On the other hand, cramped items affect the look of the test. If appearance is important, horizontal formatting should be avoided. With younger children or test anxious test-takers, the horizontal format may be more difficult to read thus needlessly depressing test performance.

9. Edit and Proof Items.

Depending on the purpose of the test and the time and other resources devoted to testing, one should always allow for editorial review. The existence of editing does not guarantee a good item. Nonetheless, we should never overlook the opportunity to improve each item by subjecting it to editing because it probably improves our chances for getting a better item.

We should note caution here. Cizek (1991) reviewed the research on editing test items. He reported findings that suggest that if an item is already being effectively used, editorial changes may disturb the performance characteristics of those test items. On the other hand, O'Neill (1986) and Webb and Heck (1991) reported no differences between items that had been style edited.

Dawson-Saunders, Reshetar, Shea, Fierman, Kangilaski, and Poniatowski (1992, 1993) experimented with a variety of alterations of items. They found that reordering options along with other editorial decisions may affect item characteristics. A prudent strategy would be to concentrate on editing the item before instead of after its use. If editing does occur after the first use of the item, these authors suggested that one consider content editing versus statistical editing. The former suggests that content changes are needed because the information in the item needs to be improved or corrected. Statistical alteration would be dictated by information showing that a distractor did not perform and should be revised or replaced. The two kinds of alterations may lead to different performances of the same item. Expert test builders consider items that have been statistically altered as new. Such items would be subject to pretesting and greater scrutiny before being used in a test. Reordering options to effect key balancing should be done cautiously.

10. Keep Vocabulary Simple for the Group of Students Being Tested.

The purpose of most MC tests is to measure knowledge, and in some circumstances, the MC format may be good for measuring problem solving, critical thinking, and other fluid abilities of a complex nature. The purpose of the test is not to measure one's ability to read. Therefore, vocabulary should be simple enough for the weakest readers in the tested group. If reading is confounded with the achievement being measured, then the test score will reflect a mixture of reading comprehension ability and the knowledge or ability you intended to measure.

11. Use Correct Grammar, Punctuation, Capitalization, and Spelling.

Errors of grammar, punctuation, capitalization, and spelling reflect on the test-maker. Such errors suggest carelessness and negligence, perhaps, the tip of a great iceberg: poor test development. You do not want to convey this impression to test-takers. Another issue is that such errors are often distracting to test-takers, particularly those who have test anxiety. By failing to be more careful in editing, these errors may prove harmful to test-takers causing them to score lower than they would have had the errors not been there.

12. Minimize the Amount of Reading in Each Item.

Items that require extended reading lengthen the time needed to complete a test. Consider an important test with alternative forms and a fixed time period. The test with wordy items requiring much reading will provide for fewer items per fixed period than the test with fewer words per item.

Thus, one benefit of reducing examinee reading time is that the number of items one can ask in a fixed time is increased. Because the number of items given in a fixed time directly affects the reliability of test scores and the adequacy of sampling of content, items need to be as brief as possible. Because reliability and validity are two very important characteristics of test scores, one should try to reduce reading time. Unless we can show that lengthy reading is necessary, such as with some complex problem solving exercises, items with high reading demand are not used.

WRITING THE STEM

13. Use Either a Question Stem or a Partial Sentence

Chapter 3 presented both the question and completion (partial sentence) formats. This rule is one that has received some recent study and has been debated (Gross, 1994). Although the two formats offer very little difference in appearance and length, the question format is a simpler and more direct tactic for eliciting a response from a test-taker. In keeping with the idea that MC question should emphasize attainment of knowledge instead of reading, we should attempt to design the item to read clearly. The question format appears to more effectively accomplish that end. But research has not shown any appreciable difference when these two formats are compared (Rodriguez, 1997).

Statman (1988) provided a logical analysis of the issue. She maintained that with the completion format, one has to retain the stem in short-term memory while completing this stem with each option, evaluating the truthfulness of each option or if short-term memory fails, the test-taker has to range back and forth from the stem to each option, making a connection and evaluating the truth of that connection. Testing is anxiety provoking, and the added stress of the completion format may contribute to test anxiety, a problem that already troubles about one in four test-takers according Hill & Wigfield (1984). The mental steps involved in answering a completion item also takes more time, which is undesirable.

The problem is great for the native speaker, but the learner with English as a second language has an even greater problem. From the standpoints of reading comprehension, administration time, anxiety, the quality of the test item, and efficiency, the question format is a more effective way to test for knowledge than the completion format.

An example in the question format is:

Which retirement investment is most recommended by investment counselors for young investors?
A.   U.S. Bonds
B.   Certificate of Deposits
C.* Fast growth stock funds

An example in the partial-sentence (completion) format is:

Regarding aging people, in other modern societies,
A.   programs for the elderly are generally a low priority item.
B.   programs for the elderly are more advanced when compared to the United States.
C.   programs for the elderly are about the same as in the United States.
D.   the elderly have been shown to have different needs, based on cultural differences.

Although logical analysis argues against the completion format, this format is and will often be used. The correct way to write a completion format is to develop the stem so that the correct answer and all distractors complete the sentence begun in the stem, shown above.

There is a popular completion format that should not be used. This format has a sentence in the stem with one part or several parts missing. The rule to apply here is to never leave a blank in the middle or at the beginning of the stem.

These "blankety-blank" formats are difficult for students to read. Such items also require more time to administer and reduce the time spent productively answering other questions. For these many reasons, the use of internal or beginning blanks in completion-type items should be avoided.

The _____ format is the best way to format a MC item.
A. completion
B. question
C. fill-in-the-blank

Child abuse is an example of _____ violence, whereas sexism is an example of _____ violence.
A. aggressive; structural
B. emotional; psychological
C. structural, emotional

14. Ensure That the Directions in the Stem are Very Clear.

The item stem should always phrase the problem to be answered by each option in a clear and unambiguous way. The test-taker should always know what is being asked in the item. When an item fails to perform with students as

Unclear Directions in The Stem
    Regarding gravitation:

Clearer Directions in the Stem
    Which of the following best shows the concept of gravitation?

intended, there are often many reasons. One of these reasons may be that the stem did not present the problem in a clear enough manner to most students. This lack of clarity is difficult to detect when items are written, but the item review or item tryout will often reveal why an item did not perform.

15. Include the Central Idea in the Stem Instead of the Choices.

One fault in item writing is to have a brief stem and most of the content in the options. The item below shows an unfocused stem. This stem provides no direction or idea about what the item writer wants to know. Unfocused stems are a frequent type of error made by novice item writers. The test-taker does not obtain the intent of the item after reading the stem. The second item in the example below takes the same idea and provides a more focused stem. Notice that the options are more alike in their structure. The test-taker knows that the item writer wants the student to show their understanding of the term *corporal punishment*.

UNFOCUSED STEM
Corporal punishment
A.   has been outlawed in many states.
B.* is psychologically unsound for school discipline.
C.   has many benefits to recommend its use.

FOCUSED STEM
What is corporal punishment?
A.* A psychologically unsound form of school discipline
B.   A useful disciplinary technique if used sparingly
C.   An illegal practice in our nation's schools

---

16. Avoid Window Dressing (Excessive Verbiage).

Some items contain words, phrases, or entire sentences that have nothing to do with the problem stated in the stem. One reason for doing this is to make the item look more lifelike or realistic, to provide some substance to it. The example on the next page shows excessive verbiage, and a version with window dressing removed follows.

There are times when verbiage in the stem may be appropriate. For example, in problems where the test-taker sorts through information and selects information to solve a problem, excessive information is necessary. (Note that the phrase *window dressing* is used exclusively for situations where useless information is embedded in the stem without any purpose or value.) In this latter instance, the purpose of excessive information is to see if the examinee can separate useful from useless information.

WINDOW DRESSING
High temperatures and heavy rainfall characterize a humid climate. People in this kind of climate usually complain of heavy perspiration. Even moderately warm days seem uncomfortable. Which climate is described?
A. Savanna
B.* Tropical rainforest
C. Tundra

NO WINDOW DRESSING
Which term below describes a climate with high temperatures and heavy rainfall?
A. Savanna
B.* Tropical rainforest
C. Tundra

In the item to follow, the student needs to compute the discount, figure out the actual sales price, compute the sales tax, add the tax to the actual sale price, and compare that amount to $9.00. The $12.00 is irrelevant, and the student is supposed to ignore this fact in the problem-solving effort. This is not window dressing.

A compact disc at the music store was specially priced at $9.99, but typically sells at $12.00. This weekend, it was marked at a 20% discount from this special price. Sales tax is 6%. Tina had $9.00 in her purse and no credit card. Does Tina have enough money to buy this compact disc?

---

17. Word the Stem Positively; Avoid Negative Phrasing.

The reason for this guideline comes from a consensus of experts in the field of testing who feel that the use of negative words in the stem have negative words effects on students and their responses to such items. Some research on the use of negative words also suggests that students have difficulty understanding the meaning of negatively phrased items. Rodriguez (1997) recently supported this guideline after his review of research.

> Which is NOT an advantage of the MC format over the CR format for measuring knowledge?
> A. Better sampling of content
> B. Greater reliability of test scores
> C. Ease of construction

According to Harasym, Doran, Brant, and Lorscheider (1992), a better way to phrase such an item is to remove the NOT and make the item a multiple true–false MTF with more options:

> Which are benefits of MC testing? Mark A if true or B if false.
> 1. Greater potential for content sampling (A)
> 2. Greater potential for high reliability (A)
> 3. More appropriate for measuring aspects of performance (B)
> 4. Objectively scored (A)
> 5. Able to measure higher level thinking (A)
> 6. Subject to guessing (A)
> 7. Free of bias (B)

Another benefit of this transformation is that because the options now become items, more items can be added, which may increase test score reliability.

Another variation of this guideline is that when a negative term is used, it should be stressed or emphasized by placing in bold type, capitalizing it, or underlining it, or all of these. The reason is that the student often reads through the not and forgets to reverse the logic of the relation being tested. This is why the use of not is not recommended for item stems.

WRITING THE CHOICES

18. Use as Many Distractors as Possible
But Three Seems to be a Natural Limit.

A growing body of research supports the use of three options for conventional MC items (Andres & del Castillo, 1990; Bruno & Dirkzwager, 1995; Downing

& Haladyna, 1997; Landrum, Cashin, & Theis, 1993; Lord, 1977; Rodriguez, 1997; Sax, & Michael, 1991; Trevisan, Sax, & Michael, 1991, 1994). One issue is the way distractors perform with test-takers. A good distractor should be selected by low achievers and ignored by high achievers. As chapters 8 and 9 show, a science of option response validation exists and is expanding to include more graphical methods.

To summarize this research on the correct number of options, evidence exists to suggest a slight advantage to having more options per test item, but only if each distractor is doing its job. Haladyna and Downing (1996) found that the number of useful distractors per item on the average, for a well-developed standardized test was between one and two. Another implication of this research is that three options may be a natural limit for most MC items. Thus, item writers are often frustrated in finding a useful fourth or fifth option because they do not exist.

The advice given here is that one should write as many good distractors as one can, but should expect that only one or two will really work as intended. It does not matter how many distractors one produces for any given MC item but it does matter that each distractor performs as intended. This advice runs counter to most standardized testing programs. Customarily, answer sheets are used with a predetermined number of options, such as four or five. However, both theory and research support the use of one or two distractors, so the existence of nonperforming distractors is nothing more than window dressing. Thus, test developers have the dilemma of producing unnecessary distractors, which do not operate as they should, for the appearance of the test, versus producing tests with varying degrees of options.

One criticism of using fewer instead of more options for an item is that guessing plays a greater role in determining a student's score. The use of fewer distractors will increase the chances of a student guessing the right answer. However, the probability that a test-taker will increase his or her score significantly over a 20-, 50- or 100-item test by pure guessing is infinitesimal. The floor of a test containing three options per item for a student who lacks knowledge and guesses randomly throughout the test is 33% correct. Therefore, administering more test items will reduce the influence of guessing on the total test score. This logic is sound for two-option items as well, because the floor of the scale is 50% and the probability of a student making 20, 50, or 100 successful randomly correct guesses is very close to zero.

19. Make Sure That Only One of These Choices is the Right Answer.

Even though a content expert writes the item and chooses the correct answer, inadvertently some items end up with more than one right answer or no right answer. The way to prevent such embarrassment is to either have other content experts verify the right answer, as suggested in chapter 7, or field test the item and determine if the correct answer has an expected performance.

20. Vary the Location of the Right Answer According to the Number of Options.

To avoid response set, the tendency of some students to follow patterns in the options, we vary the location of the right answer. If we use a three-option format, about 33 % of the time A, B, and C will be the right answer respectively. If A was the right answer most of the time, some students would notice this pattern and benefit from this knowledge, which is unfair.

21. Place Options in Logical or Numerical Order.

In the formatting of test items for a test, the options should always appear in either logical or numerical order.

WRONG	RIGHT
What is the cost of an item normally sells for $9.99 that is discounted 25%?	What is the cost of an item that normally sells for $9.99 that is discounted 25%?
A. $5.00	A. $2.50
B.* $7.50	B. $5.00
C. $2.50	C. $6.66
D. $6.66	D.* $7.50

Answers should always be arranged in ascending or descending numerical order. Remember that the idea of the item is to test for knowledge in a direct fashion. If a student has to hunt for the correct answer unnecessarily, then we unnecessarily increase the stress level for the test and we waste the test-taker's time.

Logical ordering is more difficult to illustrate, but some examples offer hints at what this guideline means. The following example illustrates illogical ordering.

> What are three most important concerns in fixing a thermofropple?
> A.* O-ring integrity, wiring, lubricant
> B.   Positioning, O-ring integrity, wiring
> C.   Lubricant, wiring, positioning

Although we may criticize such a questioning strategy for other reasons, this popular format is additionally and unnecessarily confusing because the four possible terms (Lubricant, O-ring integrity, positioning, wiring) are presented in an inconsistent order. A more logical ordering and presentation is:

> A.* Lubricant, O-ring integrity, wiring
> B.   O-ring integrity, positioning, wiring
> C.   Lubricant, positioning, wiring

The above options were placed in alphabetical order. There are instances where the logical ordering relates to the form of the answers instead of the content:

> When an item fails to perform, what is the most common cause?
> A.* The item is faulty.
> B.   Instruction was ineffective.
> C.   Student effort was inadequate.
> D.   The objective did not match the item.

In this instance, answers should be presented in order of length, short to long.

22. Keep Choices Independent; Choices Should Not Be Overlapping.

This item writing fault is very much like inter-item cuing discussed in Rule 2. If options are overlapping, these options are likely to give a clue to the test-taker about the correct answer and the distractors.

If overlapping options are correct, then the item may have two or more correct answers. The item to the right illustrates this problem. Numerical problems that have ranges that are close make the item more difficult. More important in this example, options A, B, C, and D overlap slightly. If the answer is age 25, then one can argue that both C and D are correct even though the author of the

> What age range represents the physical "peak" of life?
> A. 11-15
> B. 13-19
> C. 18-25
> D. 24-32
> E. over 32

item meant C. This careless error can be simply corrected by developing ranges that are distinctly different. The avoidance of overlapping options also will prevent embarrassing challenges to test items.

23. Keep Choices Homogeneous in Content.

The use of options that are heterogeneous in content is often a cue to the student. Such cues are not inherent in the intent of the item but an unfortunate accident. Therefore, the maintenance of homogeneous options is good advice. Fuhrman (1996) suggested another way to view the issue of option homogeneity. If the correct answer is shorter or more specific or stated in other language, perhaps more technical or less technical, these tendencies might make the item easier. A standard practice of keeping options homogeneous, avoids the possibility of giving away a right answer. The following item illustrates both homogeneous and heterogeneous options.

> HOMOGENEOUS OPTIONS
> What will make salsa hottest?
> A. Adding habanero chili peppers
> B. Adding Anaheim chili peppers
> C.* Adding jalapeno chili peppers
>
> HETEROGENEOUS OPTIONS
> What will make salsa hottest?
> A. Adding the seeds of peppers
> B. Adding spices
> C.* Adding jalapeno chili peppers

24. Keep Choice Lengths Similar.

One common fault in item writing is to make the correct answer the longest. This may happen very innocently. The item writer writes the stem and the right answer, and in the rush to complete the item adds two or three hastily written wrong answers that are shorter than the right answer.

25. Avoid Using the Choices *None of the Above*, *All of the Above*, and *I Don't Know*.

Research has increased controversy over this guideline, particularly the first part, dealing with the option none of the above. Studies by Knowles and Welch (1992) and Rodriguez (1997) do no completely concur the use of this rule as suggested by Haladyna and Downing (1989b). Gross (1994) argued that logical versus empirical arguments should determine the validity of an item-writing guideline. For this reason and the fact that most textbook authors support this guideline, *none of the above* is still not recommended.

Perhaps the most obvious reason for not using this format is that a correct answer obviously exists and should be used in the item. No advantage exists for omitting the right answer from the list of choices. One argument favoring using *none of the above* in some circumstances is that it forces the student to solve the problem rather than choose the right answer. In these circumstances, the student may work backward, using the choices to test a solution. In these instances, a constructed-response format should be used.

The use of the choice *all of the above* has been controversial (Haladyna & Downing, 1989a). Some textbook writers recommend and use this choice. One reason may be that in writing a test item, it is easy to identify one, or two, or even three right answers. The use of the choice *all of the above* is a good device for capturing this information. However, the use of this choice may help testwise test-takers. For instance, if a test-taker has partial information (knows that two of the three choices offered are correct), that information can clue the student into correctly choosing *all of the above*. Because the purpose of a MC test item is to test knowledge, using *all of the above* seems to draw students into test-taking strategies more than directly test for knowledge. One alternative to the *all of the above* choice is the use of the MTF format. Another alternative is simply avoid *all of the above* and ensure that there is one and only one right answer. For these reasons, this option should be avoided.

The intention for using *I don't know* as an choice is to minimize the role of guessing the correct choice. Unfortunately, not all children, or adults, treat this choice the same way. Sherman (1976) studied patterns of response for children answering items that had the *I don't know* choice. Differences existed for region, gender, personality variables, and ethnic background. Nnodim (1992) also studied this option but in the context of scoring that considered whether a student chose it or not. His results showed no advantage for higher achieving students over lower achieving students, as the Sherman study contended. However, the use of this option does not seem justified until the rules for scoring are clearly stated and research shows a decided advantage for *I don't know*. With respect to Sherman's results, why would anyone want to use such an choice with children knowing that it benefits some groups of test-takers at the expense of others? In other words, the *I don't know* choice appears to have great potential for producing bias in test scores. Therefore, it should be avoided.

26. Phrase Choices Positively.

We should phrase stems positively, and the same advice applies to choices. The use of negatives such as NOT and EXCEPT should be avoided in choices as well as the stem. Occasionally, the use of these words in an item stem is unavoidable. In these circumstances, we should highlight these words, boldface, capitalize, or underline, so that the test-taker will not mistake the intent of the item.

27. Avoid Various Clues to the Right Answer.

This advice pertains to a collection of common clues to item writing. Fuhrman (1996) suggested this subset of clues to right answers.

1. Specific determiners. Specific determiners are so extreme that seldom are they the correct answers. Specific determiners include such terms as *always, never, totally, absolutely,* and *completely*. A specific determiner may occasionally be the right answer. In these instances, their use is justified if the distractors also contain other specific determiners.

> Which of the following is most likely to produce the most student learning?
> A. Never assign homework on Fridays.
> B.* Homework is consistent with class learning.
> C. Always evaluate homework the next day.

2. Clang associations. Sometimes, a word or phrase that appears in the item stem will also appear in the list of choices, and that word or phrase will be the correct answer. If a clang association exists and the word or phrase is NOT the correct answer, then the item may be a trick question.

> Who were known as the Magnificent Seven?
> A.   A touring softball team
> B.* A group of seven cowboys
> C.   A rock and roll group

3. Grammatical inconsistencies. Sometimes a grammatical error in writing options may lead the test-taker to the right answer, as shown below:

> The most effective strategy in playing winning tennis for a beginner is:
> A. hit with more pace.
> B.* to keep the ball in play.
> C. volley at the net as often as possible.

For the learner of tennis, all three options may make sense, but only B is grammatically consistent with the partial-sentence stem.

4. Pair or triplets of options.
Sometimes an item contains highly related choices that provide clues to the test-taker that the pair or triplet of highly related terms are not the correct choice. Although the item may seem somewhat ridiculous, the fact that the first three choices are related points to D as the correct choice.

> Which best explains levitation?
> A. Principles of physics
> B. Principles of chemistry
> C. Principles of biology

5. Blatantly absurd, ridiculous options. When writing that third or fourth option there is a temptation to develop a ridiculous choice either as humor or out of desperation. In either case, the ridiculous option will seldom be chosen and is therefore useless.

You may not know the person in the second choice (B), but you know that it is the right answer, because the other two are absurd. If A or C are correct, then the item is a trick question.

> Who is best known for contributions to electronics?
> A. Comedian Jay Leno
> B.* Robert Sveum
> C.   Actor Bruce Willis

28. Make All Distractors Plausible.

As we know, the main use of a MC test item is to measure knowledge. Therefore, the right answer must be right, and the wrong answers must clearly be wrong. The key to developing wrong answers is plausibility.

Plausibility refers to the idea that the item should be correctly answered by those who possess a high degree of knowledge and incorrectly answered by those who possess a low degree of knowledge. A plausible distractor will look like a right answer to those who lack this knowledge. The effectiveness of a distractor can be statistically analyzed, as chapter 8 shows. Writing plausible distractors comes from hard work and is the most difficult part of MC item writing.

29. Use Common Errors of Students.

One typical suggestion is that if we gave completion items (open-ended items without choices), students would provide the correct answer and plausible wrong answers that are actually common student errors. In item writing, the good plausible distractor comes from a thorough understanding of common errors. In this example the distractor, A, is a logical incorrect answer for someone learning simple addition.

$$77 + 34 =$$
A.   101
B.* 111

30. Avoid the Use of Humor.

Although humor is a valuable tool in teaching and learning and can do much to lessen tension and improve the learning environment, we should avoid it in testing. Items containing humor can reduce the number of plausible distractors, and therefore make the item artificially easier. Humor also might encourage the student to take the test less seriously. Limited research on the use of humor shows that, in theory, humor should reduce anxiety, but sometimes highly anxious test-takers react in negative ways. Because the test measures knowledge, the use of humor detracts from this purpose and does little good. The safe practice is to avoid humor.

GUIDELINES FOR SPECIFIC MC FORMATS

The preceding pages of this chapter focused on general item-writing advice. Many of these guidelines apply equally to the various formats presented in chapter 3, including alternate-choice, matching, MTF, and item sets. However, special guidelines may be needed that are unique to each format. The next section provides some specific guidance to item writers for these other formats.

Advice for Writing Matching Items

Generally, the set of choices for a matching item set is homogeneous in terms of content. Because the benefit of a matching format is the measurement of understanding of a single learner outcome, the homogeneity of content is a characteristic of a set of matching items.

Also, the number of choices should not equal the number of items. The basis for this advice is that test-takers may try to match up items to choices believing in a one-to-one correspondence. If this is true, then there is inter-item cuing. If this is not true, students will be confused.

Advice for Writing Alternate-Choice Items

Because alternate-choice is a short form of conventional MC, no unique guidelines appear in this section. It is important to ensure that the single distractor is the most common student error, if this format is to work properly. Therefore, special effort should be given to writing the distractor for each alternate-choice item.

Advice for Writing MTF Item Clusters

1. The number of MTF items per cluster may vary within a test.
2. Conventional MC or complex MC items convert nicely to MTF items.
3. No strict guidelines exist about how many true and false items appear in a cluster, but expecting a balance between the number of true and false items per set seems reasonable.
4. The limit for the number of items in a cluster may be as few as three or as many as would fit on a single page (approximately 30 to 35).

Guidelines for True-False Testing Items

Although many experts currently do not recommend the true–false format, a body of knowledge exists on the writing of these items. In the interest of providing a balanced presentation of guidelines for various formats, this section exists.

Frisbie and Becker (1991) surveyed 17 textbooks and extracted 22 common guidelines for writing true–false items. Most of the guidelines are similar if not identical with those presented earlier in this chapter. One thing to keep in mind however is that most of these guidelines fail to reach consensus from writers of textbooks or from research. Nonetheless, Frisbie and Becker provided many excellent insights into –false item writing that are reviewed and discussed below.

Balance the Number of True and False Statements.

Key balancing is important in any kind of objectively scored test. This guideline refers to the balance between true and false statements, but it also applies to negative and positive phrasing. So, it is actually key balancing as applied to true–false items.

Use Simple Declarative Sentences.

A true–false item should be a simple, non complex sentence. It should state something in a declarative rather than interrogative way. It should not be an elliptical sentence.   Examples are provided:

Desirable:
    The principal cause of lung cancer is cigarette smoking.
Undesirable:
    The principal causes of lung cancer are cigarette smoking and
    smog.

Write Items in Pairs.

Pairs of items offer a chance to detect ambiguity. One statement can be true and another false. One would never use a pair of items in the same test, but the mere fact that a pair of items exists offers the item writer a chance to analyze the truth and falsity of related statements. Examples are provided:

Overinflated tires will show greater wear than underinflated tires.
(false)
Underinflated tires will show greater wear than overinflated tires.
(true)

Make Use of an Internal Comparison Rather Than an Explicit Comparison.

When writing the pair of items, if comparison or judging is the mental activity, write the item so that we clearly state the comparison in the item. Examples are provided:

> Desirable: In terms of durability, oil-based paint is better than latex-based paint.
> Undesirable: Oil-based paint is better than latex-based paint.

Take the Position of an Uninformed Test-taker.

This pair of items contains a true statement and a common misinterpretation.

> A percentile rank of 85 means that 85% of items were correctly answered. (false)
>
> A percentile rank of 85 means that 15% of test-takers have scored lower than people at that percentile rank. (false)

The first example is a common misunderstanding among students learning about testing. The second item is another common misinterpretation of the concept of percentile rank.

Use MC Items as a Basis for Writing True-False Items.

Good advice is to take a poor functioning MC item and convert it to several true-false items.

> The best way to improve the reliability of test scores is to
> A. increase the length of the test.
> B.* improve the quality of items on the test.
> C. increase the difficulty of the test.
> D. decrease the difficulty of the test.
> E. increase the construct validity of the test.

The items that might be extracted from the item above are as follows:

> Which actions listed below improve the reliability of test scores?
> Mark A if it tends to improve reliability, mark B if not.
> 1. Increase the length of the test. (A)
> 2. Improve the quality of the items. (A)
> 3. Substitute with more difficult items. (B)
> 4. Increase the construct validity of the test. (B)

Notice how the original item is expanded via the MTF format to increase the breadth of testing the understanding of this principle.

Advice for Writing Item Sets

Little research exists on the writing or effectiveness of item sets (Haladyna, 1992a), despite its existence in the testing literature for more than 50 years. Nonetheless, some advice is offered regarding certain aspects of the item set.

Format the Item Set So All Items are on a Single Page or Opposing Pages of the Test Booklet.

This step will ensure easy reading of the stimulus material and easy reference to the item. When limited to two pages, the total number of items ranges from 7 to 12. If the MTF or alternate-choice formats are used with the item set, then many more items can be used.

Use Algorithms if Possible.

An algorithm is a standard item set scenario with a fixed number of items. The scenario can be varied according to several dimensions producing many useful items. Haladyna (1991) presented examples for teaching statistics and art history. Chapter 6 provides illustrations and examples of these.

Use Any Format That Appears Suitable With the Item Set.

With any item set, conventional MC, matching, alternate-choice, and MTF items can be used. The item set encourages considerable creativity in developing the stimulus and using these various formats. Even CR item formats, such as short-answer essays, can be used.

SUMMARY

Since the appearance of two syntheses concerning item-writing guidelines by Haladyna and Downing (1989a, 1989b), several prominent essays and much research has contributed to a revision of the original list of 43 item-writing guidelines to a more parsimonious list of 30. Guidelines were also presented for other MC formats.

5

MEASURING HIGHER LEVEL THINKING

OVERVIEW

Defining and measuring various types of higher level thinking has been a major challenge to educators for most of this century. This chapter follows basic premises presented in the first part of the book. MC is best suited for testing knowledge and least suited for testing cognitive skills. For many fluid abilities where a strong cognitive component exists, MC has a limited role. This chapter illustrates how to use MC to measure knowledge of facts, concepts, principles, and procedures. The classification of cognitive behavior used in this chapter does not exclude the use of CR item formats. The goal of this chapter is to enable MC item writers to more effectively write MC test items that reflect knowledge and aspects of some fluid abilities that have proven difficult to measure in the past. The items that appear in this chapter as examples of different types of content and cognitive behavior are set in an instructional context, but certainly, the kind of testing suggested here could be applied to noninstructional settings, such as standardized tests for prediction, graduation, licensing, certification, selection, and placement.

THE PROBLEM WITH DEFINING HIGHER LEVEL THINKING

Frisbie, Miranda, and Baker (1993) reported a study of tests written to reflect material in elementary social studies and science textbooks. Their findings predictably indicated that most items tested isolated facts. These findings are

103

confirmed in other recent studies, for example, Stiggins, Griswold, and Wikelund (1989). Although recalling information may be a worthwhile educational objective, current approaches to teaching require more complex outcomes than recall (NCTM, 1989, Nickerson, 1989; Snow, 1989; Snow & Lohman, 1989; Stiggins et al., 1989). School reformers call for learning in various subject matter disciplines to deal with life's many challenges (*What Works*, 1985). Constructivists argue that all learning should be meaningful. Little doubt exists in this era of test reform that the measurement of higher level thinking is and will continue to be preeminent.

Cognitive Taxonomies

The best-known approach to classifying educational objectives reflecting higher level thinking is the Bloom taxonomy (Bloom, Engelhart, Furst, Hill, & Kratwohl, 1956). Sanders (1966), in his book *Classroom Questions*, provided many examples of test items based on this taxonomy. Despite the widespread popularity of this cognitive taxonomy, Seddon (1978) reported in his review of research on the validity of the taxonomy that evidence neither supports nor refutes the taxonomy. A research study by Miller, Snowman, and O'Hara (1979) suggested that Bloom's taxonomy represents fluid and crystallized intelligence. Seddon's discouraging review and the few studies existing on this subject leave those interested in developing test items that measure higher level thinking in somewhat of a quandary about what system to use to define and classify examples of complex cognitive behavior.

Other methods for classifying cognitive behavior have been proposed. Gagne's (1968) hierarchy is one, but there is little evidence of its construct validation or widespread use. Royer, Cisero, and Carlo (1993) presented a theoretical analysis of cognitive behaviors based on the learning theory of Anderson (1990). Although this promising work has a theoretical basis and a growing amount of research supporting its use, it does not seem ready for implementation. Authors of textbooks on testing routinely offer advice on how to measure higher level thinking in achievement tests. But none of these systems is widely recognized or used. In fact, we are continually reminded of the difficulty of constructing good higher level thinking items by studies such as Frisbie et al. (1993), but prescriptions for correcting the problem have been unsuccessful.

Theoretical Versus Prescriptive Methods

A distinguishing characteristic of these taxonomies is whether each is based in cognitive theory or is simply prescriptive.

Theoretically based methods for defining and measuring higher level thinking involve theoretical terms, statements of cause–effect relation, and principles governing how various types of higher level thinking are developed. Cognitive learning theories provide that basis. The proposal by Royer et al. (1993) is a good example of theory-driven higher level thinking.

Prescriptive taxonomies provide simple nontheoretical descriptions of cognitive behavior that hopefully have achieved consensus among users of the taxonomy. The Bloom taxonomy is prescriptive. As observed previously in this section, prescriptive methods also have not been successful to date, as evidenced in research studies.

In the short term, prescriptive efforts, like the Bloom taxonomy might prove useful, but in the long term, theory-based taxonomies should prove more enduring and useful because these will be integrated with instruction in a clear and understandable way.

The Definition and Measurement Dilemma

A dilemma exists when one want to measure cognitive behavior. One aspect is the definition of the construct to be measured, and the other aspect is the measurement itself. In construct validity, defining the construct is the initial step, and measuring is the second step.

In chapter 1, the problem of defining fluid abilities was described. Terms such as *creative thinking, problem solving,* and *critical thinking* are seldom described in ways that are easy to teach and test.

Each test item is designed to measure a specific behavior. Each student responds to MC items with a pattern of right and wrong answers, but no one really knows the exact mental processes used in making the correct choices in a test. For any test item, the test-taker may appear to be thinking at a higher level, but in actuality, the behavior may be remembering identical statements or ideas presented before, perhaps verbatim in the textbook or stated in class and carefully copied into the student's notes. Mislevy (1993) provided an example of a nuclear medicine physician who at one point in his or her career might detect a patient's cancerous growth in a computerized-tomography (CT) scan using reasoning, but at a latter time in his/her career would simply view the scan and recall the patient's problem. The idea is that an expert works from memory, whereas a novice has to employ more complex strategies in problem solving. In fact, the change from a high cognitive demand to a lower cognitive demand for the same complex task is a distinguishing characteristic between experts and novices in an area. The expert simply uses a well-organized knowledge network to respond to a complex problem easily, whereas the novice has to employ several higher level thought processes to arrive at the same answer. This is the ultimate dilemma with any test item. Although a consensus of content experts may agree that an item appears to measure one type of behavior, it may measure an entirely different type of behavior simply because the test-taker has a different set of experiences than the other test-takers. This may also explain our failure to isolate measures of higher level thinking, because test items intended to reflect loftier modes of thinking are often just recall to a highly experienced test-taker. Therefore, no empirical or statistical technique will ever be completely satisfactory. Whatever measures we develop will only approximate what we think the examinee is thinking when answering the test item.

With this disclaimer being given about higher level thinking, this chapter describes methods for writing and classifying MC items for types of cognitive behavior, including simple recall. Referring to an earlier distinction drawn in this chapter, the methods are descriptive. These methods do not derive from any theory of cognitive development. But the types of cognitive behavior are very common to any typology or taxonomy of cognitive behavior including the Bloom taxonomy. The methods appearing in this chapter are heuristic, intended for item writers who want to develop items beyond simple recall.

A SIMPLE TYPOLOGY

As much as possible, the advice on item development and items used to illustrate various types of content and cognitive behaviors will include conventional MC, alternate-choice, multiple true–false (MTF), and context-dependent item sets. Examples are intentionally simple and familiar as opposed to esoteric.

THE CONTENT DIMENSION

The content of a course of study or a lesson can be listed in terms of learner outcomes (objectives), textbooks or training materials, lectures, or audio or videotaped material. From these sources, all content can be classified as representing one of four categories: fact, concept, principle, or procedure.

A *fact* is a declarative statement that is undeniably true. For example:

Des Moines is the capital of Iowa.
An adverb cannot modify a noun.
A cold air mass tends to sink, whereas a hot air mass tends to rise.

As presented here, facts are singular entities, usually beyond dispute, and widely accepted by all. Testing for factual knowledge is very easy and commonplace.

A *concept* is a class of objects or events that share a common set of characteristics. For example, a chair has the intended function of seating a person, usually has four legs, a flat surface, and a backrest. The concept *chair* is noted by these distinguishing characteristics and others that may not be as important. A table might resemble a chair, but lacks the backrest, although teenagers may use a table as a chair. Other examples of concepts include:

> love, specific gravity, cash flow, pencil, student grades, validity
> insect, politician, swimming pool, plant, power, school, value

Concepts can be abstract (love) or concrete (pencil), and other distinctions have been drawn among concepts (see Markle & Tiemann, 1970); for a more thorough discussion).

A *principle* is a statement of relationship, usually between two or more concepts. A principle often takes the form: "If . . . , then . . ." Some examples of principles are shown below:

Principles come in two forms: immutable law and probable event. For instance, it is immutable that hot air rises on our planet and cold air sinks. Many principles of science are laws. On the other hand, principles exist that have either exact probabilities or subjective probabilities (guesses). A basketball player who is tall often gets more rebounds than a player

Probabilistic Principles
Overconsumption usually results in weight gain.
If you exercise a muscle, then it will likely grow.
Immutable Principles
Hot air rises, cold air sinks.
Cable TV goes out during the most exciting moment of a game.

who is short. Driving without a seat belt fastened is more likely to result in serious personal injury than driving with the seat belt fastened. With more data or a statistical model, we can estimate the probability of an event.

A *procedure* is a series of related actions with an objective or desired result. The actions may be mental or physical.

> Solving a four-step algebra problem
> Developing a plan for a company picnic
> Writing a poem or short story
> Determining how to best shop for food each week

Mental Procedures. Mental procedures are not directly observable, but we can set up observational encounters where we can see the results of a mental procedure. At best we can infer that someone has demonstrated the performance of a mental procedure. Mental procedures are illustrated on the next page.

Physical procedures. Unlike mental procedures, these are directly observable. Here are four examples.

Whether it is a mental or physical procedure, there is a mental basis in all procedures. We can easily test for knowledge of procedures, but testing for knowledge of a procedure is never a substitute for the testing for the skill of performing that procedure. The proper way to test for the acquisition of a mental or physical skill is through a performance test, usually involving direct observation.

> Performing surgery
> Batting in a softball game
> Preparing a pot of coffee
> Playing the piano

THE COGNITIVE OPERATIONS DIMENSION

In this typology of cognitive behaviors, five distinct mental operations are recalling, understanding, predicting, evaluating, and problem solving. Because the typology is two-dimensional, 20 different combinations exist (4 content classifications by 5 cognitive operations). However, it is difficult to conceptualize some combinations of content and operations, as we will see.

The next sections present items that illustrate each combination that is desirable and possible. Different formats are used as they seem appropriate. With most examples, brief discussions are offered for the item-writing strategy involved.

Recalling Behavior

Recalling refers to the simple recreation of a fact, concept, principle, or procedure. Recall is the simplest form of cognitive behavior. Each possible type of questioning strategy dealing with a type of content is presented as an example below.

    Recalling a fact. This type of question is the most common. It is easy to write. We might argue that factual knowledge is fundamental to learning, but a tendency exists for testing this far more than is justified.

    Recalling a concept. With this item, we assume that the learners have already been presented with the word *hesitant* as meaning *recalcitrant*.

    Recalling a principle. Although a principle may seem to reflect higher level thinking, the only concern here is that the test-taker can recall the principle verbatim from the original presentation. Again, we assume that the correct option was presented verbatim from reading or instruction and the learner was asked to select the correct principle exactly as presented in a class or from a textbook. Option B is actually a true statement, but it is not the answer to the question.

    Recalling a procedure. As with the other examples, procedures are presented and the correct answer is a verbatim association. A variation of recalling a procedure is recalling a specific step in a procedure.

Who put the "ram" in the "ramma lamma ding dong"?
A. Dion and the Belmonts
B. Danny and the Juniors

Which of the following defines the concept "recalcitrant"?
A. Lazy
B. Hesitant

Which of the following principles explains orographic rain?
A. Hot air rises and water vapor condenses.
B. Mountains tend to cool air resulting in transforming water vapor to rain.

Which procedure is recommended for a faulty Johnson rod?
A. Replacement
B. Repair

Recall is the simplest of behaviors. Critics of teaching and testing are well supported by studies showing that we test recalling behavior well and consistently do not test beyond recall. In initial stages of learning, recalling may be a necessary step, thus the previous examples serve to provide a complete set of examples for the typology.

Understanding Behavior

Understanding involves the identification of a paraphrased version of an original fact, concept, principle, or procedure as presented during instruction. In other words, understanding is an attempt to measure what is sometimes called *comprehension*.

Understanding can be shown in six distinct ways. Each will be described and illustrated with several examples of understanding test items. The MTF format is an excellent way to test for understanding. The alternate-choice is also an effective device for measuring understanding behavior.

1. Given a definition, ask the test-taker to identify the correct fact, concept, principle, or procedure from a list of plausible facts, concepts, principles, or procedures.

The first example shows understanding of a concept.

What is the term we use to describe the use of words to reflect sounds, such as BANG?
A.   Metaphor
B.* Onomatopoeia

The next example shows understanding of a principle:

Which of the following best explains the relationship between longevity and diet?
A.   Long life is most often associated with genetic endowment.
B.* Those living beyond their life expectancy are usually on a vegetarian diet.
C.   Those living less than life expectancy usually have a high cholesterol level.

The previous item is supposed to reflect explanation of a principle in a manner not exactly as presented in a class or a textbook. The student shows understanding by choosing the correct answer based on understanding instead of recollection.

The following item could easily be classified as *recalling a concept* if the learner had been exposed to the exact phrasing. The item has the test-taker recalling the name of a procedure.

What is the procedure for a formal hearing of an employee's complaint?
A.   Concern
B.   Protest

---

2. Given a concept, principle, or procedure, ask the test-taker to identify the correct definition from a list of plausible definitions.

This next example shows understanding of a concept:

Which represents a "typographical error?"
A.   A misspelled word
B.   Missing punctuation
C.* A typing error

This example shows understanding of a principle:

Which explains the reason for a thunderstorm in the summer?
A.   Hot and cold air masses collide along a weather front.
B.* During a humid day, rapid heating causes hot air to rise and the rapid cooling causes a rapid, violent rainstorm.
C.   Hot, moist air is pushed into a mountain; the rising air cools and

> How do you hit a spin serve in tennis?
> A.   Overhead motion
> B.   Side motion
> C.   Wrist flick

The next example shows understanding of a procedure. The student should select an answer that shows understanding of the procedure in serving a tennis ball. This is the first step in developing a skill.

3. Given several plausible examples of a concept, principle, or procedure, ask the test-taker to choose the example

> Which are examples of satellites?
> Mark A if an example and
> B if not an example.
> 1.   Earth (A)
> 2.   Sun (B)
> 3.   Moon (A)
> 4.   Asteroid (A)

that exemplifies the concept, principle, or procedure. This class of methods is very effective because many examples can be generated that are free of recall associations. With the previous two classes of methods, the threat of measuring recall instead of understanding is always present because the test-taker may have encountered the exact phrasing previously. A MTF format is very useful for understanding a concept in this instance. The example shows this format's use with a series of heavenly bodies. The student must use the definition to analyze the traits of each satellite and nonsatellite.

Understanding a Procedure. This item demonstrates what to do when a patient is admitted with a serious injury. For most practitioners, this kind of behavior is automatic and taken from memory, but for the early learner, understanding the procedure is critical to safe practice.

> A patient is taken to the emergency room after a serious auto injury.
> What is the first thing you should check?
> A.   The patient's medical insurance or ability to pay
> B.* That the patient can breathe
> C.   That the patient has suffered shock

Items like this are easy to write. However, the danger is that the item might represent recall instead of understanding. The consideration of the mental behavior shown when answering the item relates to the developmental level of persons being tested.

4. Given the concept, principle, or procedure, ask the test-taker to identify a best example from a list of several plausible examples. This differs from the previous class of understanding items in that all may be correct, but one is clearly the best. This example shows understanding a concept. This item stem is probably the most dependable for understanding a concept. The word *hyperbole* could be replaced by any other concept, which completes the item stem. Then unfamiliar examples can be generated as options. This format also can be effectively converted to multiple true–false, so that each option becomes a true–false item. This changeover will increase the number of items possible for this situation.

> Which is an example of hyperbole?
> A. It kistimary to cuss the bride.
> B. Cruel kindness
> C.* Mile- high mound of popcorn

This example shows understanding a principle. Emphysema is a concept. Causes involve principles. The test-taker must identify a cause among plausible causes. This behavior may be recalled in some instructional circumstances; here it was intended to be understanding behavior.

> Which kind of person is likely to get emphysema?
> A. Habitual drinker
> B. Chronic drug user
> C.* Habitual smoker

This example shows understanding of a procedure:

> What is liposuction?
> A. A technique for removing lipids
> B. A type of diet and exercise regimen for weight loss and toning
> C.* A surgical procedure for removing body fat

5. Given several plausible characteristics of a concept, principle, or procedure, ask the test-taker to identify the correct fact, concept, principle, or procedure. This next example shows understanding a concept:

This animal has eight legs and an external skeleton. What is it?
A.   Insect
B.* Arachnid
C.   Mollusk

This animal has eight legs and an external skeleton. What is it?
A.   Ant
B.* Spider
C.   Scallop

The two above items illustrate a general and a specific questioning strategy using the same stem.

This next example shows understanding a principle:

Which event below shows why it tends to rain in mountainous areas?
A.   Hot air mixes with cold air.
B.   Rapid evaporation saturates the air.
C.* Hot moist air condenses when it rises.

This example shows understanding of a procedure:

Which term do we use to describe the act of rapidly cooking food in a pan using cooking oil?
A.   Frying
B.   Par boiling
C.* Saute

---

6. Given a concept, principle, or procedure, ask the test-taker to identify the outstanding characteristic or distinguishing feature. The plausible list also may contain characteristics and non characteristics, distinguishing features or nondistinguishing features. This example shows understanding a concept:

Which distinguishes the albatross from most other birds?
A.*   Its size
B.   Its reputation in mythology
C.   Its tendency to protect its young

This next example shows understanding of a principle:

A piece of paper ignites in your oven. What caused this?
A.*   The temperature was above 451° Fahrenheit.
B.   Cooking oil probably covered the paper.

This example shows understanding of a procedure:

When filming an action movie, why does the director have the camera man shake the camera during an action scene?
A. The audience likes it.
B.* It creates an action effect.
C. It prevents the audience from seeing the flaws in the scene.

Understanding behavior is the simplest form of higher level thinking. In Bloom's taxonomy, understanding would probably be considered comprehension. As shown in this section, a variety of questioning techniques can be used to test one's ability to understand a fact, concept, principle, or procedure. The test items are somewhat easy to prepare. Many item stems are generic in nature. One need only identify the concept, principle, or procedure, some characteristics, and some examples and nonexamples. These are the basic materials for understanding test items.

PREDICTING BEHAVIOR

Critical thinking is characterized by several features. One of these is predicting an outcome when given some information. Predicting behavior involves the identification of consequences from a given situation. Generally, to predict an outcome, one has to use a principle. It is difficult to imagine predicting behavior based on any other type of content. With principles, predictions may be absolute or probable. We are mainly interested in probable events because they represent the uncertainty in most learning involving principles.

Item stems for predicting behavior exist in several generic forms: The following item exemplifies predicting-type, MC items. Remember that any of these items could be mistaken for a recall item, if the material had been presented to a student in this exact format. In these circumstances we are testing understanding of a principle or its application in a different setting or situation.

> If . . . , then what happens?
> What is the consequence of . . . ?
> What would happen if . . . ?

> What is the main cause of the increase in national debt from 1945 to 1985?
> A.   Increases in spending in education
> B.   Increases in defense spending
> C.   Inflation
> D.* Efforts of the congress to meet the nation's needs

This item asks the student to analyze economic history in a period and extract the cause of a condition. Causes and effects are good settings for predicting-type MC items. These kinds of questions apply in virtually any subject matter and situation. We could write such items in a multiple true–false format as appears at the top of the next page.

This is a very effective format to test the thorough understanding of a principle. In this instance, it is an absolute as opposed to a probable phenomenon. As we examine more complex behavior, the varieties of questioning strategy are fewer as are the examples. Fortunately, the use of several generic item stems provides a good basis for this kind of questioning. The next chapter provides item shells that expand this technology for systematic item writing.

When an object floats in water, what is certain?
Mark A if true or B if false.
1.   The specific gravity of the object is more than 1.00. (B)
2.   The density of the object exceeds one gram per cubic
        centimeter. (B)
3.   The object is lighter than water. (A)
4.   The pressure of water is greater than the pressure of the
        object. (B)
5.   The volume of water is greater than the volume of the object.
        (B)
6.   The weight of water for a set volume is more than the weight
        of the object for the same set volume. (A)

EVALUATING BEHAVIOR

Another aspect of critical thinking is the ability to evaluate. All evaluating
behavior requires the test-taker to choose one from among several choices based
on a criterion or criteria. There are many real-life examples of evaluating
behavior, for example, buying a box of cereal, choosing a new car, deciding
which street to take on the way to work, deciding when to go to sleep, or
deciding where to take a vacation. Evaluating behavior is also important in
problem solving. Three types of evaluating behavior are presented here that can
be tested with MC item formats.

The first is merely using a predetermined criterion to decide. For instance,
considering cost, which box of cereal among four or five should one buy? The
criterion might be changed to *taste, nutrition,* or *manufacturer's reputation.*

The second is when we present a problem, we ask the test-taker to choose
the criterion or criteria to use in making a decision. For the same cereal buying
problem, the test-taker might be asked to figure out which criterion is most
important to the health of the family members eating the cereal.

The third requires the test-taker to both select a criterion or criteria and
make a decision. Using the cereal example again, we might ask a test-taker to
choose both a criterion and a cereal in the same problem. The problem with this
third type is that when a student misses the item, it is difficult to tell if the
difficulty is in choosing a criterion or applying the criterion toward making a
decision.

Evaluating behavior is the most realistic and lifelike. Many test items can
be drawn from real life. The item maker can draw from personal experiences to

develop evaluating items or may work within the framework of case scenarios—contrived situations that provide opportunities for demonstrating evaluating behaviors. Because recent reform initiatives call for learning to be in a meaningful context (NCTM, 1989; *What Works*, 1985), evaluating questions can be easily created.

Following are examples evaluating behavior for each type of content and evaluating question strategy.

Evaluating facts. How does one evaluate facts? The following example shows how this is done.

Which is the longest way from San Francisco to San Jose?
A.   Via Interstate 5
B.   Via the Junipero Serra Freeway
C.* Via State Route 1

Although this is a fact, students who have not encountered this fact but are presented with a map and a legend can evaluate each choice to answer the test item.

Evaluating concepts. The concept of cleaning bleached hair is tested in this item. Four products are evaluated based on effectiveness.

Which is the most effective for cleaning bleached hair?
A.   Benzine
B.   Conditioner
C.* A mild shampoo

Evaluating principles. Whether the principle is absolute or probable, options can be written to set up evaluation based on a principle.

What is the most effective way to cool a home in a humid climate?
A.   Evaporative cooler
B.* Air conditioner
C.   Fan

Although all four answers are correct, the stem calls for an evaluation as to the criterion of effectiveness. The item could be modified to use the criterion of cost, which would change the answer. Or the criterion could be environmental impact, in which case air conditioner might be the worst answer among the choices.

Evaluating procedures. Given the choice of several procedures in a situation, the test-taker has to choose the best answer among the options. As with the previous example, the criterion of effectiveness could be replaced with other criteria, such as cost, long-term effectiveness, or complications. Another variation to increase the richness of this questioning strategy is to use other problems, for example, sunburn, insect bites, or skin rashes.

> What is the most effective way to treat athlete's foot?
> A. Let nature take its course.
> B. Wear sandals.
> C. Use a fungicidal foot power.
> D.* Use a fungicidal salve.

Evaluating procedures can be also treated in the format of a context-dependent item set where a vignette sets the stage for questioning and one or several items can get the test-taker to evaluate among choices in terms of a criterion. Evaluating behavior is somewhat easy to test with the array of techniques in this section. As with predicting and understanding behavior, some generic forms of questioning exist, and these are more adequately treated in the next chapter.

PROBLEM-SOLVING BEHAVIOR

This type of cognitive behavior is very complex. Several steps are involved, usually requiring combinations of recalling, summarizing, predicting, and evaluating behavior. Because there are many kinds of problem solving, this term is seldom adequately defined. Cognitive psychologists are still struggling with the defining, teaching, and measuring of problem-solving behavior (Snow, 1989; Snow & Lohman, 1989). There is little doubt that this type of behavior is important. The natural testing format for problem solving is constructed-response. It is extremely difficult to set a problem-solving experience in a MC format.

One major reason is that problem solving is often a multistep experience, and the conventional MC item does not conveniently allow for a step-by-step mental process. Evaluate the example in Fig. 5.1. It attempts to simulate the problem-solving process by asking MC questions pertaining to specific steps in the problem-solving process. The context-dependent item set is a very convenient

Molly was shopping at Superfoods and has a $0.50 double coupon for a six-pack of 12-ounce Double Bubble Cola priced at $1.49. She could also buy the same Double Bubble Cola in a 32-ounce container for $0.79. xxxIf she bought two 32-ounce containers, she could use that same coupon.

1.   What is the cost of the six-pack when applying the double coupon?
      A. $1.49
      B. $0.99
      C.*$0.49
      D. Cannot tell from information given

2.   What is the cost of the two 32-ounce containers when applying the double coupon?
      A. $0.58
      B. $0.79
      C. $1.58
      D. Cannot tell from information given

3.   Molly decides she has to buy four six-packs for the party on Friday at her house.
      Which combination below is the best value (LEAST EXPENSIVE)?
      A.*Four six-packs
      B. Nine 32-ounce containers
      C. One six-pack and seven 32-ounce containers
      D. Three six-packs and two 32-ounce containers
      E. Cannot tell from information given

FIG. 5.1. Problem-solving item set.

and effective way to test problem solving and comes close to a performance-type item where no clues are given in the choices. As a test and item designer, each of us has to compare the trade-offs in using the more efficient MC versus the more expensive and less efficient performance for measuring problem solving.

The next example of this comes from Biggs and Collis (1982) in the framework of teaching mathematical problem solving, as shown in Fig. 5.2. The stimulus condition of a test provides a basis for a variety of questions testing higher level thinking, but the item set is particularly well suited for testing problem-solving behavior. Time needed to answer this item set may be significant.

A final example of a mathematics task prototype is taken from Mislevy (1993b). In this example, which he adopted from the National Research Council, three performance items are given that require professional judgment from one or two experts. Figure 5.3 presents an adapted version. Two of the original three

This is a machine that changes numbers. It adds the number you put in three times and then adds two more. So, if you put in 4, it puts out 14.

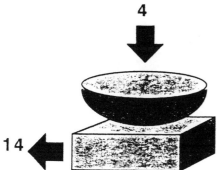

1.   If 14 is put out, what number was put in?
      A. 2
      B. 3
      C.* 4
      D. Cannot say from information given.

2.   If we put in a 5, what number will the machine put out?
      A. 4
      B. 14
      C.* 17
      D. Cannot say from information given.

3.   If we got out a 41, what number was put in?
      A. 5
      B. 12
      C.* 13
      D. Cannot say from information given.

4.   If x is the number that comes out of the machine when the number y is put in, write down the formula that will give us the value of y whatever the value of x is.
      A.*   y = 3 times x plus 2
      B. x = 3 times y plus 2
      C. y = 3 plus y plus 2 times 3
      D. x = 3 plus y plus 2 times 3

Fig. 5.2. Mathematic problem-solving.

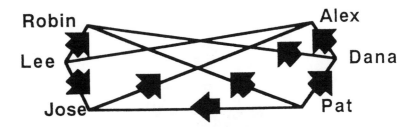

1.   Who won the game between Pat and Robin?
     A.*Pat
     B. Robin
     C. Cannot tell from this information

2.   Who is in first place?
     A. Robin
     B. Lee
     C. Jose
     D. Pat
     E. Dana
     F. Alex

3.   Dana and Lee have not yet played each other. Who do you think will win?
     A. Dana
     B. Lee
     C. Cannot tell without more information

4.   What information is needed to answer item 3?
     A. How Dana and Lee did against Alex
     B. Their won-and-loss records
     C. Who the better player is

Fig. 5.3. A mathematics task prototype.

items are easily adapted to the MC format thus eliminating the judgmental scoring task. The third task requires the student to build a table based on won/loss records. The underlying cognitive behaviors are arguably the same, no matter which format is used. Researchers are now studying similarities and differences in the cognitive processes elicited by these contrasting formats when the cognitive task appears approximately the same. Indeed Snow (1993) provided an analysis of popular arguments for and against MC and CR formats and developed a research agenda that is very much needed. Until this research leads to more definitive guidelines, the MC format is currently desirable from the many standpoints offered in chapter 2. Ultimately, we will probably learn that in most circumstances, it is immaterial whether the item format selected is MC or CR for many types of mental skills. Chapter 10 provides more discussion of this important issue. Certainly the efforts of cognitive psychologists and measurement theoreticians will likely increase the complexity and appropriateness of test formats in the measurement of these highly desired higher level thinking behaviors.

Summary

This chapter has presented some ideas for how to write MC items for various types of content and cognitive behaviors. MC is well suited for measuring recall and understanding of facts, concepts, principles, and procedures. CR is not up to this task. For mental skills, CR type items have the greatest fidelity, but MC might be viewed as a less expensive proxy, but with some risk. For higher level thinking, such as found in critical thinking and problem solving, MC can measure limited aspects. The context-dependent item set is well suited for measuring higher level thinking found in critical thinking and problem solving. A recurring theme in this chapter has been that the experience of the learner has everything to do with the type of cognitive behavior being exhibited. Therefore, our interpretations of test results are inherently flawed. Despite this frustrating dilemma, at best we can purposefully define various types of higher level thinking, and teach and test accordingly with the hope that the encounters are genuinely higher level and not simply recall.

6

ITEM SHELLS

OVERVIEW

Item writing is a very slow and painful process for most item writers. Experience shows that despite best intentions, even carefully edited items often fail to perform as intended. We need methods that accelerate the item-writing process and, also, produce higher quality items. The item shell technique provides a means for accomplishing these two goals.

Item modeling is a variation of the item shell technique that has been evolving at the National Board of Medical Examiners. Research on this method's effectiveness points to high speed production of high quality items (Shea et al., 1992). A section is devoted to item modeling. This technique has powerful implications for testing professional competence.

ORIGIN OF THE ITEM SHELL

As reported earlier in this book, attempts to make item writing a science have not yet been fruitful. An ambitious endeavor was Bormuth's (1970) algorithmic theory of item writing. He suggested a complex, item-writing algorithm that transformed prose into MC test items. His theory of achievement test item writing made item development more scientific and less subject to the caprice and whims of idiosyncratic item writers. The problem, however, was that the algorithm had too many steps making its use impractical. Others have tried similar methods with similar lack of success, including facet theory and designs, item forms, amplified objectives, among others (Roid & Haladyna, 1982).

Haladyna and Shindoll (1989) created the item shell based on the need for a systematic method of MC item writing in the direction of these earlier efforts. However, the item shell also permits item writers some freedom that, in turn, permits greater creativity in designing the item. The item shell is also seen as a more efficient process for writing MC items than any other methods that presently exist. Item shells simplify writing items that are in the desired direction of measuring higher levels of cognitive behavior.

Millman and Westman (1989) developed a computerized procedure for designing item shells. Their software elicits a series of inquiries and responses that produces item shells to match a particular type of cognitive behavior. The item writer can create a new item based on the shell provided by the computer. However, no progress has been reported in advancing this technology and no research has been reported on its use.

DEFINING AN ITEM SHELL

Haladyna and Shindoll (1989) defined an item shell as a "hollow" item containing a syntactic structure that is useful for writing sets of similar items. Each item shell is a generic MC test item.

A simple item shell is shown. One could take this blank item stem and substitute almost any concept or principle in any field or subject matter. Writing the stem is only one part of MC item writing, but often it is the most difficult part.

Which is an example of (any concept)?

A. Example
B. Plausible non-example
C. Plausible non-example

Writing a correct option and several plausible distractors is also difficult, but once we write the stem, an important part of that item-writing job is done.

A limitation of the item shell technique is that you may develop an abundance of items that all have the same syntactic structure, such as shown in the previous example. We may want greater variety in questioning strategies. Because appropriate sampling of content is a major concern in achievement and ability testing, the test items should representatively sample from different types of taught and learned content. Therefore, we recommend the use of a variety of item shells rather than generating hundreds of items from a single shell, which is entirely possible and even easy to do.

Another limitation of the item shell technique is that it does not apply equally well to all types of content and cognitive behaviors. There are many instances where the learning task is specific enough so that generalization to sets of similar items is simply not possible.

As will be shown later in this chapter, we can adapt the item shell for a variety of types of content and cognitive operations, as described in chapter 5. In fact, chapters 5 and 6 are good complements to one another.

DEVELOPING ITEM SHELLS

There are generally two ways to develop item shells. The first and easiest way is to co-opt the generic shell presented in Fig. 6.1. These shells are nothing more than item stems taken from successfully performing items. The content expert should identify the fact, concept, principle, or procedure being tested and the type of cognitive behavior wanted (i.e., recalling, defining, predicting, evaluating, or problem solving).

A second way is to transform highly successful items into item shells. To do so, one should follow certain steps. Fig. 6.2 shows a variety of item shells for medical problem solving. To transform items into shells we must meet several conditions. First, we must identify an item as a successful performer. Chapter 8 discusses the criteria for evaluating item responses. Second, the type of cognitive behavior represented by the item must be identified. Third, the content that the item tests must be identified. Fourth, we might follow a series of item-writing steps. These steps are:

1. Identify the stem of a successfully performing item.

> A 6-year-old child is brought to the hospital with contusions over the abdomen and chest as a result of an automobile accident. What should be the initial treatment?

2. Underline key words or phrases representing the content of the item.

> A <u>6-year-old child</u> is brought to the hospital with <u>contusions over the abdomen and chest</u> because of an <u>automobile</u> accident. What should be the initial treatment?

<u>Understanding—Concepts</u>.
Which is the best definition of this (concept)?
Which is the meaning of this (concept)?
Which is synonymous with this (concept)?
Which is like this (concept)?
Which is characteristic of this (concept)?
Which is an example of this (concept)?

<u>Understanding—Principles</u>.
Which is the best definition of ...?
Which statement below exemplifies the principle of ...?
Which is the reason for or cause of ...?
Which is the relationship between ... and...?
Which is an example of the principle of ...?

<u>Critical Thinking—Predicting Using a Principle</u>.
What would happen if ...?
If (there is an action), then what happens?
What is the consequence of (an action)?
What is the cause of a (result)?
Information given. What is the expected result?
Which distinguishes (one concept from another concept)?

<u>Critical Thinking—Evaluating Using Facts and Concepts</u>.
Which is the most or least important, significant, effective ...?
Which is better, worse, higher, lower, farther, nearer, heavier, lighter ...?
Which is most like, least like ...?
What is the difference between ... and ...?
What is a similarity between ... and ...?

<u>Critical Thinking—Evaluating Using a Principle</u>.
Which of the following principles applies to evaluating something?
What is the most important factor contributing to ...?

<u>Evaluating—Procedures</u>.
Which of the following procedures best applies to the solution of a problem?

<u>Problem Solving—Concepts, Principles, Procedures</u>.
Problem presented. What is the best way to solve this problem?
Problem presented. What is the solution?

FIG. 6.1. Generic item shells.

Defining

What are the main symptoms of ... ?

What is the most common (cause, complication, symptom, or consequence) of (a procedure, disorder, or action)?

Comment: These item shells provide for the generation of a multitude of items dealing with the symptoms of patient illnesses.

Predicting

What is the most common (cause, or symptom) of a (patient problem)?

Comment: This very general item shell provides for a variety of combinations that mostly reflects anticipating consequences or cause-and-effect relationships arising from principles. Understanding of concepts is also important for successful performance on such items.

Evaluating

Patient illness is diagnosed. Which treatment is likely to be most effective?

Comment: This item shell provides for a variety of patient illnesses, according to some taxonomy or typology of illnesses and treatment options. Simply stated, one is the best. Another questioning strategy is to choose the reason that a particular treatment is most effective.

Applying

Information is presented about a patient problem. How should the patient be treated?

Comment: The item shell provides information about a patient disease or injury. The completed item will require the test-taker to make a correct diagnosis and to identify the correct treatment protocol, based upon the information given.

FIG. 6.2. Examples of item shells for medical problem solving Adapted from Haladyna and Shindoll (1989).

3. **Identify variations for each key word or phrase.**

> Age of person: infant, child (ages 3 to 14), adolescent (ages 13 to 18), young adult (ages 19 to 31), middle age (ages 32 to 59), elderly (ages 60 and over).
>
> Trauma injury and complications: Cuts, contusions, fractures, internal injuries.
>
> Type of accident: Automobile, home, industrial, recreational

4. **Select an age, trauma injury or complication, and type of accident, from personal experience.**

> Infant   Abrasion   Home

5. **Write the item stem.**

> An infant is brought to the hospital with severe abrasions following a bicycle accident involving the mother. What should initial treatment be?

6. **Write the correct answer.**

> A.   Conduct a visual examination.

7. **Write the required number of distractors, or as many plausible distractors as you can with a limit of four, because most automated scoring devices permit up to five options comfortably.**

> B. Treat for infection
> C. Administer pain killers to calm the infant.
> D. Send for laboratory tests.
> E. Clean the wounds with an antiseptic.

Steps 4 through 7 can be repeated for writing a set of items dealing with a physician's treatment of people coming to the emergency department of a hospital. The effectiveness of the item comes with the writing of plausible distractors. However, the phrasing of the item, with the three variations, makes it possible to generate many items covering many combinations of ages, trauma injuries and complications, and types of injuries. The item writer need not be concerned with the "trappings" of the item but can, instead, concentrate on content. For instance, an experienced physician who is writing test items for a certification examination might draw heavily from clinical experience and use the item shell to generate a dozen different items representing the realistic range of problems encountered in a typical medical practice. In these instances, we can transform the testing events into context-dependent item sets.

An item shell for eighth-grade science is developed to illustrate the process. The unit is on gases and its characteristics:

Step 1: Identify the stem.

> Which is the distinguishing characteristic of hydrogen?

Step 2: Underline the key word or phrase.

> Which is the distinguishing characteristic of <u>hydrogen?</u>

Step 3: Identify variations for each key word or phrase.

> Which is the distinguishing characteristic of
> (any gases studied in this unit)?

Step 4: Select an instance from the range of variations.

> Oxygen

Step 5: Write the stem.

> Which is the distinguishing characteristic of oxygen?

Step 6: Write the correct answer.

> A. It is the secondary element in water.

Step 7: Write the distractors.

> B. It has a lower density than hydrogen.
> C. It can be fractionally distilled.
> D. It has a lower boiling point than hydrogen.

The last word in the stem can be replaced by any of a variety of gasses, easily producing many item stems. The difficult task of choosing a right answer and several plausible distractors, however, remains.

Although the process of developing item shells may seem laborious, as illustrated on the preceding pages, keep in mind that many of these seven steps become automatic in the development of item shell. In fact, once a good item is discovered, several steps can be done simultaneously arriving at a new item soon after the original item is identified.

Item shells have the value of being used formally or informally, as part of a careful item development effort, or informally for classroom testing. The value of the item shell is its versatility to operate at different cognitive operations with the four types of content (facts, concepts, principles, and procedures) and in different subject matter areas.

EVALUATION OF ITEM SHELLS

According to Haladyna and Shindoll (1989), the item shell has several attractive features:

1. The item shell helps inexperienced item writers phrase the item in an attractive and effective manner because the item shell is based on previously used, successfully performing items.

2. Item shells can be applied to a variety of types of content (facts, concepts, principles, and procedures), types of cognitive behaviors (recalling, summarizing, predicting, evaluating, and problem solving), and various subject matters.

3. Item shells are easily produced, and lead to the rapid development of useful items.

4. Item shells can be used in item-writing training, as a teaching device.

5. Item shells can be used to help item writers polish good ideas for items. Once they have ideas, they can select from generic shells, as Fig. 6.1 shows, or from a specially prepared set of shells, as Fig. 6.2 shows.

6. Item shells complement traditional methods of item writing, so that a variety of item formats exist.

7. Finally, item shells help crystallize our ideas about the content of a test. The item shell provides the most basic, operational definition of what is really measured. In fact, the item shell comes close to resembling instructional objectives or other types of content identifiers.

In summary, the item shell is a very useful device for writing MC items because it has an empirical basis and provides the structure for the content expert who wishes to write items. The technique is flexible enough to allow a variety of shells fitting the complex needs of most formal and informal testing programs. Millman and Westman (1989) showed that this technique can be computerized, thus even further streamlining the process. Thus, the future of the item shell as an item-writing aid seems bright.

GENERIC ITEM SETS

Chapter 3 presents and illustrates the context-dependent item set as a means for testing various types of higher level thinking with meaningful scenarios or vignettes. This format is becoming increasingly popular because of its versatility. Testing theorists are also developing new models for scoring item sets (Thissen, Steinberg, & Mooney, 1989). This section uses the concept of item shells in a more elaborate format, the item set. This work is derived principally from Haladyna (1991) but also has roots in the earlier theories of Guttman and Hively (discussed in Roid & Haladyna, 1982).

ITEM SHELLS FOR ITEM SETS

The production of test items that measure various types of higher level thinking are problematic, as noted in previous chapters. Item shells presented in this chapter lessen this problem. With the problem-solving type item set introduced in chapter 3, a systematic method for producing large numbers of items for item sets using shell-like structures has been developed (Haladyna, 1991). This section provides the concept and methods for developing item shells for item sets.

Generic Scenario

The generic scenario is a key element in the development of these items. A scenario (or vignette) is a short story containing relevant information to solve a problem. Sometimes the scenario can contain irrelevant information, if the intent is to have the examinee discriminate between the relevant and irrelevant information.

These scenarios can have the general form, as shown for a beginning graduate statistics course:

> Given a situation where bivariate correlation is to be used, the student will (1) state or identify the research question/hypothesis; (2) identify the constructs (Y and X) to be measured; (3) write or identify the statistical null and alternate hypotheses, or directional, if indicated in the problem; (4) identify the criterion and predictor variables; (5) assess the power of the statistical test; (6) determine alpha; (7) draw a conclusion regarding the null/alternate hypotheses, when given results; (8) determine the degree of practical significance; (9) discuss the possibility of Type I and Type II errors in this problem; and (10) draw a conclusion regarding the research question/hypothesis.

The above example involved one statistical test, product–moment correlation. A total of 18 common statistical tests are taught. With the use of each test, four variations exist: (a) statistical and practical significance, (b) statistical but no practical significance, (c) no statistical but potentially practical significance, and (d) neither statistical nor practical significance. Thus, the achievement domain contains 72 possibilities. Once a scenario is generated, the four conditions may be created with a single scenario.

For example:

> Two researchers studied 42 men and women for the relationship between amount of sleep each night and calories burned on an exercise bike. They obtained a correlation of .28, which has a two-tailed probability of .08.

This problem can be varied as to its sample size and its correlation to simulate the four conditions described in the previous paragraph. Thus, with the writing of a single scenario, four scenarios are actually developed.

With each scenario, a total of 10 test items is possible. With the development of this single scenario and its four variants, the item writer has created a total of 40 test items. Some item sets can be used in an instructional setting for practice, whereas others should appear on formative quizzes and summative tests. For formal testing programs, item sets can be generated in large quantities to satisfy needs without great expense.

Fig. 6.3 presents a fully developed item set. This set is unconventional, because it contains a subset of multiple true–false items. Typically, not all possible items from an item-set domain would be used in a test for several reasons. First, too many items are possible and it might exceed the need called for in the test specifications. Second, item sets are best confined to a single page or facing pages in a test booklet. Third, item sets are known to have inter-item cuing, so the use of all possible items may enhance undesirable cuing. With the scenario presented in Fig. 6.3, minor variations in the sample size, the correlation and its associated probability, and a directional test can create essentially a new problem.

Evaluation of Generic Item Sets

This method provides a basis for testing complex, multistep thinking that may be scenario based. In most circumstances, such thinking would be tested using an open-ended response format. In fact, the generic item set makes no assumption about the test item format. However, the generic item set technique is very well suited to simulating complex thinking with the objectively scorable multiple-choice format.

This method is rigid in the sense that it has a structure and organization. However, this is important in easing the development of many relevant items. On the other hand, the item writer has the freedom to write interesting scenarios and identify factors within each scenario that may be systematically varied. The

Two researchers were studying the relationship between amount of sleep each night and calories burned on an exercise bike for 42 men and women. They were interested in whether people who slept more had more energy to use during their exercise session. They obtained a correlation of .28, which has a two-tailed probability of .08.

1. Which is an example of a properly written research question?
    A.* Is there a relationship between amount of sleep and energy expended?
    B.   Does amount of sleep correlate with energy used?
    C.   What is the cause of energy expended?

    What is the correct term for the variable amount of sleep?
    Mark A if correct or B if incorrect
2. Criterion (A)
3. Independent (B)
4. Dependent (A)
5. Predictor (B)
6. y (A)
7. x (B)

8. What is the correct statistical hypothesis?
    A.   There is no correlation between sleep and energy expended.
    B.* Rho equals zero.
    C.   r equals zero.
    D.   Rho equals r.

9. If power is a potentially serious problem in this study, what remedies should you take?
    A.* Set alpha to .10 and do a directional test.
    B.   Set alpha to .05 and do a directional test.
    C.   Set alpha to .01 and do a nondirectional test.
    D.   Set alpha to .05 and do a nondirectional test.

10. What conclusion should you draw regarding the null hypothesis?
    A.* Reject
    B.   Accept
    C.   Cannot determine without more information.

FIG. 6.3. A fully developed scenario-based problem solving item set.

generic questions also can be a creative endeavor, but once developed they can be used for variations of the scenario. The writing of the correct answer is somewhat straightforward, but the writing of distractors requires some inventiveness.

As noted earlier and well worth making the point again, item sets have a tendency for inter-item cuing. In technical terms, this is called *local dependence* (Hambleton & Swaminathan, 1987), and the problem is significant for item sets (see Haladyna, 1992a; Thissen, Steinberg, & Mooney, 1989). When writing these items, Item writers have to be careful to reduce the tendency for examinees to benefit from other items appearing in the set. This is why it is recommended that not all possible items in the set should be used for each set at any one time.

The generic item set seems to apply well to quantitative subjects, such as the statistics examples. However, how well does it apply to nonquantitative content? These item sets have been successfully used in national licensing examinations in accountancy, medicine, nursing, and pharmacy, among others. Haladyna (1991) provided an example in art history. So it seems that this method can be used for other types of content.

This method derives from the earlier work with item forms by Hively and with facet theory by Guttman, whose theories are discussed by Roid and Haladyna (1982). These earlier efforts failed because the methods were too cumbersome to use and the items did not perform as desired. Nonetheless, these earlier methods provide a theoretical rationale for this method, and, I hope, for other proposals that will be discussed in chapter 10.

ITEM MODELING

Although item modeling has many traits in common with item shells, it is distinguished in several important ways. This section presents a case of an operational definition of professional practice, justifies the use of item modeling as a basis for the content validation of resulting test scores, and illustrates the item-modeling procedure.

Operational Definition Versus Construct Definition

As presented earlier in this book, construct validation is recommended when developing measures of a construct (Messick, 1989). However, Cronbach (1987), among others, maintained that operational definitions are preferable to constructs because such definitions leave no doubt about what we are trying to measure. Unfortunately, we have few instances where we can operationally define constructs and thus avoid the necessity of construct validation.

In the operationist perspective, there is one and only one measure of a concept. Independent test builders working from the same understanding will build identical tests, if an operational definition is adequate. In contrast, construct validity admits that this is not possible; that we have to build alternative measures and collect evidence regarding their similarities. For example, two measures of a construct should be highly correlated, and measures of unrelated constructs should not be highly correlated. The observation of this behavior is one aspect of what is done in construct validation.

A Rationale for Item Modeling

Traditional tests of ability and achievement view cognitive behavior as existing in discrete parts. Each test item systematically samples a specific class of behavior. A domain-referenced interpretation results when a test score reflects the amount of learning from a representative sampling of items. Mislevy (1993) referred to this mode of construct definition and the resulting tests as representing *low-to-high proficiency*. Some writers maintain that this view is outmoded and inappropriate for most professions (Shepard, 1991; Snow, 1993).

This point of view is consistent with modern reform movements in education calling for greater emphasis on higher level thinking (Nickerson, 1989). For nearly two decades, mathematics educators have promoted a greater emphasis on problem solving, in fact, arguing that problem solving is the main reason for studying mathematics (Prawat, 1993). Other subject matters are presented as fertile for problem-solving teaching and testing. In summary, the impetus of school reform coupled with advances in cognitive psychology are calling for a different view of learning and, in this setting, competence. LaDuca (1994) submitted that competent practice resides in appropriate responses to the demands of the encounter.

LaDuca proposed that licensure tests for a profession ought to be aimed at behavior that unimpeachably relates to effective practice. The nature of each encounter presents a problem that needs an effective solution to the attending physician. Conventional task analysis and role delineation studies identify knowledge and skills that tangentially relate to competence, but the linkage is not so direct. In place of this approach is problem-solving behavior that hinges on all possible realistic, professional encounters.

LaDuca's ideas apply directly to professional licensing and competency testing, but it may be adapted to other settings. For instance, item modeling might be used in consumer problems (e.g., buying a car or appliance, food shopping, painting a house or a room, remodeling a house, fixing a car, or planning landscaping for a new home).

An Example of Item Modeling

This section briefly presents the structural aspects of LaDuca's item-modeling procedures. (Readers interested in the fuller discussion should refer to LaDuca, 1994; LaDuca, Downing, & Henzel, 1995; LaDuca, Staples, Templeton, & Holzman, 1986; and Shea et al.,1992).

For clinical encounters, several faceted dimensions exist for the development of the vignette (clinical encounter) driving the content of the item. These facets are used by the expert physician in writing a content-appropriate test item. The existence of these facets makes item writing more systematic.

The first facet identifies five major settings involving patient encounters. The weighting of these settings may be done through studies of the profession or through professional judgment about the criticalness of each setting.

FACET ONE: SETTING
1. Unscheduled patients/clinic visits
2. Scheduled appointments
3. Hospital rounds
4. Emergency department
5. Other encounters

The second facet provides the array of possible physician activities in sequential order. The last activity, applying scientific concepts, is somewhat disjointed from the others, because it connects patient conditions with diagnostic

---

FACET TWO: PHYSICIAN TASKS
1. Obtaining history and performing physical examination
2. Using laboratory and diagnostic studies
3. Formulating most likely diagnosis
4. Evaluating the severity of patient's problem(s)
5. Managing the patient
6. Applying scientific concepts

---

data and also disease or injury patterns and their complications. In other words, it is the complex step in treatment that the other categories do not conveniently describe.

The third facet on the top of the next page provides patient encounters in three discrete categories with two variations in each of the first two categories. A sample question follows that provides the application of these three facets:

Facet One: Setting-2. Scheduled appointment
Facet Two: Physician Task-3. Formulating most likely diagnosis
Facet Three: Case Cluster-1a. Initial workup of new patient, new problem

---

FACET THREE: CASE CLUSTER

1a. Initial workup of new patient, new problem
1b. Initial workup of known patient, new problem

2a. Continued care of known patient, old problem
2b. Continued care of known patient, worsening old problem.

3.   Emergency care

A 19-year-old archeology student comes to the student health service complaining of severe diarrhea, with 15 large-volume watery stools per day for 2 days. She has had no vomiting, hematochezia, chills or fever, but she is very weak and very thirsty. She is just returned form a 2-week trip to a remote Central American archeological research site. Physical examination shows a temperature 37.2 degrees Centigrade (99.0 degrees Fahrenheit), pulse 120/min, respirations 12/min and blood pressure 90/50 mm Hg. Her lips are dry and skin turgor is poor. What is the most likely cause of the diarrhea?

A.   Anxiety and stress from traveling
B.   Inflammatory disease of the large bowel
C.   An osmotic diarrheal process
D.* A secretory diarrheal process
E.   Poor eating habits during her trip

Interestingly, the item pinpoints a central task (3) of diagnosis, but necessarily involves the successful completion of the first two tasks in the task taxonomy. The vignette could be transformed to a context-dependent item set that includes all six physician tasks. The genesis of the patient problem comes from the rich experience of the physician/expert, but systematically fits into the faceted vignette so that test specifications can be satisfied.

Evaluation of Item Modeling

This approach to automated item writing has many virtues to recommend its use.

These include the following:

1. Its foundation is in generating an operational definition. In many settings, particularly in a profession, encounters seem appropriate and realistic. The ability to define a domain consisting of all encounters is at the heart of item modeling.
2. The method is flexible and adaptable to many settings and situations.
3. The method has a high degree of credibility because it rests on the judgments of experts in a field of study or profession.
4. The method accelerates the item-writer's ability to write test items, something that nonprofessional item writers greatly need.
5. In its most sophisticated form, distractors are systematically created.
6. Item specifications are created that are standardized and uniform.
7. The method can provide a basis for instruction and also formative testing because the item model can be used in teaching just as easily as in testing.
8. Although not explicit, item modeling can be revised to the item set format that more closely models multistep thinking.

Its greatest difficulty may be that a lack of imagination would render it useless. Experts in a selected field will need to collectively use that expertise and invent vignettes that systematically define the domain of possible encounters in a field of study. For instance, in auto mechanics, using vignettes to define all possible electrical problems that may occur in the training and licensing of a certified automotive mechanic may be possible.

SUMMARY

Item shells, generic item shells for item sets, and item modeling were discussed, illustrated, and evaluated. These methods have much in common. The item shell technique is merely prescriptive, and depends on using existing items. The generic item set approaches item modeling in concept, but has a fixed questioning structure. Item modeling has a fixed structure of item stems that allows for a domain definition of encounters. Although these are somewhat new methods, each seems to have great potential for improving both the quality and efficiency of item writing as we know it. The greatest reservation in using either method is the preparation required at the onset of item-writing training. Experts need to identify a vignette structure and systematically define the facets varied. Although item shells and item modeling have much in common, further developments will probably favor item modeling because of its inherent theoretical qualities that strike at the foundation of professional competence. But the greatest efficiency and hope for modeling problem solving will come from the merging of item modeling with item sets.

III

VALIDATING ITEM RESPONSES

OVERVIEW

How valid is it to interpret a test score or to use a test score for a specific purpose? The answer to this question rests on validity evidence. Kane (1992) has used the phrase *validity argument* for collecting and integrating validity evidence to support a specific test score interpretation or use. The strength of the argument rests on this validity evidence.

For test scores, Downing and Haladyna (1997) suggested a variety of validity evidence that derives from studies and test development procedures. This list is impressive about what is needed to support any test score interpretation or use. They also drew a parallelism between test score validation and item response validation. Validity evidence forms an argument supporting test score interpretation and use. Item validity evidence also forms an argument supporting item response interpretation and use. We expect item performance to mimic test score performance. The laws of consistency we expect in test scores should be mirrored in item responses. Using this parallelism, chapters 7, 8, and 9 are complementary.

Chapter 7 discusses the kinds of validity evidence that comes from following well-established procedures in test development governing item development. Chapter 8 discuss studies of item responses. Chapter 9 provides more advanced topics in studies of item responses. The procedures of chapter 7 coupled with the studies described in chapters 8 and 9 provide a body of evidence that forms this validity argument supporting test score interpretation and use.

7

VALIDITY EVIDENCE ARISING FROM
ITEM DEVELOPMENT PROCEDURES

OVERVIEW

After an item is written, several item improvement activities should be completed. Both research and experience has shown that many MC items are flawed in some way at the initial stage of item development, so these activities are much needed. The time invested in these activities will reap many rewards. The more polish applied to items, the better the items become. However, some of these activities are more important than others and deserve more attention.

A RATIONALE FOR ITEM IMPROVEMENT ACTIVITIES

Because the science of writing test items is emerging, the practice of item writing is not yet a highly scientific endeavor, such as the practices of analyzing and scoring item responses. In a formal testing program, the activities to be recommended are essential, whereas in classroom testing such reviews are desirable but often impractical. Nonetheless, the improvement of testing hinges on the ability of test makers to design and write test items properly and to review and improve these items.

Messick (1989) made a very important point about the value of these reviews. Any factor contributing to the increased or reduced difficulty of the test is a form of bias. It contaminates the inferences we require from test results.

145

Thus, the various activities that comprise item review are essential in construct validation. *The Standards for Educational and Psychological Testing* (APA, 1985) also support this important practice in Standard 3.10. Downing and Haladyna (1997) viewed the collection of validity evidence from a variety of sources. Their 11 types of evidence provide the basis for the procedures that can become part of this validity evidence.

CONTENT DEFINITION

This process was traditionally termed *content validity* because of the focus on content of the test and test items. Messick (1989) has argued that because content is not a property of tests but of test scores, content validity has no relevance. Content-related evidence seems more appropriate (Messick, 1995).

Classroom testing. For this type of testing, the instructional objective has long served as a basis for both defining learning and directing the content of tests. States' have developed content standards replete with lists of instructional objectives. Terminology may vary. Terms such as *content standards, performance indicators*, and *outcomes* are used, but the traditional Mager (1962) objective remains:

Anatomy of an Objective	Example
TSW (The student will)	TSW
action verb	identify examples of invertebrates.
conditions for performance	Animals will be described in terms of characteristics, habitats, and behaviors. Some will be invertebrate.

Some interest has been expressed in developing fluid abilities, such as reading and writing. Whereas there is still heavy reliance on teaching and testing atomistic aspects of reading and writing, among other subjects, the fluid ability requires integrated performance that may involve reading, writing, critical thinking, problem solving, and even creative thinking. MC items cannot bear the load for such complex behavior.

Large-scale testing. Formal testing programs often have different bases for defining content. In certification and licensing testing in the professions, knowledge and skills may dominate, favoring MC. Nevertheless, role delineation, job analysis, task analysis, or professional practice analysis studies are recommended. These surveys yield information about the knowledge and skills viewed as critical to professional practice. MC tests measure this knowledge and knowledge of skills, but the resulting test scores are used with other evaluations related to actual performance in the profession under supervision.

The heart of content definition is expert judgment. No matter what type of testing, consensus among content experts is a critical piece of evidence in test score interpretation and item response validation.

TEST SPECIFICATIONS

A systematic process is used to take test content and translate it into quantitative test specifications stating how many items will be used and which content topics will be tested. Kane (1997) discussed ways that we can translate from content definition to test specification. Although this process is not well established in traditional literature, it is practiced widely. Generally, the effort to create test specification again rests on expert judgment. As Messick (1995) expressed, test specifications provide boundaries for the domain to be sampled. This content definition is actualized through test specifications. Most measurement textbooks discuss test specifications. They generally have two dimensions: content and behavior. Chapter 5 provides four content dimensions, but these are far too general for test specifications. The behavior dimensions offer in chapter 5 provide a sound basis for classifying items. However, the behavior dimension should not be too complex. The well-known Bloom taxonomy has never reached the success it might have reached had it been simpler and more accessible to the great variety of test developers.

ITEM-WRITER TRAINING

For low-stakes testing, the item writers should be trained in the principles of item writing, as expressed throughout this book. This training need not take a long time, as content experts can learn the basics of item writing in a short time, and the many reviews of items described in this chapter provide a quality control for the development of these items. The training should be based on a set of item-writing guidelines, formats that will be used, test specifications, and the manner in which items are classified by content and cognitive behavior. Participants in this training should have supervised time to write items and engage in collegial review. Generally volunteer or paid item writers are kept for periods, as once they are trained their expertise grows, and the pool of items prospers.

For high-stakes testing, one might argue that such training is crucial to the appointment of item writers. Downing and Haladyna (1997) argued that a key piece of validity evidence is the expertise of these item writers. Not only must a case be made for adequate training, but the credentials of these item writers should enhance the reputation of the testing program, as one of high quality.

One useful piece of evidence is the *Item Writing Guide*, which is the instructional booklet that every item writer receives. These booklets contain the instructional material and also examples and blank item-writing forms, so that all items can be drafted and correctly coded and classified for item banking and later for review.

REVIEW OF ITEMS FOR ITEM-WRITING ERRORS

Chapter 4 presented item-writing guidelines and examples of the use or misuse of each guideline. Every test item should be subjected to a review to decide if items were properly written. The guidelines are really advice based on a consensus, so we should not think of these rules as rigid laws of item writing. As noted previously in this book and in other sources (e.g., Haladyna & Downing, 1989a, 1989b) the degree of consensus about many rules is questionable and the amount of empirical research supporting many rules is lacking. Nonetheless, once these rules are mastered, the detection of item-writing errors is a skill that can be developed to a high degree of proficiency. Items should be revised accordingly. Violating these rules does not necessarily lead to bad items. On the other hand, following these rules probably will result in a test that not only looks better but is more likely to perform according to expectations.

Table 4.1 (in chapter 4) summarizes these rules. A convenient and effective way to use Table 4.1 in reviewing items is to use each rule number as a code for items that are being reviewed. The people doing the review can read each item and enter the code on the test booklet containing the offending item. Such information can be used by the test developers to consider redrafting the item, revising it appropriately, or retiring the item. As mentioned previously, these rules are not especially well grounded in expert opinion or research, thus they should be viewed more as guidelines or advice.

COGNITIVE BEHAVIOR

The Bloom taxonomy was discussed in chapter 5 as the impetus for many attempts to classify objectives and test items. Whereas studies failed to support the Bloom taxonomy, other attempts at classification systems also proved futile. As chapter 5 pointed out, it is difficult to discover the cognitive behavior being displayed because the experience of the test-taker is not well known. The test-taker may be responding from memory, based on extensive experience, or may be reasoning to get the right answer. Thus, any classification of an item by cognitive behavior is still a speculation.

Nonetheless, chapter 5 provided a simple basis for classifying items: recall, understanding, and higher level thinking that included critical thinking, problems solving, and creative thinking. Any classification system rests on the ability of content experts to independently agree about the kind of behavior elicited by its test-takers.

CONTENT REVIEW

The central issue in content review is relevance. Messick (1989) stated:

> *Judgments of the relevance of test items or tasks to the intended score interpretation should take into account all aspects of the testing procedure that significantly affect test performance. These include, as we have seen, specification of the construct domain of reference as to topical content, typical behaviors, and underlying processes. Also needed are test specifications regarding stimulus formats and response alternatives, administration conditions (such as examinee instructions or time limits), and criteria for item scoring.* (p. 276)

As Popham (1993) pointed out, the expert judgment regarding test items has dominated validity studies. Most classroom testing and formal testing programs seek a type of test score interpretation related to some well-defined content (Fitzpatrick, 1981; Kane, 1982; Messick, 1989). Under these conditions, content is believed to be definable in terms of a domain of knowledge (e.g., a set of facts, concepts, principles, or procedures). Under these circumstances, each test is believed to be a representative sample of the total domain of knowledge. As Messick noted, the chief concerns are clear construct definition, test specifications that call for the sample of content and behaviors desired, and attention to the test item formats and response conditions desired. He further added administration and scoring conditions to this area of concern.

The technology, as noted by Popham previously, is use of content experts, persons intimate with the content who are willing to review items to ensure that each item represents the content and level of cognitive behavior desired. The expert or panel of experts should ensure that each item is relevant to the domain of content being tested, and properly identified as to this content. For example, if auto mechanics' knowledge of brakes is being tested, then each item should be analyzed to figure out if it belongs to the domain of knowledge for which the test is designed and if it is correctly identified.

Although this step may seem very tedious, it is sometimes surprising to see items misclassified by content. With classroom tests designed to measure student achievement, students can easily identify items that are instructionally irrelevant. In formal testing programs, many detection techniques inform users about items that may be out of place. This chapter discusses judgmental review, whereas chapters 8 and 9 discuss statistical methods.

Methods for performing the content review were suggested by Rovinelli and Hambleton (1977). In selecting content reviewers, these authors make excellent points:

1.   Can the reviewers make valid judgments regarding the content of items?
2.   Is there agreement among reviewers?
3.   What information is sought in the content review?
4.   What factors affect the accuracy of content judgments of the reviewers?
5.   What techniques can be used to collect and analyze judgments?

Regarding the last point, the authors strongly recommend using the simplest method available.

Toward that end, the review of test items can be done in formal testing programs by asking each content specialist to classify the item according to an item classification guide. Rovinelli and Hambleton (1977) recommended a simple three-point rating scale:

1.   Item is correctly classified.
2.   Uncertain.
3.   Item is incorrectly classified.

These authors also provided an index of congruence between the original classification and the content specialists' classification. The index can be used to identify those items having content classification problems. A simpler index might be any item with a high frequency of ratings of 2 or 3 as determined from the above scale. If the cognitive level of each item is of concern, the same kind of rating can be used.

Figure 7.1 provides a simplified example of ratings from content experts using the mythical Azalea Growers' Certification Test. As shown at the top of the figure, the test specifications provide the proportions of items required in the test, whereas the bottom provides the actual ratings of content. In most testing programs, the four topics shown would be further subdivided into subtopics in outline fashion, and content experts would be asked to provide a more exacting type of review than simply to identify the main topic.

The science of content review has been raised beyond merely expert judgment and simple descriptive indicators of content agreement. Crocker, Llabre, and Miller (1988) proposed a more sophisticated system of study of content ratings involving generalizability theory. They described how theory can be used to generate a variety of study designs that not only provide indices of content-rater consistency, but also identify sources of inconsistency. In the context of a high-stakes testing program, procedures such as the one they recommend are more defensible than simplistic content review procedures.

Content review has been a mundane aspect of test design. As Messick (1989) noted, although most capable test development includes these important

Behavior	Topics				
	Watering	Fertilizer	Light	Soil	Total
Recalling	10%	5%	5%	10%	30%
Understanding	10%	5%	5%	10%	30%
Problem Solving	5%	10%	10%	15%	40%
Total	25%	20%	20%	35%	100%

Item	Original Classification	Reviewers		
		#1	#2	#3
82	Watering	3	3	3
83	Fertilizer	1	1	1
84	Soil	1	2	1
85	Soil	2	3	2
86	Light	1	1	1

FIG. 7.1. Excerpt of reviews from three content reviewers against original classification for the *Azalea Growers Certification Test.*

steps, we do not have much systematic information in the literature that informs us about what to use and how to use it. Hambleton (1984) provided the most current and comprehensive summary of methods for validating test items.

EDITORIAL REVIEW

No matter the type of testing program or the resources available for the development of the test, having each test professionally edited is desirable. The editor is someone who is usually formally trained in the canons of English grammar and composition.

There are several good reasons for the editorial review. First, edited test items present the cognitive tasks in a clearer fashion than unedited test items. Not only is this an item-writing rule, it is common sense. Items should clearly and accurately present the problem and the options. Second, editorial errors tend to distract test-takers. Because great concentration is needed on the test, such errors detract from the basic purpose of testing, to find the extent of knowledge of the test-taker. Third, errors reflect badly on the test maker. Face validity is the tendency for a test to look like a test. If there are many editorial errors, the test-takers are likely to think that the test falls short in the more important areas of content and item-writing quality. Thus, the test maker loses the respect of test-takers. There are several areas of concern of the editorial review:

Areas of Concern	Aspects of the Review
1. Mechanics	Spelling, abbreviations and acronyms, punctuation, and capitalization
2. Grammar	Complete sentences, correct use of pronouns, correct form and use of verbs, and correct use of modifiers
3. Clarity	Item stem clearly presents the problem, and options provide coherent and plausible responses.
4. Style	Active voice, conciseness, positive statements of the problem in the stem, consistency

A valuable aid in testing programs is an editorial guide, which is normally several pages of guidelines about acceptable formats, abbreviations, style conventions, and other details of item preparation, such as type font and size, margins, etcetera. For informal testing, where no editorial guideline is feasible, consistency of style is very important.

There are some excellent references that should be part of the library of a test maker, whether professional or amateur. Some of these are:

Achtert, W. S., & Gibaldi, J. (1985). *The MLA style manual.* New York, NY: Modern Language Association of America.

American Psychological Association. (1994). *Publication manual of the American Psychological Association* (4th ed.). Washington, DC: Author.

Strunk, W., Jr., & White, E. B. (1959). *The elements of style.* New York, NY: MacMillan.

The Chicago manual of style (13th ed.). (1982). Chicago, IL: University of Chicago Press.

Warriner, J. E., & Griffith, F. (1957). *English grammar and composition.* New York, NY: Harcourt, Brace, & World.

A spelling checker on a word processing program is also very handy. Spelling checkers have resident dictionaries for checking the correct spelling of many words. However, the best feature is the opportunity to develop an exception spelling list, where specialized words not in the spelling checker's dictionary can be added. Of course, many of these types of words have to be first verified from another source before each word can be so added. For example if one works in medicine or in law, the spelling of various medical terms can be checked in a specialized dictionary, such as Stedman's *Medical Dictionary* or Black's *Law Dictionary.* The former has more than 68,000 medical terms and the latter uses more than 16,000 legal terms.

SENSITIVITY REVIEW

Bias is a complex concept relating to unfairness of test score interpretations. Bias can be observed at the test score and item response levels. Evidence of bias comes in different forms. One is a judgmental process that called *sensitivity review.* Another process involves statistical procedures involving item responses and is termed *differential item functioning (DIF).* Study of both types of bias is highly recommended and, in fact, complementary (Clauser & Mazor, 1998; Cole & Moss, 1989; Messick, 1989; Ramsey, 1993). This section deals with the sensitivity review. Chapter 9 treats the statistical process for studying item bias.

Sensitivity review has received very little scholarly attention. Few primary references in the field of educational measurement provide more than a paragraph to a page of general discussion. *The Standards for Educational and Psychological Testing* (APA, 1985) provided in Standard 3.10 a single paragraph of commentary that explains the nature of item bias and the responsibility of test-makers:

When previous research indicates the need for studies of item or test performance differences for a particular kind of test for members of certain age, ethnic, cultural, and gender groups in the population of test-takers, such studies should be conducted as soon as is feasible. Such research should be designed to detect and eliminate aspects of test design, content, or format that might bias test scores for a particular groups. (p. 27)

This standard emphasizes empirical forms of item bias at the expense of judgmental forms. A stronger standard would include the sensitivity review as standard practice for standardized testing programs, particularly those with "high stakes" interpretations and uses. Classroom testing should routinely be monitored for insensitive references as mentioned in this standard. In fact, school district policies might exist for this purpose.

According to Ramsey (1993), the earliest publication on sensitivity review was the Educational Testing Service. This publication was part of an effort by ETS to provide testing content that reflected the diversity of our nation without perpetuating negative and unfair stereotypes. Later revisions of this document included disabled persons. Although ETS did not publicize their efforts to develop sensitivity reviews, ETS has exerted a steadying influence on the testing industry to be more active in watch guarding the content of test in an effort not to offend subgroups who take these tests or perpetuate stereotypes.

Current textbooks on educational measurement give very little attention to this topic. However, there are several good reasons for more concern. First and foremost, Zoref and Williams (1980) noted a high incidence of gender and ethnic stereotyping in several prominent intelligence tests. They cited several studies done in the 1970s where similar findings existed for achievement tests. To what extent this kind of bias exists in other standardized tests currently can only be speculation, but any incidence of this stereotyping is to be avoided in the future. Two, for humanistic concerns, all test makers should ensure that items do not stereotype diverse elements of our society. Three, such stereotyping is inaccurate, due to overgeneralization. Fourth, stereotyping may cause adverse reactions during the test-taking process.

Table 7.1 provides some criteria for judging item bias, adapted from Zoref and Williams (1980). Despite the attempt in that table to categorize forms of item bias, this area is in much need of more systematic and extensive study than it has received in the past. We lack both a complete rationale and a technology for doing judgmental item bias reviews.

Ramsey (1993) urged testing personnel to identify committees to conduct sensitivity reviews of test items and to provide training to committee members.

TABLE 7.1
A Typology for Judgmental Item Bias Review

Gender	Race/Ethnic
Representation: Items should be balanced with respect to gender representations. Factors to consider include clothes, length of hair, facial qualities, and make-up. Nouns and pronouns should be considered (he/she, woman/man).	Representation: Simply stated, if the racial or ethnic identity of characters in test items is present, it should resemble the demographics of the testing taking population.
Characterization: Two aspects of this are role stereotyping (RS) and apparel stereotyping (AS). RS would include any verbal or pictorial referring to qualities such as intelligence, strength, vigor, ruggedness, historical contributions, mechanical aptitude, professionalism, and/or fame being assigned to males exclusively. Female examples of RS include depicting women in domestic situations, passiveness, weakness, general activity, excessive interest in clothes or cosmetics, and the like. AS is viewed as the lesser of the two aspects of characterization. AS refers to clothing and other accouterments that are associated with men and women, for example, neckties, cosmetics. This latter category is used to support the more important designation of the former category in identifying gender bias in an item.	Characterization: White characters in test items may be stereotypically be presented in leadership roles, wealthy, professional, technical, intelligent, academic, and the like. Minority characters are depicted as unskilled, subservient, undereducated, poor, or in professional sports.

He recommended four questions to pose to committee members:

1. Is there a problem?
2. If there is, which guideline is violated?
3. Can a revision be offered?
4. Would you sign off on the item if no revision was made? In other words how offensive is the violation?

As a contrast to Table 7.1, Ramsey listed these criteria for sensitivity review from the ETS guidelines: balance in gender and eliminating sexist language, avoiding negative stereotypes, even in the distractors, avoiding controversial material, such as abortion, homosexuality, religion, and politics, eliminating words or phrases that may appeal of socioeconomic or social subgroups at the expense of other groups, referred to as *elitism* and *ethnocentrism*.

There is little doubt that sensitivity reviews are vital in testing programs involving the public. The sensitivity review provides a useful complement to statistical studies of item responses in Chapter 9.

9. TEST-TAKER REVIEW

A good source of information about the quality of a test item is the test-taker. In fact, one of several good sources of evidence in construct validation is the collection of qualitative data regarding test item performance. If the setting for testing is based on instruction, than this review is strongly recommended because each student's analysis of wrong answers can actually aid in the learning process. If the setting for testing is a formal testing program, this type of inquiry is more problematic and logistically difficult. Nonetheless, several compelling reasons exist to recommend this practice.

Classroom Testing

The next class period following a classroom test should be spent discussing test results. The primary purpose is to help students learn from their errors. If learning is a continuous process, a post-test analysis can be very helpful in subsequent learning efforts. A second purpose, however, is to detect items that fail to perform as intended. The expert judgment of classroom learners can be marshaled for exposing ambiguous or misleading items.

After a classroom test is administered and scored, it is recommended that students have an opportunity to discuss each item and provide alternative reasoning for their wrong answers. Sometimes, they may prove the inherent weakness in the item and the correct rationale for their answer. In these circumstances, they deserve credit for their responses. Such informal polling also may determine that certain items are deficient because the highest scoring students are chronically missing the item or the lowest scoring students are chronically getting an item right. Standard item analysis also will reveal this, but the informal polling method is practical and feasible. In fact, it can be done immediately after the test is given, if time permits, or at the next class meeting. Furthermore, there is instructional value to the activity, because students have the opportunity to learn what they did not learn before being tested. An electronic version of this polling method using the S–P chart is reported by Sato (1980), but such a technique would be difficult to carry out in most instructional settings because of cost. On the other hand, the informal polling method can simulate the idea behind the S–P process and simultaneously provide appeals for the correct scoring of the test and provide some diagnostic teaching and remedial learning.

An analysis for any single student can reveal the nature of the problem. Sometimes, a student may realize that overconfidence, test anxiety, lack of study or preparation, or other factors legitimately affected performance, or it may reveal that the items were at fault. In some circumstances, a student can offer a correct line of reasoning that justifies an answer that no one else in the class or the teacher thought was right. In these rarer circumstances, credit could be given. This action rightfully accepts the premise that item writing is seldom a perfect process and that such corrective actions are sometimes justified.

Another device for obtaining answer justification is the use of a form where the student writes out a criticism of the item or the reasoning used to select his or her response. The instruction might read:

> Present any arguments favoring the answer you chose on the test.

Such written commentary often reveals the thought processes of students in arriving at a wrong answer. If the process were valid, perhaps the item was flawed and prevented the student from choosing the desired answer. It is surprising how flaws are discovered by the test-taker even after the items passed through all other reviews.

Formal Testing

In formal testing programs, the *think-aloud* procedure has been used to study the thought processes of students during a test. The *developmental field test* is also designed to accomplish a similar end, to analyze student behavior during a test to decide if an item is working as intended. The procedures for the think-aloud and the developmental field test are essentially the same. Students are grouped at a table and asked to answer a set of questions. During the time allotted, the administrator sits at the table and talks to the students, probing to find out what prompted certain answers. The setting is friendly and collegial, and each student is urged to talk about the test.

The basis for the think-aloud procedure comes from studies of cognitive behavior. Norris (1990) provided an excellent review of both the history and the rationale for verbal reports of test-taking behavior. However, seeing the link to construct validity, test specialists have recommended this practice. Indeed, test-taker reports of students' perceived thought processes involved in answer selection or answer creation can be very revealing about the actual thought processes involved. Some impetus for this kind of test score validation comes from cognitive psychology, where information processing theory can be studied au naturel. Norris provides a useful taxonomy of elicitation levels, shown in Table 7.2.

One conclusion that Norris drew from his experimental study of college students is that the use of the six levels of elicitation of verbal reports did not affect cognitive test behavior. Some benefits of this kind of probing, he claimed, include detecting misleading expressions, implicit clues, unfamiliar vocabulary, and alternative justifiable answers.

Another recent study by Farr, Pritchard, and Smitten (1990) shed more light on verbal reports of test-takers. Their study involved reading comprehension of passages, involving the context dependent item set for measuring comprehension, as discussed in chapter 3. Their interest was to find out if the MC format controls the kind of cognitive behavior wanted. Various critics of using MC to measure reading comprehension claim that this format encourages test-takers to perform surface reading as opposed to the more desired in-depth reading. They experimented with 26 college students using a standardized reading comprehension test and planned probes to obtain verbal reports of their thinking processes. Four distinctly different strategies were identified for answering these context dependent passages. The most popular of these strategies was to read the passage, then read each question, then search for the answer in the passage. Without any doubt, all test-takers manifested question-answering behaviors. In other words, they were focused on answering questions, as opposed to reading the passage for surface or deep meaning. Although these researchers concluded that the MC reading comprehension test is a special type of reading comprehension task, it seems to have general value to the act of reading comprehension. These researchers concluded that this study answers critics who contend that surface thinking only occurs in this kind of test. Further, they say that the development of items (tasks) actually determines the types of cognitive behaviors being elicited. Their sample includes highly able adult readers who used effective reading skills in finding the correct answers. Descriptive studies like this one are rare but they help us understand better the underlying cognitive processes actually used to answer questions. Norris (1990) summarized verbal reports of test taking:

> *Verbal reports of thinking would be useful in the validation of MC critical thinking tests, if they could provide evidence to judge whether good thinking was associated with choosing keyed answers and poor thinking was associated with unkeyed answers. (p. 55)*

TABLE 7.2
Descriptions of Elicitation Levels

Elicitation Level	Description
Think Aloud	Subjects were instructed to report all they were thinking as they worked through the items and to mark their answers on a standardized answer sheet.
Immediate Recall	Subjects were instructed to mark their answers to each item on a standardized answer sheet and to tell immediately after choosing each answer why they chose it.
Criteria Probe	Subjects were instructed to mark their answers to each item on a standardized answer sheet, and were asked immediately after marking each answer whether a piece of information pointed out in the item had made any difference to their choice.
Principle Probe	Subjects were treated as in the criterion problem group with an additional question asking whether their answer choice was based on particular general principles.
No Elicitation	Subjects were not interviewed, but were instructed to work alone and to mark their answers on a standardized sheet.

Although this method is time consuming and logistically difficult, it seems well worth the effort if one is serious about validating test results.

10. KEY CHECK (VERIFICATION)

Why is it necessary to check the key? Because several possibilities exist:

1. There may be no right answer for an item.
2. There may be a right answer, but it is not the one that is keyed.
3. There may be two or more right answers.

The key check is a method for ensuring that there is one and only one correct answer. Checking the key is an important step in test development, and never should be done superficially or casually. Two opportunities exist for the key check. Both opportunities should be explored.

Performing the Initial Key Check

The initial key check is done as an item is being developed. When the author of the item identifies the key, one or two other content experts should independently review the item and determine what their correct answer is. If there is disagreement, then the item needs to be revised or retired.

Another way to verify a key is to provide a reference to the right answer from an authoritative source, such as a textbook or a journal. This is a common practice in medical certification testing and other professional licensing and certification tests. The practice of providing references for test items also ensures a faithfulness to content that may be part of the test specifications.

Performing the Statistical Key Check

In any testing program where important decisions are made based on test scores, the failure to deal with key errors is unfair to test-takers. An item analysis is completed after the test is given and before students are assigned test scores. Chapter 8 provides information about evaluating options in terms of test-takers' performances. If an item's correct choice fails to perform as expected, this fact should be called to the attention of the person responsible for the test and a decision should be made about the item. The principle at stake is that test-takers must be treated fairly. The item with the questionable key should be removed from the test or the key should be changed. In some circumstances, the key will remain the same, despite its poor performance because the person making the decision will insist that the key is correct. After all questionable items have been considered, the test results can be scored, and test-takers can be assigned their score.

These two actions, the initial key check and the statistical key check, ensure that only right answers are scored as correct.

11. TEST SECURITY

In high-stakes testing program, there is an active effort to obtain copies of tests or test items for the express purpose of increasing performance. This kind of zeal is evident in standardized testing in public schools, where a variety of tactics are used to increase performance. Although the problem with such testing may be misinterpretation and misuse of test scores by policymakers, including legislators and school boards, lack of test security makes it possible to obtain and compromise legitimate uses of the test. In high stakes certification and licensing tests, poor security may lead to exposed items that weaken the valid interpretation and uses of test scores.

Downing and Haladyna (1997) recommended a test security plan that details how items are prepared and guarded. If security breaches occur, are replacement items available? If so, a replacement test needs to be assembled to replace the compromised test. As they pointed out, the test security issue cuts across all other activities mentioned in this chapter because test security is an overarching concern in test development, administration, and scoring.

SUMMARY

This chapter emphasized the benefits of many complementary reviews of test items. The *item-writing rule review* is desirable because it allows reviewers the chance to look for obvious item-writing violations that may lead to faulty performance. The *editorial review* is essential to preserving the "looks" and clarity of the test items. The *key check* is essential to ensure that the keyed options are correct. If experts cannot agree on the correct answer to the test item, then the item probably should not be used. The *content classification review* is also essential in preserving the fidelity between the choice of items for a test and the test specifications. A *judgmental item bias review* is essential for high-stakes testing programs and desirable for all other testing programs, including informal testing. However, the judgmental item bias review is only part of a total study of bias because statistical methods for detecting bias also may be used and are described and reviewed in chapters 8 and 9. The *test-taker review* is very desirable in all types of testing programs and testing situations and has many good qualities. Answer justification is useful in a classroom setting where teacher-made tests may be evaluated by the consumer, the student. Think-aloud procedures can be used to validate test items in formal testing programs.

8

ANALYZING ITEM RESPONSES

OVERVIEW

Two aspects of item response validation are procedural and quantitative/statistical. Chapter 7 discussed procedural activities that provide one type of validity evidence. This chapter complements chapter 7. Specifically, we are concerned with the tabulation of responses to MC items, statistical analyses that provides descriptions of item characteristics and test score properties, and graphical methods for displaying the results. The objective of analyzing item responses is to collect another type of validity evidence that supports using item responses to create test scores.

THE NATURE OF ITEM RESPONSES

Responses to test items usually develop patterns. Items with desirable response patterns contribute to developing an effective test. Items with undesirable item response patterns weaken the validity of our test score interpretations. Thus, the primary objective in this chapter is to learn how to tabulate, analyze, and evaluate item responses. Once we evaluate item responses, we can discard items, retain items for future use, or revise items and then see if the changes produce patterns that we expect in item responses. The particular test theory we use complicates the attainment of this objective. We address the problem of analyzing item response patterns using classical test theory (CTT), but then later in this chapter we shift to item response theory (IRT). Both are statistical theories of test scores and item responses. Although these rivaling theories have much in common, they have enough differences to make one arguably preferable to the other, although which one is preferable is a matter of continued debate. Some statistical methods are not theory-based but are useful in better understanding the dynamics of item responses.

Weighted or Unweighted Scoring

A complication we face is the choice of the scoring method. For nearly a century, test analysts have treated distractors and items equally. That is, all right answers score one point each and all distractors score no points. Should some options have more weight than others in the scoring process? If the answer is no, then the appropriate method of scoring is *zero-one* or *binary*. With the coming of dichotomous IRT, the weighting of test items is realized with the two- and three-parameter logistic response models. With polychotomous IRT, we gain the ability to weight MC options.

When comparing unweighted item scoring with weighted item scoring, the sets of scores are highly correlated. The differences between unweighted and weighted scores are very small and usually observed in the upper and lower tails of the distributions of test scores.

Response-weighted Scoring

In both CTT and IRT frameworks, theoreticians have developed polychotomous scoring models that consider the differential information offered in distractors (Haladyna & Sympson, 1988). Methods described in this chapter show that distractors differ in information about the ability or knowledge being tested. By studying distractor performance, one can eliminate useless distractors or identify specific distractors that may need revision. Another implication of differential distractor information is that items can be scored with this in mind. Later in this chapter, we further develop this implication.

Instruction or Training Context

To understand how to use item response patterns to evaluate items, we must place the item in a context, which is what the test is supposed to measure and how test scores will be used.

One prominent context is instruction or training. In these settings, a test is intended to measure student learning. With instruction or training, a certain domain of knowledge is to be learned. A test is a sample of that domain. If the test measures status in a domain for certifying competence in a profession, licensing a professional, certifying completion of a course of study, or the like, we are again interested in accomplishment relevant to a domain. An added responsibility is to decide if the test score truly falls above or below the passing score. This matter involves test score reliability, or more specifically, the precision of a test score. Item quality is a major factor in determining the precision of test scores.

ITEM PERFORMANCE PATTERNS

There are several ways to study item response patterns and draw inferences about the effectiveness of each item. Each is presented and discussed. These methods are usually complementary, but some interesting and important distinctions exist among these methods that may lead to different results. Some of these variations deal with the statistical test theory used, whereas other variations deal with whether results are dichotomously or polychotomously scored. Readers who are conversant with traditional and IRT item analyses will find this section to be a review of familiar concepts and procedures. However, some additional and innovative procedures are introduced and illustrated. This section has two parts. The first part examines characteristics test item responses, and the second part examines distractor characteristics.

CHARACTERISTICS OF TEST ITEM RESPONSES

Item Difficulty

The natural scale for item difficulty is percentage of examinees correctly answering the item. The ceiling of any MC item is 100% and the probability of a correct response determines the floor when examinees with no knowledge are randomly guessing. With a four-option item, the floor is 25%, and with a three-option item the floor is 33%. One term for item difficulty is *p-value*, which stands for the proportion or percentage of examinees correctly answering the item.

Every item has a natural difficulty; one that is based on the performance of all persons for whom we intend the test. This *p-value* is very difficult to estimate accurately unless a very representative group of test-takers is being tested. This is one reason that CTT is criticized, because the estimation of the *p-value* is potentially biased by the sample on which the estimate of item difficulty is based. If the sample contains well instructed, highly trained, or highly able people, then the tests and its items appear very easy, usually above .90. If the sample contains uninstructed, untrained, or low-ability people, then the test and the items appear very hard, usually below .40, for instance.

IRT allows for the estimation of item difficulty without consideration of exactly who is tested. With CTT, as just noted, the performance level of the sample strongly influences the estimation of difficulty. With IRT, the composition of the sample is generally immaterial, and item difficulty can be estimated without bias. There are many IRT models. Most are applicable to large testing programs, involving 500 or more test-takers. If a testing program is that large and the content domain is unidimensional, IRT can be very effective for constructing tests that are adaptable for many purposes and types of examinees. The one-, two-, and three-parameter binary-scoring IRT models typically lead to similar estimates of difficulty, and these estimates are highly correlated to classical estimates of difficulty. The ability to accurately estimate parameters, such as difficulty, provide a clear advantage for IRT over classical test score theory.

   Controlling item difficulty. What causes an item to be difficult or easy? Studies of factors that control item difficulty are scarce. Green and Smith (1987), Smith (1986), and Smith and Kramer (1990) conducted some interesting experiments on controlling item difficulty. This aspect of item design is a promising research topic. The production of items at a known level of difficulty provides an advantage over the current hit or miss methods typically used. If we could grade tasks deductively before item development, we would have more intelligent control of item difficulty and, perhaps, overall item quality as well. Another possible cause of a *p-value* is the extent to which instruction, training, or development has occurred with those being tested. Consider an item with a p-value of .66. Was it the composition of the group being tested, or the effectiveness of instruction or training that caused this *p-value*? One clue is to examine test performance of instructed and uninstructed, trained or untrained, developed or undeveloped individuals and groups. This is the concept of instructional sensitivity, and it is more fully discussed in a subsequent section of this chapter. Another possible cause of a *p-value* is that the item is really not relevant to the knowledge domain being tested. In this circumstance, we would expect the item performance pattern to be unintelligible or the p-value to be very low because the item does not deal with the instruction or training.

Item Discrimination

Item discrimination is an item characteristic that describes the item's ability to sensitively measure individual differences that truly exist among test-takers. If we know test-takers to differ in their knowledge or ability, then each test item should mirror the tendency for test-takers to be different. Thus, with a highly discriminating item, those choosing the correct answer must necessarily differ in total score from those choosing any wrong answer. This is a characteristic of any measuring instrument where repeated trials (items) are used. Those possessing more of the trait should do better on the items comprising the test than those possessing less of that trait.

   Item discrimination can be estimated in several ways. Pitfalls exist in its estimation. Some major differences exist depending on which statistical theory of test scores is used. In CTT, for instance, item discrimination is the

TABLE 8.1

**Examples of the Average (Mean) Scores of
Those Answering the Item Correctly and Incorrectly
for Four Types of Item Discrimination**

Those Answering	Mean Score Item One	Mean Score Item Two	Mean Score Item Three	Mean Score Item Four
Correctly	90%	70%	65%	65%
Incorrectly	30%	60%	65%	75%
Discrimination	Very high	Moderate	Zero	Negative

product-moment (point-biserial) relationship between item and test performance. The biserial correlation (a sister to the point-biserial) may also be used, but it has a less direct relationship to alpha, the reliability coefficient typically used for MC test scores.

Table 8.1 provides information about four items of varying levels of discrimination. A good way to understand item discrimination is to note that those who choose the correct answer should have an overall high score on the test, and those who choose the wrong answer should have an overall low score on the test. In Table 8.1, the first item is a good discriminator, the second item is less of a discriminator, the third item fails to discriminate, and the fourth item discriminates in a negative way. Such an item may be miskeyed.

The size of the discrimination index is informative about the relation of the item to the total domain of knowledge, as represented by the total test score. It can be shown both statistically and empirically that test score reliability depends on item discrimination. The weakness of using classical item discrimination in instructional testing is that if the range of scores is restricted, when instruction is effective and student effort is strong, the discrimination index is greatly underestimated. In fact, if all performers answer correctly, the discrimination index is zero. Nevertheless, this is misleading. If the sample included nonlearners, we would find out more about the ability of the item to discriminate. One can obtain an unbiased estimate of discrimination in the same way as one can obtain an unbiased estimate of difficulty—by obtaining a representative sample that includes the full range of behavior for the trait being measured. Restriction in the range of this behavior is likely to affect the estimation of discrimination.

With IRT, there are a variety of traditional, dichotomous scoring models as well as newer polychotomous scoring models from which to choose. The one-parameter item response model (referred to as the *Rasch model*) is not concerned with discrimination, as it assumes that all items discriminate equally. The Rasch model has one parameter—difficulty. The model is popular because applying it is simple, and it provides satisfactory results despite this implausible assumption about discrimination. Critics of this model appropriately point out that the model is too simplistic and ignores the fact that items do vary with respect to discrimination. With the two-parameter and three-parameter models, item discrimination is proportional to the slope of the option characteristic curve at the point of inflexion (Lord, 1980). This shows that an item is most discriminating in a particular range of scores. One item may discriminate very well for high-scoring test-takers, whereas another item may discriminate best for low-scoring test-takers.

Fig. 8.1 illustrates a trace line (also known as an *option characteristic curve*) for the correct choice and all incorrect choices taken collectively. The trace line for the correct choice is monotonically increasing as a function of the achievement level of the group. The trace line for the collective incorrect choices is a reverse mirror image of the trace line for the correct answer, monotonically decreasing. Thus, we graphically see how a successfully discriminating item performs.

Trace Lines for Right and Wrong Answers

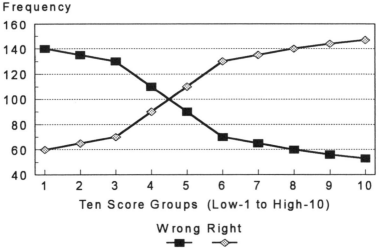

FIG. 8.1. Trace lines for the right answers and the combined information from all wrong choices (distractors).

A test consisting of items with the same discrimination would provide a very precise estimate of test scores at that point of inflexion. In Fig. 8.1, this slope is not so steep but steadily increases. In designing tests guided by IRT, discrimination pays handsome dividends. Interested readers should consult one of many books on this topic that provide more complete discussions (e.g., Hambleton & Swaminathan, 1987; Hulin, Drasgow, & Parsons, 1983; Lord, 1980).

Several excellent computer programs are available for a variety of computer environments that provide estimates of parameters. These include *Rascal* (Assessment Systems Corporation, 1992), *Ascal* (Assessment Systems Corporation, 1989), *Bigsteps*, (Wright & Linacre, 1992), and *Bilog MG* (Muraki, Mislevy, & Bock, 1992), *Rumm* (Sheridan, Andrich, & Luo, 1996), to name a few that are easily obtainable. The latter program is especially good at providing trace lines and using innovative scoring methods.

A third method to estimate item discrimination is the *eta coefficient*. This statistic can be derived from the one-way analysis of variance, where the dependent variable is the average score of persons selecting that option (choice mean), and the independent variable is the option choice. In analysis of variance, three estimates of variance are obtained: sums of square between, sums of squares within, and sums of squares total. The ratio of the sums of squares between and the sums of squares total is the squared eta coefficient. In some statistical treatments, this ratio is also the squared correlation between two variables (R^2). The eta coefficient is similar to the traditional product-moment discrimination index. In practice, the eta coefficient differs from the product-moment correlation coefficient in that the eta considers the differential nature of distractors, whereas the product-moment makes no distinction among item responses to distractors.

Table 8.2 illustrates a high discrimination index but a low eta coefficient. Notice that the choice means are closely bunched. The second item also has a high discrimination index but also a high eta coefficient, owing to the fact that the choice means of the distractors are more separated. In dichotomous scoring, point-biserial may also be appropriate, and the discrimination parameter in the two- and three-parameter models may be appropriate. However, with polychotomous scoring, the eta coefficient provides different information that is appropriate for studying item performance relative to polychotomous scoring.

What we can learn from this section is that with dichotomous scoring, one can obtain approximately the same information from using the classical discrimination index (the product-moment correlation between item and test performance) or the discrimination parameter from the two- or three-parameter item response models. But with polychotomous scoring these methods are inappropriate, and the eta coefficient provides unique and more appropriate

TABLE 8.2

Point-biserial and Eta Coefficients for Two Items

	Item 1	Item 2
Point-Biserial	.512	.552
Eta Coefficient	.189	.326
	Choice Mean	Choice Mean
Option A-correct	33.9%	33.4%
Option B-incorrect	23.5%	24.8%
Option C-incorrect	27.0%	29.6%
Option D-incorrect	26.4%	30.7%

information because the size of the coefficient depends on the differential nature of the options, as shown with Item 2 in contrast with Item 1.

Dimensionality and discrimination. A problem that exists with estimating discrimination is the dimensionality of the set of items chosen for a test. Generally, any test ought to be as unidimensional as possible with the present theories and methods in use. Nunnally (1967) described the problem as fundamental to validity. Any test should measure an attribute of student learning, such as a specific body of knowledge or a cognitive ability. Items need to have the same core to function appropriately. This lack of a common attribute clouds our interpretation of the test score.

With the existence of several factors on the test, item response patterns are likely to be odd or nondiscriminating. Deciding which items are working well is difficult because items discriminate with a common attribute in mind. With two or more attributes present in the test item discrimination has no criterion.

With IRT, unidimensionality is a prerequisite of test data. Hattie (1985) provided an excellent review of this issue, and Tate (1998) provided a timely update of this earlier work. When using the two- or three-parameter logistic response model, the computer program will fail to converge if multidimensionality exists. With the use of classical theory, discrimination indexes, obtained from product-moment correlations or biserial correlations, will be lower than expected and unstable from sample to sample. Thus, one has to be cautious that the underlying test data is unidimensional when estimating discrimination. A quick-and-dirty method for studying this problem is to obtain a KR-20 internal consistency estimate of reliability. If it is lower than expected for the number of items in the test, then this is a clue that the data may be multidimensional. A more dependable method is to conduct a factor analysis, but this action has some difficulties as well (Gorsuch, 1983; Hambleton & Swaminathan, 1987; Hattie, 1985). Chapter 9 provides more discussion of this problem.

Instructional Sensitivity

If instruction or training has been successful, students instructed or trained should perform at the upper end of the test score scale, whereas those not instructed or trained will perform at the lower end of the scale, as illustrated in Fig. 8.2. This is not true in instances where bias exists, or the test-taker is performing erratically, or the test is in some way inappropriate, for example, too hard or too easy or the test simply does not represent that domain.

In Fig. 8.2, the uninstructed group displays low performance on a test and its items, and the instructed group displays high performance on a test and its items. This idealized performance pattern shows effective instruction, good student effort, and a test that is sensitive to this instruction. Other terms used to describe this phenomenon are *instructional sensitivity* or *opportunity to learn* (Haladyna & Roid, 1981). Instructional sensitivity can be estimated using classical or IRT. The concept of instructional sensitivity incorporates the concepts of item difficulty and item discrimination (Haladyna, 1974; Haladyna & Roid, 1981; Herbig, 1976).

Item difficulty varies because the group of students tested has received differential instruction. Advanced students perform well on an item, whereas less advanced students do not perform very well. Therefore, it is possible to observe several conditions involving item difficulty that help us find which items are working as predicted and which items have performance problems that require closer analysis.

xx	*xx*
Xxx	*xxx*
Xxxxxx	*xxxxxxx*
xxxxxxxxxx	*xxxxxxxxxx*

Low performance   High performance
Before instruction   After Instruction

FIG. 8.2. Idealized performance of instructed and uninstructed students.

The simplest of the instructional sensitivity indexes is now used to illustrate several possible conditions. Then, we can see how instructional sensitivity can be measured in several ways.

Instructional sensitivity is a helpful concept in analyzing several important instructional conditions. These conditions include effective instruction, ineffective or lack of instruction, and unneeded instruction or an item is too easy. With each condition, several plausible, alternate explanations exist. The index must be interpreted by someone who is intimate with the instructional setting.

Pre-to-post difference index (PPDI). This index, first introduced by Cox and Vargas (1966), provides the simple difference in item difficulty based on two samples of test-takers known to differ with respect to instruction. For instance, the first group can be typical students who have not yet received instruction, whereas the second group can be typical students who have received instruction.

Pre-Instruction	Post-Instruction	PPDI
40%	80%	40

This simple illustration suggests that the item is moderately difficult (60%) for a typical four-option MC item, when the sample has an equal number of instructed and uninstructed students. The change in difficulty for the two conditions represents how much learning was gained from instruction, as reflected by a single item.

Because a single item is a somewhat undependable measure of overall learning, and because a single item is somewhat biased by its intrinsic difficulty, aggregating several items across the test to make an inference about instructional effectiveness or growth is far better. Other conditions exist for this index that provides useful descriptive information about item performance:

Pre-Instruction	Post-Instruction	PPDI
40%	40%	0

This kind of performance suggests ineffective instruction or lack of treatment of the content on which the item was based. A second plausible and rivaling explanation is that the item is so difficult that few can answer it correctly, despite the effectiveness of instruction. A third plausible hypothesis is that the item is unrelated to the purposes of the test. Therefore, no amount of instruction is relevant to performance on the item. The instructional designer and test designer must be careful to consider other, more plausible hypotheses and reach a correct conclusion. Often this conclusion is augmented by studying the performance patterns of clusters of items. Having a single item perform like the previous one is a different matter, but having all items perform as just shown is entirely another matter. A single item may be unnecessarily difficult, but if all items perform similarly, then the problem may lie with instruction, or the entire test may not reflect the desired content.

Pre-Instruction	Post-Instruction	PPDI
90%	90%	0

Like the previous example, the PPDI is zero, but unlike the previous example, the performance of both samples is high. Several rivaling hypotheses explain this performance. First, the material may have already been learned, and both uninstructed and instructed groups perform well on the item. Second, the item may have a fault that is cuing the correct answer; therefore, most students are picking the right answer regardless of whether they have learned the content represented by the item. Third, the item is inherently easy for everyone. The item fails to reflect the influence of instruction because the item fails to discriminate what content is to be measured due to the inherent easiness of the item.

These three examples show the interplay in instruction with items specifically designed or chosen to match instruction. Knowing how students perform before and after instruction informs the test designer about the effectiveness of the items as well as instruction.

Other indexes. Obtaining a sample of test behavior from a preinstructed or uninstructed group is often impractical. Thus, the PPDI is not an easy index to obtain. Haladyna and Roid (1981) examined a set of other instructional sensitivity indexes, including one derived from the Rasch model and a Bayesian index. They found a high degree of relation among these indexes. They also found that the post-instruction difficulty is a very dependable predictor of PPDI, but this difficulty is limited because the use of this index will be incorrect in the condition reported above where pre- and post-instruction performance of test-takers is uniformly high. Thus, this short-cut method for estimating PPDI is useful but one should always consider this inherent weakness in analyzing the instructional sensitivity of items by using post-instruction difficulty alone.

In this setting, the validity of these conclusions is not easy to prove based on statistical results alone. Analysis of performance patterns requires close observation of the instructional circumstances and the judicious use of item and test scores to draw valid conclusions. Instructional sensitivity is a useful combination of information about item difficulty and discrimination that contributes to the study and improvement of items designed to test the effects of teaching or training.

Guessing

With the use of MC test items, an element of guessing exists. Any test-taker, when encountering the item, answer either knows the right answer, has partial knowledge that allows for the elimination of implausible distractors and a guess among the remaining choices, or simply guesses in the absence of any knowledge.

In CTT, one can ignore the influence of guessing completely. To do so, one should consider the laws of probability that influence the degree to which guessing might be successful. The probability of getting a higher-than-deserved score by guessing is very small as the test gets longer. For example, even in a four-option, 10-item test, the probably of getting 10 correct random guesses is .0000009. Some test developers have used correction-for-guessing formulas.

Statistical indicators exist for studying the extent and influence of guessing with each item. Specifically, in the three-parameter item response model, the third parameter is guessing. Hambleton and Swaminathan (1987) described the guessing parameter as a pseudochance level. This parameter is not intended to model the psychological process of guessing, but merely to establish that a reasonable floor exists for the difficulty parameter. This guessing parameter is used along with item difficulty and discrimination to compute a test-taker's score. The influence of the guessing parameter is small in relation to the influence of the discrimination parameter. Several polychotomous scoring models that also use correct and incorrect responses also incorporate information about guessing into scoring procedures (Sympson, 1983, 1986; Thissen & Steinberg, 1984).

Distractor Evaluation

Previous sections dealt with characteristics of test items that depend on the correct answer, without regard for distractors. This section treats the evaluation of distractors. Because we know that distractors are functionally related to the trace lines, the development of good distractors will show up in corresponding trace lines.

Traditional treatments of distractor evaluation in the authoritative *Educational Measurement* are brief (Millman & Greene, 1989; Wesman, 1971). Textbooks seldom provide an in-depth treatment of this subject, probably because not much is known about how to evaluate distractors.

Thissen, Steinberg, and Fitzpatrick (1989) stated that test users and analysts should consider that the distractor is an important part of the item. Indeed, nearly 50 years of continuous research has revealed a relationship between distractor choice and total test score (Haladyna & Sympson, 1988; Levine & Drasgow, 1983; Nishisato, 1980). In fact, there is a compelling rationale and more recent evidence to suggest that the study of distractors is necessary for sound item and test development. Schultz (1995) used a non-IRT method for increasing the reliability of test scores using option weighting. Experiments by Drasgow, Levine, Tsien, Williams, and Mead (1995) with a variety of polychotomous IRT methods resulted in some models emerging as more robust. Andrich, Styles, Tognolini, Luo, and Sheridan (1997) used partial credit with MC with some promising results. As polychotomous IRT methods become more accessible, the scoring of MC responses using distractor information may become more common place.

Many factors govern performance of the test item, one being the quality of the distractors. Although it may be obvious that the correct answer must be correct, it is equally important that the distractors must be incorrect. Experience has shown that there may accidentally be more than one correct answer for a test item, and that item response patterns for distractors seldom reflect what is expected (Haladyna & Downing, 1993). Distractor response patterns occasionally resemble correct answer response patterns or often will have no interpretable response pattern. Expert, consensus judgment is critical in determining the rightness and wrongness of options. But this is not enough. Option analysis provides insights into potential errors of judgment and inadequate performances of distractors. Distractors that fail to perform can be revised, replaced, or removed. Thus, the objective should be to detect poorly performing distractors and then take remedial action.

Three different yet complementary ways exist to study responses to distractors. First, there is the frequency table (Levine & Drasgow, 1983; Wainer, 1989) that provides a tabulation of option choices as a function of ordinal score groups. Second, trace lines provide a graphical image of item response. Third, a family of statistical indexes can be used to determine which distractors are working and which are not working.

To summarize, the conceptual rationale underpinning the creation of a distractor is that it should appeal to low scorers, those who have not mastered the domain of knowledge, whereas high scorers, who have shown a high degree of mastery of the domain of knowledge should avoid distractors. Distractors that are seldom chosen by any test-taker should be removed or replaced. These kinds of distractors are likely to be so implausible to all test-takers that hardly anyone would choose one of these. Distractors essentially unrelated to test performance should be replaced, because they fail to contribute to the functioning of the item as illustrated in Fig. 8.1. As we examine the three approaches to studying distractor performance, the main idea is that distractors should appeal to low-scoring test-takers and not appeal to high scoring test-takers. Any contradiction to this state of affairs signals an ineffective distractor.

Frequency table. The frequency table is a distribution of responses for each option according to score groups. Each score group represents an ordered fractional part of the test score distribution. Table 8.3 shows the frequency tables for two items. In this table, there are five score groups, representing five distinctly ordered ability levels. For small samples of test-takers, 5 score groups can be used, whereas with larger samples, 10 to 20 score groups might prove useful. The sum of frequencies (in percent) for each score group is the fractional equivalent of the number of test-takers in that score group to the total sample. Because we have five score groups, each row equals about 20%, one fifth of the total sample. (Sometimes, because more than one person received the same score, having exactly 20% in each score is not possible.) The column totals represent the frequency of response to each option.

For the first item, the correct answer, option A, was chosen 55% of the time, 17% by the highest score group, 14% by the next highest score group, and 6% by the lowest score group. This is a typical and desirable pattern of response for a correct answer.

Option B, a distractor, has a low response rate for the higher groups and a higher response rate for the lower groups. This is a desirable pattern for a good performing distractor. As described earlier, all distractors should have a pattern like this.

Option C illustrates a low response rate across all five score groups. Such distractors are useless, probably due to extreme implausibility. Such distractors should either be removed from the test item or replaced.

Option D illustrates a rather unchanging performance across all score groups. No orderly relation exists between this distractor and total test performance. We should remove or replace such a distractor from the test item because it is not working as intended.

The second item exhibits a distractor pattern that presents problems of interpretation and evaluation. Option D is more often chosen by the middle group and less often chosen by the higher and lower groups. This pattern is nonmonotonic, in the sense that it increases as a function of total test score and then decreases. Is this pattern a statistical accident or does the distractor attract middle achievers and not attract high and low achievers? Distractors are not designed to produce such a pattern, because the general intent of a distractor is to appeal to persons who lack knowledge. The nonmonotonic pattern shown in Option D implies that the information represented by Option D is more attractive to middle performers and less attractive to high and low performers. The nonmonotonic pattern appears to disrupt the orderly relation between right and wrong answers illustrated in Options A and B. For this reason, nonmonotonic trace lines should be viewed as undesirable.

TABLE 8.3
Frequency Tables for Two 4-Option Multiple-Choice Items

Item 1	OPTIONS			
Score[1] Group	A*	B	C	D
80-99%ile	17%	1%	0%	2%
60-79%ile	14%	2%	0%	4%
40-59%ile	10%	2%	0%	4%
20-39%ile	8%	9%	1%	2%
1-19%ile	6%	13%	3%	0%
Total	55%	27%	4%	14%

Item 2	OPTIONS			
Score[1] Group	A*	B	C	D
80-99%ile	19%	1%	0%	0%
60-79%ile	14%	3%	1%	2%
40-59%ile	8%	4%	2%	6%
20-39%ile	8%	9%	1%	2%
1-19%ile	6%	12%	1%	1%
Total	55%	29%	5%	11%

*Correct Answer
[1]In percentile ranks

Trace lines. The trace line is a graphical depiction of option performance as a function of total performance (Nunnally, 1967). Fig. 8.3 shows four trace trace lines. A four-option item can have up to five trace lines. One trace line

Frequency of Occurence for Each Score Group

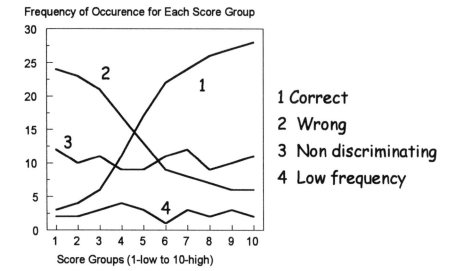

FIG. 8.3. Four types of trace lines.

exists for each option, and one for nonresponse. Because nonresponse is seldom a problem in modern tests, this trace line may be unnecessary. Where correction-for-guessing is employed, nonresponse is significant and a trace line for nonresponse is necessary because test-takers are encouraged not to guess.

An effectively performing item contains a trace line for the correct choice that is monotonically increasing, as illustrated in Fig. 8.1 and again in Fig. 8.3. These figures show that the probability or tendency to choose the right answer increases with the person's ability. The collective performance of distractors must monotonically decrease in opposite corresponding fashion, as illustrated in Fig. 8.1. That figure shows that any examinee's tendency to choose any wrong answer decreases with the person's ability/achievement.

As stated previously, the correct answer should have a trace line that is monotonically increasing, as Fig. 8.1 and Fig. 8.3 show. This trace line is lower with low-achieving test-takers and increases as total test scores increase. This is a desirable pattern for a correct answer. Correspondingly, a distractor should have a monotonically decreasing trace line. Lower scoring test-takers tend to choose this option, whereas moderate and higher scorers tend to avoid it. The third trace line in Fig. 8.3 shows a somewhat flat performance across score groups. This option simply does not discriminate in the way it is expected to discriminate. This kind of option probably has no use in the item. The fourth type of trace line in Fig. 8.3 shows low response rates for all score groups. This kind of distractor is one that is probably implausible and therefore is typically not chosen.

Trace lines can be constructed by using a standard computer graphics program, such as found with word processing programs. Statistical packages also are useful for constructing trace lines. Some of these computer programs have the option of taking the data from the frequency tables and providing smoothed curves for easier interpretation of the trace lines. An item analysis and scaling program, RUMM, introduced by Sheridan, Andrich, & Luo (1996) provides trace lines for both MC items and rating scales. Wainer (1989) and Thissen, Steinberg, and Fitzpatrick (1989) favored using trace lines. They argued that trace lines make item analysis more meaningful and interpretable. Statistical approaches can be daunting to many practitioners, and trace lines offer a valid method for studying distractor performance.

Statistical methods. Several statistical methods can be used to study distractor performance. These methods do not necessarily measure the same characteristic (Downing & Haladyna, 1997). Among these methods, two have serious shortcomings and probably should not be used, whereas the last, based on the trace line, is probably the best.

The first is the product-moment correlation between distractor performance and total test score. This is the point-biserial discrimination index that is found in most item analysis computer programs. This index considers the average performance of those selecting the distractor versus the average of those not selecting the distractor. A statistically significant positive correlation is expected for a correct choice, whereas a statistically significant negative correlation is expected for a distractor. Low-response distractors are eliminated from this analysis; the low response would suggest that such distractors are so implausible that only a few random guessers would select this option. Nonmonotonic distractors would produce negative correlations, but are subject to the test for statistical significance. This correlation is more likely to *not* be statistically significant, because the nonmonotonic trace line mimics the trace line of a correct answer in part. Also, because the number of test-takers choosing distractors is likely to be small, the statistical tests lack the results to reject the null hypothesis that the population correlation is zero. To increase the power, a directional test should be used and alpha should be set at .10. Distractors should be negatively correlated with total test score, and correct choices should be positively correlated with total test score. A bootstrap method is suggested for overcoming any bias introduced by the nature of the sample (de Gruijter, 1988), but this kind of extreme measure points out an inherent flaw in the use of this index. It should be noted that the discrimination index is not robust. If item difficulty is high or low, the index is attenuated. It maximizes when difficulty is moderate. The sample composition has much to do with the estimate of discrimination. Distractors tend to be infrequently chosen, particularly when item difficulty exceeds .75. Thus, the point-biserial correlation is often based on only a few observations, which is a serious limitation. Henrysson (1971) provided additional insights into the inadequacy of this index for the study of distractor performance. Because of these many limitations, this index probably should not be used.

Another related method is the choice mean for each distractor. As noted earlier in this chapter, the choice mean of distractors should be lower than the choice mean of the correct answer. The eta coefficient informs us about the degree of discriminability among distractors, but it does not provide a clear answer to the question of how well each distractor works. Referring to Table 8.4, however, we note that the choice mean for each distractor differs from the choice mean of the correct answer. The difference in these choice means can serve as a measure of distractor effectiveness; the lower the choice mean, the better the distractor. This difference can be standardized by using the standard deviation of test scores, if a standardized effect-size measure is desired.

The choice mean seems useful for studying distractors. The lower the choice mean, the more effective the distractor. Yet, it should be noted that a bias exists in this procedure, because when the right answer is chosen by most high-scoring test-takers, the low-scoring test-takers divide their choices among the three distractors plus the correct answer. So, distractors will always have lower choice means, and statistical tests will always reveal this condition. Any exception would signal a distractor that is probably a correct answer.

TABLE 8.4
Choice Means for Two Items from a Test

Options	Item 32	Item 45
A*	66%	88%
B	54%	86%
C	43%	84%
D	62%	85%
F-Ratio	22.44	1.04
Probability	.000...	.62
R-Squared	.12	.02

*Correct choice

As indicated earlier, the trace line has many attractive characteristics in the evaluation of item performance. These characteristics apply equally to distractor analysis. Haladyna and Downing (1993) also showed that trace lines reveal more about an option's performance than a choice mean. Whereas choice means reveal the average performance of all examinees choosing any option, the trace line accurately characterizes the functional relationship between item and total test performance as is inferred by the concept of item discrimination. For example, a distractor may have a low choice mean but a flat trace line, showing that it fails to discriminate among the score groups. So, the trace line is superior to the choice mean for evaluating a distractor.

Up to this point, the trace line has not been evaluated statistically. Haladyna and Downing (1993) showed that the trace line can be subjected to statistical criteria using a chi-square test of independence. Table 8.5 illustrates a contingency table for option performance. Applying a chi-square test to these categorical frequencies, a statistically significant result would signal a trace line that is not flat. In the above case, it is monotonically increasing, which is characteristic of a correct answer.

Thus, with the notion of option discrimination for the right choice, we expect monotonically increasing trace lines, positive point-biserial discrimination indexes, positive discrimination parameters with the two- and three-parameter models, and choice means that exceed the choice means for distractors. For the wrong choice, we expect monotonically decreasing trace lines, negative discrimination, negative discrimination parameters for the two- and three-parameter models (which are very unconventional to compute), and choice means that are lower than the choice mean for the correct option.

The trace line appears to offer a sensitive and revealing look at option performance. Trace lines can be easily understood by item writers who lack the

TABLE 8.5

Contingency Table for Chi-Squared Test for an Option

	First Score Group	Second Score Group	Third Score Group	Fourth Score Group	Fifth Score Group
Expected	20%	20%	20%	20%	20%
Observed	6%	14%	20%	26%	34%

statistical background needed to interpret option discrimination indexes. The other statistical methods all have limitations that suggest that they should not be used.

SUMMARY

This chapter has focused on the task of examining item response patterns to evaluate item performance. A variety of perspectives and methods have been described and illustrated. Tabular methods provide clear summaries of response patterns, but graphical methods are easier to understand and interpret. Statistical indexes with tests of statistical significance are necessary to distinguish between real tendencies and random variation. Binary scoring suggests one set of procedures, whereas polychotomous scoring suggests another.

9

USING ITEM RESPONSE PATTERNS TO
STUDY SPECIFIC PROBLEMS IN TESTING

OVERVIEW

C hapter 8 provided basic information about analyzing item response patterns. That chapter included both traditional and innovative methods for studying and evaluating item responses, for the purpose of revising or rejecting MC items for use in a test or adding to an item bank.

Several problems are the focus of this chapter. Each problem is unique and significant enough to deserve attention. Each problem requires resolution in most testing programs.

One of these problems is *item bias (equity)* and the associated statistical procedure known as *differential item functioning* (DIF). The existence of DIF in item responses diminishes the validity of test score interpretations and uses. The study of DIF is essential for any test with significant consequences.

Another problem is the study and detection of item response patterns that may be leading to an invalid test score interpretation. This topic is *person fit*. Another name for this is *appropriateness measurement*.

A third problem is the *dimensionality* of a set of items proposed for a test. Since the appearance of a major review of this problem by Hattie (1985), several new, interesting developments have helped us study dimensionality of test scores. Tate (1998) contributed to synthesizing recent progress in this area.

A fourth problem deals with the limitation of using dichotomous scoring for MC when we have *polychotomous scoring* tools. Specifically, in this section, we assert that information contained in distractors is both differential and advantageous in computing test scores.

Each of the four sections of this chapter provides a brief treatment of the topic, seminal references on the problem, and recommendations for use.

SECTION 1: ITEM BIAS

Test results may be used in many ways, including placement, selection, certification, licensing, or advancement. These uses have both personal and social consequences. Test-takers are often affected by test score uses. In licensing and certification, the public benefits or loses according to decisions made to license or certify professionals based on test scores.

Bias is a threat to valid interpretation or use of test scores, because bias favors one group of test-takers over another. Bias also has dual meanings. Bias is a term that suggests unfairness or an undue influence. In statistics, bias is systematic error as opposed to random error. A scale that "weighs heavy" has this statistical bias. Although bias has two identities, the public is most likely to identify with the first definition of bias rather than the second (Dorans & Potenza, 1993). We need to be mindful of the value of both definitions and act accordingly. Although the discussion has been limited to bias of test scores, in this section, the concern is with bias in item responses, thus the term item bias.

As discussed in chapter 7, sensitivity review involves a trained committee that subjectively identifies and questions items on the premise that test-takers might be distracted or offended by the item's test content or some wording. Therefore, sensitivity item review is concerned with the first meaning of item bias.

DIF refers to a statistical analysis that intends to reveal systematic differences among groups on a test score or test item response that is attributable to group membership instead of true differences in the construct being measured.

Several important resources contributed to this section. The first is an edited volume by Holland and Wainer (1993) dedicated to DIF. This book provides a wealth of information about this rapidly growing field of item response analysis. The second source is an instructional module on DIF by Clauser and Mazor (1998). Readers looking for more comprehensive discussions of DIF should consult both sources and other references provided here.

A Brief History

A barbering examination in Oregon in the late 1800s is one of the earliest examples of testing for a profession. Since then, test programs for certification, licensure, or credentialing have proliferated (Shapiro, Stutsky, & Watt, 1989). These kinds of testing programs have two very significant consequences. First, those persons taking the test need to pass to be certified or licensed to practice. Second, these tests are intended to filter competent and incompetent professionals, assuring the public of safer professional practice.

Well-documented racial differences in test scores led to widespread discontent, culminating in a court case, the Golden Rule Insurance Company versus Mathias case in the Illinois Appellate Court in 1980. Federal legislation led to policies that promoted greater monitoring of Black–White racial difference in test performance. The reasoning was that if a Black–White difference in item difficulty was greater than the observed test score difference, this result was taken as evidence of DIF. We have witnessed an explosion in the quantity and variety of DIF methods.

Methods for Studying DIF

Following a proliferation of methods and studies of them, research shows that these methods share much in common. We can delineate the field of DIF using five discrete methods with the understanding that items detected via one method are likely to be identified via other methods.

1. IRT methods. This class of methods feature comparisons of trace lines for different groups of examinees or item parameters. Normally, there is a reference group and a focal group from which to make comparisons. A statistically significant difference implies that the item is differentially favoring one group over another (Thissen, Steinberg, & Wainer, 1993). However, it matters which IRT model is used, because the simplest (Rasch) involves difficulty, but DIF may occur with discrimination or the guessing (pseudochance) parameters as well. These methods have large sample size requirements and users must have a good understanding of how parameters are estimated and compared.

2. Mantel-Haenzel (MH) statistic. Introduced by Holland and Thayer (1988), this method is one of the most popular. Frequency counts are done using a contingency table based on the reference and focal groups. This statistic considers the odds of two different groups correctly answering an item when ability of the groups is already statistically controlled. Specific details on its calculation and uses can be found in Holland and Thayer (1988) or Dorans and Holland (1993). The statistic is evaluated using a chi-square test. Holland and Thayer suggested that the MH statistic is similar to the procedure for DIF associated with the Rasch model. This fact also supports the idea that the many DIF statistics proposed do share this ability in common. However, the MH statistic is considered one of the most powerful for detecting DIF, which explains its popularity.

3. Standardization. This method is the simplest to understand and apply and has the most common appeal among practitioners. However, this method lacks a statistical test. Dorans and Holland (1993) and Dorans and Kullick (1986) provided good accounts of the development of this method, which is based on empirical trace line analysis and a standardized difference in difficulty for the focal and reference groups. They pointed out the proximity of this method to the MH.

4. SIBTEST. This computer program introduced by Shealy and Stout (1993) reflects the standardization method but has a statistical test. It produces results similar to the MH statistic and does well with small samples. This approach has many features that are attractive to users. One can experiment with the elimination of DIF items to obtain a shorter test that is free of differentially performing items. Despite its newness, research on this method has increased its visibility as a DIF method.

5. Logistic regression. One might consider this method as a unifying idea for the other methods provided. It operates from a contingency table but uses total score as the criterion measure. Although it approximates results found with MH, it is superior for nonuniform DIF situations. Thus, this method is more adaptable to a greater variety of situations.

Conclusions and Recommendations

DIF is a healthy and actively growing field of study. The emerging DIF technology assisted by user-friendly software gives test users important and necessary tools to improve test items and therefore improve the validity of test score interpretations and uses. For formal testing programs, especially when the stakes for test-takers and the test sponsor are moderate to high, DIF studies are essential validity evidence. The *Standards for Educational and Psychological Testing* (APA, 1985) are specific about the need to examine bias and deal with it accordingly. Therefore, DIF studies of item responses seem unavoidable.

Clauser and Mazor (1998) provided a comprehensive discussion of these methods and situations when one might be preferred to another. They described several conditions to be considered before choosing a DIF method. Although these methods share much in common, detailed discussion of these conditions before choosing a method. Overall, it seems the choice of any method could be justified.

As Ramsey (1993) pointed out, however, the use of DIF requires human judgment. Statistics alone will not justify the inclusion or rejection of any item. Thus, the process of studying item bias via DIF is a an more involved process that includes judgment along with the use of one of these five DIF methods.

SECTION 2: PERSON FIT

Person fit is an emerging field of item response study that examines item response patterns on a person by person basis to detect if something is happening that would lead us to conclude that test scores cannot be validly interpreted. This field also applies to groups of persons who have some common problem. Another term used in this new and growing field is *appropriateness measurement*.

The objective of person fit is statistical detection of invalid test scores. Such invalid test scores can arise in many ways, and there are many detection methods. In this section, types of test performance problems that might be encountered are identified. Then, theories and methods are discussed. An entire issue of *Applied Measurement in Education* (Meijer, 1996) was devoted to person-fit research and applications. Readers looking for more comprehensive discussions should consult the contributing authors' articles and the many references they provided as well as those provided in this section.

Types of Person Item Response Misfits

In this section, types of item response patterns that might lead to misfitting interpretation of item response data are discussed. The intent in this section is to support person-fit analysis as a standard procedure in testing programs where the stakes are significant for the test-taker or the sponsor of the testing program. This section is derived from several sources including Wright and Stone (1979), Meijer (1996), Meijer, Muijtjens, and van der Vleuten (1996), and Drasgow, Levine, and Zickar (1996).

Cheating

Cheating inflates estimates of knowledge or ability thus leading to invalid interpretations and uses of test scores. In many circumstances, the use of test scores inflated by cheating may have harmful effects on the public. In licensing testing, a passing score obtained by an incompetent physician, pharmacist, nurse, architect, or automotive mechanic might negatively affect the public.

The problem of cheating is significant. Cannell (1989), Haladyna, Nolen, and Haas (1991), and Mehrens and Kaminski (1989) discussed aspects and ramifications of cheating in standardized testing. They reported on the extensiveness of this problem in American testing.

According to Frary (1993), methods to combat cheating in high-stakes testing programs involve scrambling of test items from form to form, multiple test forms each consisting of different sets of items, or careful monitoring of test-takers during test administration. Given that these methods may fail to prevent cheating, test administrators need to identify potential instances of cheating and obtain evidence in support of an accusation.

An extensive literature exists for the detection of patterns of answer copying by test-takers. For example, Bellezza and Bellezza (1989) reported in their review of this problem, that about 75 % of undergraduate college students resort to some form of cheating. They suggested an error-similarity pattern analysis based on binomial probabilities. Bellezza and Bellezza's index resembles earlier indexes suggested by Angoff (1974) and Cody (1985). They offered a FORTRAN computer program that can be used with a personal computer. Such a program could be written for a mainframe computer to deal with larger testing programs. The method identifies outliers, performances so similar with respect to wrong answers, that it may have occurred through copying. SCRUTINY (*Advanced Psychometrics*, 1998) is another computer program designed to screen test results for possible copying. This program has a report called *suspicious similarities report* that identifies those examinees who may have copied someone else's answers. Such programs are well within the capabilities of most current personal computers.

It is important to note that the study of patterns of right answers may be misleading because it is possible for two persons studying together to have similar patterns of right answers, but it is unlikely that wrong answer patterns will be similar because distactors have differential attractiveness and most tests have three or four distactors per item.

Test Anxiety

A persistent problem in any standardized and classroom testing setting is anxiety that depresses test performance. Hill and Wigfield (1984) estimated that about 25% of the population has some form of test anxiety. Test anxiety is treatable. One way is to prepare adequately for the test. Another strategy is to provide good test-taking skills that include psychological preparation and time-management strategies.

Inattention

Test-takers who are not well motivated or easily distracted may choose MC answers carelessly. Wright (1977) called such test-takers *sleepers*. If sleeper patterns are identified, test scores might be invalidated. The types of tests that come to mind that might have many inattentive test-takers are standardized achievement tests given to elementary and secondary students. Many students have little reason or motivation to sustain a high level of concentration demanded on these lengthy tests. This point was demonstrated in a study by Wolf and Smith (1995) with college students. With consequences in a course test, student motivation and performance was higher than a comparable nonconsequences condition. This point was also well made by Paris, Lawton, Turner, and Roth (1991) in their analysis of the effects of standardized testing on children. They pointed out that older children tend to think that such tests has less importance, thus increasing the possibility for inattention.

Omitting Versus Guessing

Under conditions of guessing when the correct answer cannot be identified, testwise examinees usually answer all items on a test, so that nonresponse is not a problem. In some testing situations, test-takers are encouraged to omit an answer instead of guessing. Personality factors interplay here with test-taking (testwiseness) strategies. This area is much understudied (Hutchinson, 1994; Wisner & Wisner, 1997). And the debate about penalties for guessing has not been resolved. Nonetheless, most testing programs permit guessing without any formal training or orientation about how to guess.

Idiosyncratic Answering

Under conditions where the test does not have important consequences to the test-taker, some test-takers may mark in peculiar patterns, to give the appearance that they are seriously taking the test. Such behavior produces a negative bias in scores, affecting both individual and group performances. Some examples could be pattern marking, for example, ABCDABCDABCD..., or BBBCCCBBBCCC... The identification and removal of offending scores helps improve the accuracy of group results. Tests without serious consequences to older children will be more subject to idiosyncratic pattern marking. A tendency among school-age children to mark idiosyncratically has been documented in several studies (e.g., Paris et al., 1991). Thus, the problem seems significant in situations where the test-takers have little reason to do well.

Plodding

As described under the topic of nonresponse, some students under conditions of a timed test, may not have enough time to answer all items due to their plodding nature. These persons are very careful and meticulous in approaching each item and also may lack test-taking skills that encourage time management strategies. Thus, they do not answer items at the end of the test. The result is a lower score than deserved. It is not possible to extend the time limit for most standardized tests; therefore, the prevention of the problem lies in better test-taking training. The detection of plodders can be done by methods discussed in the next section.

Coaching

In testing situations where the outcomes are especially important, such as licensing examinations, there are many test coaching services that provide specific content instruction that may be articulated with part of the test. Another context for coaching is with college admissions testing. Reviews of the extant research on admissions testing coaching by Becker (1990) and Linn (1990a) provided evidence that most coaching gains are of a small nature, usually less than one fifth of a standard deviation. Linn made the important point that the crucial consideration is not how much scores have changed, but how much the underlying trait that the test purportedly measures has changed. If coaching involved item-specific strategies, then interpretation of any gain should be that test behavior does not generalize to the larger domain that the test score represents. If coached test-takers are compared with uncoached test-takers, the subsequent interpretations might be flawed. Haladyna, Nolen, and Haas (1991) called this practice *test score pollution*, arguing that such coaching may boost test performance without substantially affecting the domain that a test score represents.

The detection of coaching can be using any of the techniques identified and discussed in the section on differential item functioning in this chapter. The necessary precondition to using these techniques is to identify two groups, one coached and one uncoached. Items displaying DIF provide evidence of the types of items, content, and cognitive demand that affect test scores. But research of this type about coaching effects has not yet been reported. In fact, Becker (1990) stated that the quality of most research on coaching is inadequate.

Another important issue about coaching is what action to take with test-takers who have received specific coaching. Because such scores may be argued to be invalid in some circumstances, should sponsoring organizations invalidate scores of people who have been coached for a test, or should interpretations of coached results be tempered?

Creative Test-takers

Someone may find test items so easy that they will reinterpret and provide answers that only they can intelligently justify. These students may also provide correct answers to more difficult items. Statistics can identify these persons. This pattern also resembles a lazy test-taker who might "cruise" through an easy part of a test until challenged.

Language Deficiency

Test-takers may have a high degree of knowledge about a domain but fail to show this knowledge because the test-taker's primary language is not English. In these instances, any interpretation or use of a test score should be declared invalid. Standard 6.10 in the *Standards for Educational and Psychological Testing* (APA, 1985) urged caution in test score interpretation and use when the language of the test exceeds the linguistic abilities of test-takers. The problem of language deficiency might also fall in two previously discussed categories, non response and plodding. But because we have so many second-language learners in the United States, emphasizing the problem this way seems justified. Testing policies seldom recognize that language deficiency introduces bias in test scores and leads to faulty interpretations of student knowledge or ability.

Marking or Alignment Errors

Test responses are often made on optically scannable answer sheets. Sometimes, in the midst of this anxiety-provoking testing situation, test-takers may mark in the wrong places on the answer sheet. Marking across instead of down, or down instead of across, or skipping one place and marking in all other places, so that all answers are off by one or more positions. Such detection is possible. The policy to deal with the problem is again another issue. Mismarked answer sheets produce invalid test scores. Therefore, it seems reasonable that these mismarked sheets must be detected and removed from the scoring and reporting process, and the test-taker might be given an opportunity to correct the error if obtaining a validly interpreted score is important.

Methods of Detecting Person Fit and Research

The field of person fit seems bifurcated. One road follows traditional IRT methods (Drasgow, Levine, & Zickar, 1996), another following nonparametric methods (Meijer, Muijtjens, & van der Vleuten, 1996). Each is briefly discussed and some research will be reported bearing on the success of these methods. This field is ripe for further study, as the theoretical groundwork has been laid and computer software is appearing that handles detection of person fit problems.

IRT Solutions to Person Fit

IRT methods are useful because they can detect a variety of test performance problems, but IRT is limited by the need for large samples. The chief characteristic of these methods is the use of an explicit statistical IRT model. Appropriateness measurement should offer evidence that a test score may be invalid. This array of uses shows the application of appropriateness measurement to greater problems than is the object of this section.

The context or purpose for an index for person fit is important. Drasgow and Guertler (1987) stated that several subjective judgments are necessary. For example, if one is using a test to make a pass/fail certification decision, the location of a dubious score relative to the passing score and the relative risk one is willing to take have much to do with these decisions. Other factors to consider in using these indexes are (a) the cost of retesting, (b) the risk of misclassification, (c) the cost of misclassification, and (d) the confidence or research evidence supporting the use of the procedure.

According to Drasgow, Levine, and Williams (1985), aberrant response patterns are identified by first applying a model to a set of normal responses and then using a measure of goodness of fit, an appropriateness index, to find out the degree to which anyone deviates from normal response patterns. Levine and Rubin (1979) showed that such detection was achievable, and since then there has been a steady progression of studies involving several theoretical models (Drasgow, 1982; Drasgow, Levine, & Zickar, 1996; Levine & Drasgow, 1982, 1983). These studies were initially done using the three-parameter item response model, but later studies involved polychotomous item response models (Drasgow et al., 1985). Drasgow et al. (1996) provided an update of their work. They indicated that appropriateness measurement is most powerful because it has the higher rate of error detection when compared to other methods. With the coming of better computer programs, more extensive research can be conducted, and testing programs might consider employing these methods to identify test-takers whose results should not be reported, interpreted, or used.

Nonparametric Person Fit

Whereas the first approach to person fit employs actual and ideal response patterns using one- or three-parameter IRT models, the nonparametric person fit statistics derive from the use of nonparametric models. Like the field of DIF, a proliferation of methods has resulted in a large array of choices and little research to gain guidance about which is best. According to Meijer et al. (1996), three methods that stand out here are the Sato Caution Index, and the Modified Caution Index, and the U3 statistic.

The student-problems (SP) chart. Sato (1975) introduced a simple pattern analysis for a classroom based on the idea that some scores deserve a cautious interpretation. Like appropriateness measurement, the caution index and its derivatives have a broad array of applications, but this section will be limited to only those problems discussed earlier. The focus of pattern analysis is the S–P chart that is a display of right and wrong answers for a class. Table 9.1 is adapted from Tatsuoka and Linn (1983), and contains the right and wrong responses to 10 items for 15 students. Not only does the S–P chart identify aberrant scores, but it also identifies items with aberrant item response patterns. The S–P chart is based on two boundaries, the *S–curve* and the *P–curve*, and a student/item matrix of item responses. Students are ordered by scores, and items are placed from easy on the left side of the chart to hard on the right. The *S–curve* is constructed by counting the number correct for any student and constructing the boundary line to the right of the item response for that student. For the 15 students, there are

TABLE 9.1
Students/Problems (SP) Chart for a Class of 15 Students
on a 10-Item Test

Student	Items										
	1	2	3	4	5	6	7	8	9	10	Tot.
1	1	1	1	1	1	1	1	1	1	1	10
2	1	1	1	1	1	1	1	1	1	0	9
3	1	1	1	1	1	0	1	1	0	1	8
4	1	0	1	1	1	1	0	1	0	0	6
5	1	1	1	1	0	1	0	0	1	0	6
6	1	1	1	0	1	0	1	0	1	0	6
7	1	1	1	1	0	0	1	0	0	0	5
8	1	1	1	0	1	1	0	0	0	0	5
9	1	0	0	1	0	1	0	1	1	0	5
10	1	1	0	1	0	0	1	0	0	1	5
11	0	1	1	1	1	0	0	0	0	0	4
12	1	0	0	0	1	1	0	0	0	0	3
13	1	1	0	0	0	1	0	0	0	0	3
14	1	0	1	0	0	0	0	0	0	0	2
15	0	1	0	0	0	0	0	0	0	0	1
Item Diff.	13	11	10	9	8	8	6	5	5	4	
p-value	87	73	67	60	53	53	40	33	23	27	

Note. Based on "Indices for detecting unusual patterns: Links between two general approaches and potential applications." by K. K. Tatsuoka and R. L. Linn, 1983, *Applied Psychological Measurement, 7*, 81-96.

are 15 boundary lines that are connected to form the *S–curve*. If a student answers items correctly outside of the *S–curve* (to the right of the *S–curve*), this improbable result implies that the score should be considered cautiously. Similarly, if a student misses an item inside of the *S–curve* (to the left of the *S–curve*, this improbable result implies that the student failed items that a student of this achievement level would ordinarily answer correctly. In the first instance, the student passed items that would normally be failed. Referring to Table 9.1, Student 9 answered Items 6, 8, and 9 correctly, which would normally be missed by students at this level of achievement. Student 9 also missed two easy items. A total of 5 improbable responses for Student 9 points to a potential problem of interpretation of this student score of 5 out of 10 (50%). The *P–curve* is constructed by counting the number right in the class for each item and drawing a boundary line below that item response in the matrix. For example, the first item was correctly answered by 13 of 15 students so the *P–curve* boundary line is drawn below the item response for the 13th student. Analogous to the *S–curve*, it is improbable to miss an item above the P–curve and answer an item below the *P–curve* correctly. Item 6 shows that three high-scoring students missed this item whereas three low-scoring students answered it correctly. Item 6 has an aberrant response pattern that causes us to look at it more closely. A variety of indexes is available that provides numerical values for each student and item (see Meijer et al., 1996; Tatsuoka & Linn, 1983).

U3

The underlying assumption for this method is that for a set of examinees with a specific total score, their item response patterns can be compared. If number correct is identical, examinees with aberrant score patterns are subject to further consideration for misfitting. Van der Flier (1982) derived this person-fit statistic and studied its characteristics. The premise of U3 is the comparison of probabilities of an item score pattern in conjunction with the probability of the pattern of correct answers. The index is zero if the student responses follow a Guttman pattern. An index of one is the reverse Guttman pattern. Meijer, Molenaar, and Sijtsma (1994) evaluated U3, finding it to be extremely useful for detecting item response problems. In a series of studies by Meijer and his associates, a number of positive findings were reported for U3. One important finding was that this method works best under conditions of higher reliability, longer tests, and situations where a high proportion of examinees have aberrant patterns. U3 can also be applied to group statistics of person fit. Meijer and Sijtsma (1995) concluded that U3 was the best among a great many proposed indices available because the sampling distribution is known, facilitating interpretation of results.

Conclusions and Recommendations

Although the study by Rudner, Bracey, and Skaggs (1996) suggested that person-fit was nonproductive for a high quality testing program, it seems prudent to consider person-fit studies as part of the overall validation effort. In their study, only 3 % of their sample had person-fit problems. Although this percentage may seem small, consider that these few instances may have led to negative consequences for the test-takers. This concern echoes the current and appropriate consideration of social consequences that Messick (1989) originally championed.

Several of the testing specialists in the field of person-fit have stated that the statistical procedure leads to establishing a signal of a problem and further investigation is warranted (e.g., Meijer & Sijtsma, 1995). It would be inappropriate to eliminate or invalidate scores simply on the basis of person-fit statistics alone. Also, they suggested using person fit to study instructional patterns and problems. If a group of test-takers has a misfit problem, one can consider removing this group in an effort to improve the inference or interpretation we make for test scores. Finally, the concept of person fit actually applies to classroom testing, but the technology for how to do this is not very well developed. Skillful teachers who understand the principles discussed in this section can informally study item responses, perhaps using the kind of logic expressed in the Sato student-item matrix.

SECTION 3: DIMENSIONALITY

The underlying structure of item responses is fundamental to construct validity. Indeed, the history of cognitive measurement has focused on the making and interpreting of homogeneous tests consisting of items that share a common factor or dimension (MacDonald, 1985). For instance, Nunnally (1977) stated:

> *Each test should be homogeneous in content, and consequently the items on each test should correlate substantially with one another.* (p. 247)

Messick (1989) stated that a single score on a test implies a single dimension. If a test contains several dimensions, a multidimensional approach should be used. A total test score from a multidimensional test is subject to misinterpretation or misuse because differential performance in any dimension might be overlooked by forming a composite score. Item and test characteristics may go awry. That is because classical and traditional IRT methods assume unidimensionality among item responses. Violations of the unidimensionality assumption play strange tricks on our computer software and give us bad results.

A seminal review by Hattie (1985) provided one of the best syntheses of thinking about dimensionality to that date. Since then, a host of test analysts and researchers have improved methods of study and increased our ability to study item responses from a number of perspectives. In this section, we review four of these recent trends, suggest fruitful further research, and encourage more use of these methods in everyday test and item analyses.

Definition of Dimensionality

Fundamentally, any definition of dimensionality should focus on what a test measures. In construct validity, the formulation of the construct identifies whether we intend a unidimensional or multidimensional character to our test.

Tate (1998) defined test dimensionality as "the minimum number of dimensions of a test for a specified examinee population resulting in responses that are locally independent." (p. 3) The concept of local independence means that items are not related in such a way that the probability of a correct response on one item is strongly influenced by the probability of a response on the other item. Practically speaking, item sets are well known to suffer from local dependence (Haladyna, 1992a). Also, some items may cue other items, and by that, become locally dependent. Statistically, the joint probability of correct answers for any pair of items is equal to the product of the probability of a correct response for each item.

Methods of Study

Factor analysis is the primary means for studying item response structure . About the time of the review by Hattie (1985), it was widely understood that traditional linear factor analysis was inappropriate for analyzing item responses. Its limitation resides mainly with the use of phi or point-biserial correlations among items. Factor analysis based on these correlation coefficients may result in a difficulty factor or too many factors due to the range of item difficulties. A tetrachoric correlational approach is preferred because it assumes that the underlying trait in dichotomously scored items is continuous, not binary. Thus, the methods discussed in this section improve on traditional linear factor analysis. Computer programs are available for these methods. In this section, we briefly review the four methods, but readers seeking more detailed discussion should consult Tate (1998) and other references provided here.

Nonlinear Factor Analysis

The computer program NOHARM (Fraser, 1986) allows the use of nonlinear factor analysis in both exploratory and confirmatory modes. The user can then employ orthogonal or oblique rotations. The program provides a test for local independence. A method for assessing model fit is available that derives from successively more complex solutions regarding dimensionality. A manual is provided with NOHARM regarding procedures for performing this analysis.

An adjunct program was developed by DeChamplain and Tang (1997) called CHIDIM (chi-squared test of the fit of the estimated model). This program looks at changes in fit statistics as the factor analysis results increase in factorial complexity. When the fit statistic is sufficiently small, the current factor structure is taken as true.

Full-Information Factor Analysis

The computer program TESTFACT developed by Wilson, Wood, and Gibbons (1992) provides a factor analysis with a complete or partial matrix of student-item responses. The procedure starts with a principal component analysis using the tetrachoric correlation matrix. Like NOHARM, TESTFACT provides for orthogonal or oblique rotations. TESTFACT also has several tests, one of which allows for increasing the complexity of the solution. These two factor analysis methods share much in common. TESTFACT is an considered exploratory approach.

Confirmatory Factor Analysis

Exploratory factor analysis has existed as a tool to determine possible factor structures as an aid to clarifying the nature of data. Confirmatory factor analysis is generally considered advantageous when researchers or test developers have a good understanding of the structure of data intended. However, the distinction between confirmatory and exploratory is somewhat vague, and might be considered along a continuum.

In testing, we have argued that unidimensionality is important in measuring constructs. The computer programs PRELIS 2.14 and LISREL 8.14 (Joreskog & Sorbom, 1989) provide factor solutions for item responses. This procedure has large sample size requirements. For example, with 50 items, the sample size would have to be 1,225. A number of tests are provided for assessing unidimensionality. The range of global indexes and statistical tests is impressive. This procedure provides test researchers with a wealth of information. One feature is the ability to test for a one-factor model and then determine if the structure is hierarchical. Direct tests of such hierarchy are possible.

Nonparametric Analyses of Item Covariances

This fourth method works from item associations that are analogous to covariance residuals in factor analysis. Although this method is not strictly factor analytic, it comes close. Conditional item association involves item covariances. For any pair of items, residual covariance can exist after the influence of a single factor has been extracted. Although this methods differs from the factor analysis methods just discussed, this method answers the same question that factor analysis answers. The procedure can work within or outside IRT. DIMTEST and DETECT are recommended computer programs representing this fourth method (Stout, Nandakumar, Junker, Chang, & Steidlinger, 1993). DIMTEST is intended as the formal test of unidimensionality, whereas DETECT is recommended as a follow-up procedure. The data is multidimensional DETECT is considered exploratory, although a confirmatory version is forthcoming (Tate, 1998).

Research on These Four Methods

Tate (1998) also provided results of a study of both real and simulated data involving these four procedures. The first data set was presumed to be unidimensional but included 2 days of testing which was detected as a factor with each of these procedures. The first data set also included item sets, which are known to have a local dependence problem. The consistent finding was two factors, reflecting the 2 days of testing. Each method detected the two factors attributed to testing days, with two procedures isolating some passage-dependent items. The fourth method appeared to be the most sensitive to nuances of this first data set.

The second data set was simulated to have both unidimensional and multidimensional subsets. Results were very complex, but showed that these methods performed very well under a variety of conditions with the exception of the confirmatory factor analysis, which failed to detect some conditions of multidimensionality and has the sample size restriction.

Conclusions and Recommendations

The role of factor analysis in the study of the structure of item responses has been underappreciated in test development and validation. For example, the authoritative *Educational Measurement* (Linn, 1989) provided few references to the role that factor analysis plays in test development. But recent research, as evidenced by references in this section, provides a strong rationale for the use of any of these procedures as a vital step in test development and interpretation.

Hambleton (1989) provided a useful summary of procedures that should be employed in assessing goodness of fit. Under unidimensionality in his chart, he mentioned two of the procedures described here (involving NOHARM and TESTFACT). Research about the efficacy of these alternate models under various conditions is still needed, because Tate's study showed some variations among methods as a function of certain conditions.

The reader should not be deceived into thinking that studies of dimensionality are simply a matter of running computer programs as described here. Thorough understanding of the underpinnings of factor analysis and of each method is crucial to its successful use. Tate (1998) provided rich details of these considerations. Coupled with the manuals, users of any of these computer programs might be pleased with the results they get and will be better able to defend their definition of the what their tests measure.

SECTION 4: POLYCHOTOMOUS SCALING OF MC ITEM RESPONSES

MC items are usually scored in a binary fashion, zero for an incorrect choice and one for a correct choice. A total score is the sum of correct answers. With the one-parameter IRT model, there is a transformation of the total score to a scaled score. With the two- and three-parameter models, the transformation to a scaled score is more complex, because items are weighted so that any raw score can have different scaled scores based on the pattern of correct answers. With the traditional binary-scoring IRT models, no recognition is given to the differential nature of distactors. Polychotomous IRT models permit scoring as a function of distactors chosen. This section deals with the potential of using information from distactors for scoring MC tests.

Are MC Distractors Differentially Discriminating?

The answer is yes. Traditional methods for studying distractor functioning are rare, but the few studies reported are convincing of this fact (Haladyna & Downing, 1993; Haladyna & Sympson, 1988; Levine & Drasgow, 1983; Thissen, 1976; Thissen, Steinberg, & Fitzpatrick, 1989; Thissen, Steinberg, & Mooney, 1989; Wainer, 1989).

As indicated in chapter 8, one of the best ways to study distractor performance is via the trace line (item response plot or option characteristic curve). Desirable distactors have a natural monotonically decreasing as a function of ability. A negative discrimination index results. Other types of distractor trace lines that were discussed in chapter 8 are increasing—indicating a key error, flat—indicating no pattern, and close to zero frequency—indicating implausibility.

Seldom are all distactors alike in this characteristic. If discriminations among distactors can be made, it is possible to use responses to distactors to score tests. The next sections deal with some scoring methods for using distactors to score MC tests.

1. Linear Option Weighting and the Method of Reciprocal Averages

Richardson and Kuder (1933) suggested a method whereby coefficient alpha is maximized, and Guttman (1941) proposed this method for MC item responses. Lord (1958) showed the relationship of this method to the first principal component in factor analysis. Indeed, the method of reciprocal averages does maximize coefficient alpha. Haladyna and Sympson (1988) reviewed the extant research on reciprocal averages and concluded that studies generally supported the premise that methods such as reciprocal averages tended to purify traits, eliminating construct irrelevant variance. Evidence of this came from increases in the alpha coefficient and increases in the eigenvalue of the first principal component in factor analysis. Weighting options seems to yield a more homogeneous test score. In other words, the alpha reliability of the option-weighted score is higher than the alpha of the binary score.

The method of reciprocal averages involves computing the average score for all examinees who chose any option. The option weights are used to compute a test score. Then the procedure is repeated. A new set of weights are computed and used to compute a test score. This process continues until improvement in coefficient alpha maximizes. A test score is simply the sum of products of weights and responses. Cross validation is recommended regarding weights. Although the method has this iterative feature, experience shows that a single estimation is very close to the iterative result (Haladyna, 1990). In the framework of a certification/licensing examination, the procedure produced positive results but the computational complexity brings to our attention a major limitation of this method. Haladyna (1990) and Schultz (1995) provided predictable results showing the option weighting performs better than simple dichotomous scoring with respect to alpha estimates of reliability and decision making consistency.

2. Polychotomous IRT Scaling of MC Responses

Polychotomous IRT models proposed by Bock (1972), Masters (1982), and Samejima (1979) led to the development of promising computer programs such as MULTILOG, BIGSTEPS, and PARSCALE that permitted the analysis of rating scale data. But the application of these models to MC items has been slow to develop. Perhaps a major reason for slow development is the discouraging finding that polychotomous scaling of MC item responses usually leads to small gains in internal consistency reliability at the high cost of a complex and cumbersome procedure (Haladyna & Sympson, 1988).

The most current, comprehensive, and thorough review of IRT scaling was done by Drasgow et al. (1995). They fitted a number of proposed models to three large standardized cognitive tests. They concluded that fitting MC responses to these polychotomous IRT models was problematic, especially when examinees omitted responses.

Andrich, et al. (1997) proposed a graded response method for scaling MC items based on distractor information, the Rasch extended logistic model. This model is suitable for multicategory scoring such as that seen with rating scales and MC when distactors are considered. The computer program RUMM developed by Andrich, Luo, and Sheridan (1996) provides a user-friendly method for scaling MC. Research comparing results obtained by RUMM with other methods, such as reciprocal averages has yet to be reported, but should help us understand the influence of distactors in polychotomous MC scaling and practicality of IRT approaches to polychotomous MC scaling.

Conclusions and Recommendations

A revival of research on polychotomous scoring of MC item responses has been prompted by new IRT software. This research should continue to show that distactors provide different degrees of information about the latent trait that a test measures, and that it is possible to score MC item responses using the information provided by distactors. This scoring is much more complicated than simply summing correct answers or using dichotomous IRT software. But if the benefit is increased precision of test scores, then it could be argued in high-stakes testing such as for graduation or certification/licensure, that such precision is justified.

However, a major limitation of this research and its implications for test development is that writing MC items is still more art than science. Distractors must have a monotonically decreasing trace line. All other types of distactors essentially are unusable or contribute little to scoring. The U-shaped trace line is especially problematic. Even though we can score U-shaped distributions, the interpretation of this event is difficult to make.

The objective of improving scoring is not the only reason for promoting polychotomous scoring of MC item responses. The continued study of trace lines should help us develop strategies for writing better distactors. As item writing improves, polychotomous scoring will be more productive.

SUMMARY

This chapter has focused on four problems that have received recent attention by theorists and researchers. All four problems have strong implications for test practices involving item responses that should improve the validity of test score interpretations and uses. As we think of these four problems, studies related to each become part of the validity evidence can be used to support interpretations and uses of test scores.

IV

The Future of Item Development

10

THE FUTURE OF ITEM DEVELOPMENT

OVERVIEW

Item writing has been characterized in this book as a science much in need of nourishing theory and research. The promising theories of item writing discussed in Roid and Haladyna (1982) have not resulted in further research and development. In fact, these theories have been virtually abandoned. However, statistical methods for the study of item response have thrived.

In this final chapter, the science of item development is discussed in the contexts that affect its future. These contexts include (a) the role of policy at national, state, and local levels, politics, and educational reform, (b) the emergence of cognitive psychology and the retrenchment of behaviorism, (c) changes in the way we define outcomes of schooling and professional training, and (d) emergence of statistical test score theories and computer programs that are more in step with recent cognitive psychology. These four contexts should greatly influence the future of item development.

FACTORS AFFECTING THE FUTURE OF ITEM DEVELOPMENT

Policy, Politics, and School Reform

Education consists of various communities. These communities provide educational opportunities to millions of people in a variety of ways and at difference levels of learning that include preschool, elementary and secondary schools, undergraduate university and college education, graduate programs, professional, military, and business training, professional development, and adult continuing education that reflects recreational, personal, or human development.

Policymakers represent a very important community within education. Policymakers include elected and appointed federal and state officials and school board members. They have political philosophies, constituencies, advisors, and specific objectives that affect how tests are developed and used. Their main responsibilities are to make policy and then allocate resources.

Although many of these policy makers may not be well informed about schools, schooling, theories, research on schooling, cognitive psychology, or statistical test score theories, they have considerable influence on educational practice. These policymakers will continue to make decisions affecting testing in their jurisdictions.

House (1991) characterized educational policy as heavily influenced by economic and social conditions and political philosophies. He traced recent history regarding the status of schools, concerning our economic and social conditions, to two rivaling political positions—liberal and conservative. In the liberal view, increases in spending on education will lead to better trained people who will be producers as opposed to consumers of our resources. In the conservative view, the failure of education to deal with the poor has resulted in undisciplined masses who have contributed heavily to economic and social woes. Thus, political education platforms and their policies affect educational policy, and, more specifically, educational testing. With respect to changes in testing in the nation, states, and local school districts, the education platforms of political parties have a major influence on the testing policies and practices in each jurisdiction.

School reform appears to have received its impetus from the report *A Nation At Risk* (National Commission on Educational Excellence, 1983). Another significant movement is restructuring of schools, which is more systemic and involves decentralized control of schools by parents, teachers, and students. One of many forces behind the reform movement has been the misuse of standardized test scores. In recent years, test scores have been used in ways unimagined by the original developers and publishers of these tests (Haladyna, Haas, & Allison, 1998; Mehrens & Kaminski, 1989; Nolen, Haladyna, & Haas, 1992). The need for accountability has also created a ruthless *test score improvement* industry where vendors and educators employ many questionable practices to raise test scores in high stakes cognitive tests (Cannell, 1989; Nolen et al., 1992).

With respect to school reform, traditional ideas and practices must be reexamined and reevaluated. This reform movement will lead to new testing paradigms where some of these traditional ideas and practices will survive, but others will not. Indeed, this is already underway. Performance testing has had a profound effect on educational testing in the nation, in states, in classrooms, and on teaching.

MC testing has enjoyed a renaissance as policymakers and educators realize that the foundation of most education and training is acquisition of knowledge. MC is still the best way to measure knowledge. Also, MC is useful in approximating many types of higher level thinking processes. As we get better in using new MC formats, our ability to design better MC tests is increasing.

Cognitive Psychology

Behaviorism has been well established in teaching and testing. Most varieties of systematic instruction have behaviorist origins and characteristics. Included in this list of behaviorally based examples are objective-based learning, outcome-based learning, mastery learning, the personalized system of instruction, competency-based instruction, and the Carroll model for school learning. These teaching methods have the common elements of unit mastery, well-defined learning outcomes, and criterion-referenced tests closely linked to learner outcomes. However, the focus on knowledge and skills falls short of the need to use knowledge and skills in complex ways to solve problems, think critically, and create. Behavioral approaches to teaching may diminish in stature as we develop better ideas about developing complex cognitive abilities such as reading, writing, problem solving, and critical thinking.

Cognitive psychology has still not emerged as a unified science of human learning. Snow and Lohman (1989) described cognitive psychology as a loose confederation of scientists studying various aspects of cognitive behavior. Terminology among cognitive psychologists varies considerably. For instance, knowledge structures are variously called mental models, frames, or schemas (Mislevy, 1993). Despite this heterogeneity in the theoretical bases for research, many cognitive psychologists are working on the same problems in much the same way with a common theoretical orientation, namely that (a) learners develop their working internal models to solve problems, (b) these models develop from personal experience, and (c) these models are used to solve other similar situations encountered in life. The most intelligent behavior consists of a variety of working models (schemas, the building blocks of cognition) that have greater generality. The issue of learning task generality to other problems encountered is critical to learning theory and testing.

Dibello, Roussos, and Stout (1993) proposed a unified theory drawing heavily from earlier work by Tatsuoka (1985) and her colleagues. An emergent unified theory of school learning, such as this one, hopes to explain how students find, organize, and use knowledge. An emerging theory will:

1. likely derive from current and past information processing theories.
2. incorporate ideas of declarative, procedural, and strategic knowledge, as opposed to the more traditional dichotomy of knowledge and skills. Dibello et al. (1993) also proposed schematic and algorithmic knowledge.

3. provide a basis for organizing both declarative and procedural knowledge using schemata, and a complete understanding of how these will lead to more effective teaching methods.

4. place emphasis on problem solving and other types of higher level thinking. Problem solving will be more complex than we realize. In fact, there is evidence to suggest that a variety of problem solving methods are content bound (see Snow & Lohman, 1989).

5. be confirmed or disconfirmed by both qualitative and quantitative inquiry.

6. focus on practical applications of principles and procedures to classroom instruction. In this context, the instructional program becomes the focus; its constituent parts are curriculum, instruction, and integrated testing.

7. include a way to diagnose learning difficulties using a student's incorrect responses.

8. incorporate a componential conceptualization of abilities into the curriculum. Abilities will be developed over longer periods of time (Gardner & Hatch, 1989; Sternberg, 1985). Test scores reflecting these abilities will not be dramatic in showing growth because such growth is irregular and slow.

9. involve the idiosyncratic nature of each school learner, a condition that has direct implications for individualized instruction and individual education plans.

10. recognize the context of exogenous factors. The personal/social context of each learner has a strong influence on the quality and quantity of learning. Such factors as test anxiety, economic status, parental support for schooling, nutrition, personal or social adjustment, physical health, and the like become critical aspects of both theory and technology of school learning.

11. Have a component consisting of a statistical theory of option response patterns that will be more compatible with complex, multi step thinking.

Although we are far from having a unified learning theory, the groundwork is being laid. Given these 11 qualities of this emerging unified theory of school learning, present-day teaching and testing practices seem almost obsolete. The futures of item development and item-response validation in the context of measuring student learning should be quite different from current practices.

Barriers to Redefining of the Outcomes of Schooling and Professional Competence

Two related but different barriers exist that affect the future of item development. The two are related, but are different problems. Cognitive psychologists and others have used a plethora of terms representing higher level thinking, including metacognition, problem solving, analysis, evaluation, comprehension, conceptual learning, critical thinking, reasoning, strategic knowledge, schematic knowledge, and algorithmic knowledge, to name a few. The first stage in construct validity is construct definition. These terms are seldom adequately defined so that we can identify or construct items that measure these traits. Thus, the most basic step in construct validity, construct definition, continues to inhibit both the development of many higher level thinking behaviors and its measurement. As the focus changes from knowledge and skills to fluid abilities, we will have to identify and define these abilities better than we have in the past.

A second barrier is the absence of a validated taxonomy of complex cognitive behavior. Studies of teachers' success with using higher level thinking questions lead to inconclusive findings due to a variety of factors, including methodological problems (Winne, 1979). Many other studies and reports attest to the current difficulty of successfully measuring higher level thinking with the kind of scientific rigor required in construct validation. Royer, Cisero, and Carlo (1993) proposed a taxonomy of higher level behavior and reviewed research on its validity. This impressive work is based on a cognitive learning theory proposed by Anderson (1990). Although the taxonomy is far from being at the implementation stage, it provides a reasonable structure that invites further study and validation.

Item writing in the current environment cannot thrive due to the existence of these two barriers. Advances in learning theory should lead to better construct definitions and organization of types of higher level thinking that will sustain more productive item development leading to higher quality teacher-produced and standardized tests of higher level thinking.

Statistical Theories of Test Scores

Once constructs are defined and variables are constructed, testing provides one basis for the empirical validation of test score interpretations and uses. In this context, a statistical theory of test scores is adopted, and this theory can be applied to item responses with the objective of evaluating and improving items until they display desirable item-response patterns.

Classical test theory has its roots settled in the early part of this century and has grown substantially. It is still widely accepted and used in testing programs despite the rapid and understandable emergence of item-response theories. For many reasons enumerated in chapter 8 and in other sources (e.g., Hambleton & Jones, 1993; Hambleton & Swaminathan, 1987), classical theory has enough deficiencies to limit its future use. Nonetheless, its use is encouraged by its familiarity to the mainstream of test users.

Generalizability theory is a neoclassical theory that gives users the ability to study sources of error in cognitive measurement using familiar analysis of variance techniques. Brennan (1993) showed how generalizability theory can be used to study the influences of context in test development. However, generalizability theory suffers from the same limitations as classical test theory. Thus, its use might diminish as other approaches are introduced.

Dichotomous (binary) item-response theories have developed rapidly in recent years, largely due to the efforts of theorists like Rasch, Birnbaum, Lord, Bock, and Wright, to name a few. These theories are increasingly applied in large-scale testing programs. Computer software is very user-friendly. However, Linn (1990b) observed that item-response theories do not seem to produce more valid test score interpretations. However, item-response theories have changed the way we think about test design and scaling. Although dichotomous item-response theory receives a high degree of support among theoreticians and some practitioners, its complexity and dependence on unidimensional test data and large samples limit its applications. The applicability of item-response theory to classroom instruction is problematic, for several reasons. First, because item-response theory requires large samples, it is seldom useful at the classroom level, unless tests are designed for many classrooms. Second, the construct represented by a test must be unidimensional if item-response theory is used. Third, item parameter estimates may fluctuate because of differential instruction, where some concepts, principles, and procedures are taught and other content is not taught. If a test contains taught and untaught material, unidimensionality fails, and estimates of item parameters in the two- and three-parameter model will fail to converge. Thus, administration of achievement tests closely linked to ongoing instruction is likely to lead to unstable parameter estimates.

Linear polychotomous scoring (option weighting) procedures discussed in chapter 9 have been supported by more than 50 years of intermittent research that consistently shows slightly higher reliability when compared with dichotomous scoring (Haladyna & Sympson, 1988). More recently, polychotomous item-response theories have been developed by Bock (1972), Samejima (1979), Sympson (1983, 1986), and Thissen and Steinberg (1986). This theoretical work has led to the development of computer software that initiates studies bearing on the comparative effectiveness of these proposed models, as chapter 9 discussed. However, is the effort needed to produce these scales and test scores worth the small gains in reliability?

In *Test Theory for a New Generation of Tests*, Frederiksen, Mislevy, and Bejar (1993) assembled an impressive and comprehensive treatment of ongoing theoretical work, representing a new wave of statistical test theory. This collection of papers is aimed at realizing the goal of unifying cognitive and measurement perspectives with emphasis on complex learning. Mislevy (1993a) distinguished much of this recent work as departing from low-to-high proficiency testing in which a total score has meaning to pattern scoring where wrong answers have diagnostic value. In this setting, the total score does not inform us about *how* a learner reached the final answer to a complex set of activities. An appropriate analysis of patterns of responses may inform us about the effectiveness of a process used to solve a problem. In other words, patterns of responses, such as derived from the context-dependent item set, may lead to inferences about optimal and suboptimal learning. Theoretical developments by Bejar (1993), Embretsen (1985), Fischer (1983), Haertel and Wiley (1993), Jannarone (1988), Tatsuoka (1990), and Wilson (1989) captured the rich array of promising new choices. Many of these theorists agree that traditional classical test theory and even present-day item-response theories may become *passe*, because they are inadequate for handling complex cognitive behavior. As with any new theory, extensive research leading to technologies will take considerable time and resources. Thus, it will be a while before these theories become practice.

These new statistical theories have significant implications for item-response validation. Traditional item analysis was concerned with estimating item difficulty and discrimination. Newer theories will lead to *option-response theories*, where right and wrong answers provide useful information, and patterns of responses also provide information on the success of learners on complex tasks.

THE FUTURE OF ITEM DEVELOPMENT

In this section, two topics are addressed. First, the status of item writing is described. Then the characteristics of future item development are identified and described. A worthwhile goal should be to abandon the current prescriptive method for writing items and work within the framework of an item-writing theory that integrates with cognitive learning theory.

The Legacy of Item-Writing

Critics have noted that item writing is not a scholarly area of testing (e.g., Cronbach, 1970; Nitko, 1985). Item writing is characterized by the collective wisdom and experience of measurement experts who often convey this knowledge in textbooks. Another problem is that item writing is not especially well-grounded in research. Previous discussions of item development in *Educational Measurement* (Lindquist, 1951; Linn, 1989; Thorndike, 1970) have treated item writing in isolation of other topics, such as validity, reliability, and item analysis, among other topics. Cronbach (1971), in his classic chapter on validation, provided scant attention to the role of items and item responses in test validation. Messick (1989), on the other hand, referred to the importance of various aspects of item development and item-response validation on construct validity. The current unified view of validity explicitly unites many aspects of item development and item-response validation with other critical aspects of construct validation. But this is only a recent development.

The criterion-referenced testing movement brought sweeping reform to test constructors at all levels by focusing attention on instructional objectives. Each item needed to be linked to an instructional objective. Test items were painstakingly matched to objectives, and collections of items formed tests that putatively reflected these objectives. The integration of teaching and testing produced predictable results: high degree of learning, if student time for learning was flexible to fit slow learners. The dilemma was how specific to make the objective. Objectives too specific limited the degree to which we could generalize; objectives too vague produced too much inconsistency in item development resulting in disagreement among context experts about the classifications of these items. No single test item or even small sample of test items was adequate for measuring an objective. The widespread use of instructional objectives in education and training is remarkable. But the criticism of this approach is that learning can seem fragmented and piecemeal. What fails to happen is that students do not learn to use knowledge and skills to perform some complex cognitive operation.

The current reform movement and the current emphasis on performance testing has caused a reconsideration of the usefulness of the instructional objective. Because criterion-referenced testing is objective-driven, it may be replaced by statements that convey a different focus: one on the development of fluid abilities.

Current knowledge about item writing was kernelized by Haladyna and Downing (1989a) into a taxonomy of 43 item-writing rules. Haladyna, Downing, and Rodriguez (1999) updated this study and reduced the list of rules to a smaller set, as shown in chapter 4. Research on item writing is still asystematic and limited only to several rules. Encouraging research continues to be done, showing that there is some interest in advancing the science of item writing.

Theories of item writing provide a more systematic basis for generating items that map content domains of ability and achievement. However, the appearance of item writing theories by Roid and Haladyna (1982), no developments have been reported.

A series of integrative reviews by Albanese (1992), Downing (1992), Frisbie (1992), and Haladyna (1992a) provided guidance about the variety of MC formats available for item writing. This work provided an important basis for the use of some formats and the discontinuation of other formats, such as the complex MC and true–false.

This legacy of item writing is characterized by a checkered past, consisting of many thoughtful essays and chapters in textbooks about how to write items. Although most of this advice is good, it fails to qualify as a science. Attempts at theory building have been ambitious but have failed due to neglect and other factors. However, these failures provide a basis for planning new theories. The next section describes desirable aspects of new item-writing theories.

CHARACTERISTICS OF NEW THEORIES OF ITEM WRITING

This section addresses some characteristics that these new item-writing theories must possess to meet the challenge of measuring complex behavior. These characteristics draw heavily from current thinking in cognitive psychology but also rely on this item-writing legacy.

New Kinds of Tasks and Scoring

Computers now present examinees with tasks to examinees of a complex nature, with interactive components that simulate real-life, complex decision making. Scoring can offer several pathways to correct answers, and scoring can be automated. The fidelity of such creative testing is being demonstrated in computer-delivered licensing tests in architecture. Mislevy (1996b) made a good point about this emerging technology. If the information provided is no better than provided by conventional MC, then the innovation seems pointless. These innovations must provide something well beyond what is available using formats presented in chapter 3.

The Breakdown of Standardization in Testing

Whereas outcomes of educational or training may be uniform, the means by which the outcomes are achieved may be diverse. Mislevy (1996) also observed that in graduate education, a student might be expected to have foundation knowledge, but thesis or dissertation research is creative and hardly the same from graduate to graduate. Also, not all students have the same background experiences and capability. The generalizability of one test may be little, but very relevant to an immediate goal. Thus, in future test design, more will have to be considered than simply defining a domain of tasks and computing a test score based on a sample of these tasks. Within instruction or training, the use of computers allows for more individualization, which may nonstandardize the test but will standardize the result of instruction or training. In other words, students will follow different paths in their instruction or training, perhaps, reaching different ends to fit their personal educational plan. Uniform teaching and testing might end.

Inference Networks

Traditional item writing focuses on a single behavior. The stem communicates a single task; the options provide the correct and several plausible choices. Theorists such as Royer et al. (1993) portrayed this type of testing as representing micro skills, simple cognitive behaviors that, although often important, are not as important as macroskills. The latter represents the various types of higher level thinking.

Although the instructional objective was the basis for writing the item in the teaching technology in the 1970s and 1980s, defining and measuring macroskills using the objective is quite difficult, perhaps contributing to this extensive failure by practitioners to write this type of test item.

Cognitive psychology is working toward an opposite end. Constructs are more complicated, reflecting how we learn instead of what we learn. Instead of aggregating knowledge, like filling a storeroom, learning is viewed as more patchwork or mosaic. The schema is the mental structure for organizing this knowledge. Mislevy (1993b) provided examples of inference networks, which are graphical representations that reflect the cluster and connectedness of microtasks that comprise a complex cognitive behavior. These networks have a statistical basis, reflecting the reasoning about the causality of factors that we can observe. The inference network may contain both MC and CR elements, each providing for a certain kind of inference. Mislevy described both a causal model of reasoning about observations and an appropriate statistical theory that can be used to model student behavior during learning. This is how the unification of cognitive learning theory and statistical test score theory takes place. Such inference networks can illustrate the pattern of behavior in a complex process or simple proficiency—the outcome of the process.

Inference networks provide a new way to view content and cognitive behavior in a complex type of learning. The inference network can be expanded to include the instructional strategy needed for each micro skill and the formative and summative aspects of learning. Item writing becomes an interesting challenge, because items must model the range of behaviors that distinguish students with respect to the trait being learned and measured. Mislevy provided several examples from different fields, illustrating that inference networks will help develop effective measures of complex behavior in a variety of settings.

Item-Generating Ability

Present-day item writing is a slow process. Item writers can expect that about 50% of their items will fail to perform as intended. This state of affairs characterizes even further how item writing needs to improve. Ideally any new item-writing theory should lead to the easy generation of many content-relevant items. A simple example shows how item-generating schemes can benefit item writing. In dental education, an early skill is learning to identify tooth names and numbers using the Universal Coding System. Two objectives can be used to quickly generate 104 test items:

> Given a letter code, identify the tooth name.
> Given the tooth name, identify the code letter.

Because there are 32 teeth in the adult dentition, a total of 64 items defines the domain. The primary dentition has 20 teeth, so 40 more items are possible. Each item can be MC, or we can authentically assess a dental student's actual performance using a patient. Also, a plaster or plastic model of the adult or child dentition can be used. If domain specifications were this simple in all educational settings, the problems of construct definition and item writing would be trivial. Unfortunately, we have not cleverly devised enough useful tasks like this to use such algorithms.

Chapter 6 discusses three distinctly different approaches to item-generating procedures. The item shell provides a syntax for item writers based on successfully performing items. The algorithmic context-dependent item set attempts to measure higher level thinking through realistic encounters, portrayed in scenarios (vignettes) with key facets to vary that systematically change each scenario. Item modeling is a more systematic process that resembles Guttman's facet theory but appears more workable. Reports of its productivity are impressive. None of these methods are particularly based on an item-writing theory, but item modeling comes closest. Subsequent work on it may distinguish it as a highly useful item-writing theory for tapping clinical problem solving in the professions.

With respect to new item-writing theories, Bejar (1993) proposed response generative model (RGM) as a form of item writing that is superior to these earlier theories because it has a basis in cognitive theory, whereas these earlier generative theories have behavioristic origins. The RGM proposes to generate items with a predictable set of parameters, from which clear interpretations are possible. Bejar presented some evidence from a variety of researchers, including in areas such as spatial ability, reasoning, and verbal ability. The underlying rationale of the RGM is that item writing and item response are linked predictably. Every time an item is written, responses to that item can confirm the theory. Failure to confirm would destroy the theory's credibility. Bejar maintained that this approach is not so much an item-writing method, a content-specification scheme, or a cognitive theory but a philosophy of test construction and response modeling that is integrative.

The RGM has tremendous appeal to prove or disprove itself as it is used. It has the attractive qualities of earlier generative item-writing theories, namely (a) the ability to operationalize a domain definition, (b) the ability to generate objectively sufficient numbers of items, and (c) the ease with which relevant tests are created with predictable characteristics. Additionally RGM provides a basis for validating item responses and test scores at the time of administration. What is not provided in Bejar's theory thus far, are the detailed specifications of the use of the theory and the much needed research to transform theory into technology. Like earlier theories, significant research will be needed to realize the attractive claims for this model.

Misconception Strategies

A third characteristic of new item-writing theories will be the diagnostic value of wrong choices. Current item-writing wisdom suggest that distractors should be based on common errors of students (Haladyna & Downing, 1989a; Haladyna, Downing, & Rodriguez, 1999). Although this method of creating distractors may seem simplistic, one has only to administer items in an open-ended format to appropriately instructed students to develop credible distractors. This process applies to open-ended performance testing. The scoring rubric for open-ended tests would derive from an analysis of student errors, thus making the process very much like the design of a MC item.

Tatsuoka (1985) and her colleagues proposed a model for diagnosing cognitive errors in problem solving. This impressive research uses her rule space model based on task analyses of mathematics skills. Mathematics seems the most readily adaptable to these theoretical developments. We lack applications to more challenging subject matters, for example, biology, philosophy, history, political science, speech, reading, literature studies, psychology, and art. Because a desirable feature of achievement tests is diagnostic information leading to reteaching, these misconception methods are highly desirable.

Lohman and Ippel (1993) presented a general cognitive theory that examines processes that uncover misconceptions in student learning. The nature of complex learning compels cognitive psychologists to reject traditional test models that focus on the meaning of total test scores. These researchers go further to assert that even measures of components of process that are often quantitative may be inappropriate, because step-by-step observations do not capture the essence of what makes individuals different in the performance of a complex task. Lohman and Ippel looked to understandings based on developmental psychology. Instead of using quantitative indicators in a problem-solving process, they looked for qualitative evidence. Although this work is very preliminary, it shows that cognitive psychologists are sensitive to uncovering the precise steps in correct and incorrect problem solving. This work directly affects item writing in the future. Also conventional item writing does not contribute to modeling complex behavior as it emerges in these cognitive theories.

An urgent need exists to make erroneous response part of the scoring system in testing, and, at the same time, provide information to teachers and learners about the remedial efforts needed to successfully complete complex tasks. Future item-writing theories will need this component if we are to solve the mystery of writing items for higher level thinking.

Conclusion

This section has treated the future of item writing. Item writing lacks the rich theoretical tradition that we observe with statistical theories of test scores. The undervaluing of item writing has resulted in a prescriptive technology instead of workable item-writing theories. The item-writing theory of the future will feature a workable method for specifying content. Perhaps the inference networks suggested by Mislevy (1993b) or the diagnostic error classification systems developed by Tatsuoka (1985) will serve this purpose. Future item-writing theory will permit the ability to rapidly generate items that completely map ability or achievement domains. Finally, any emergent theory must provide a basis for creating distractors that reveal misconceptions in learning so that diagnosis and remediation can occur.

THE FUTURE OF ITEM-RESPONSE VALIDATION

Item analysis has been a somewhat stagnant field in the past, limited to the estimation of item difficulty and discrimination using classical or item-response theory, and the counting of responses to each distractor. Successive editions of *Educational Measurement* (Lindquist, 1951; Linn, 1989; Thorndike, 1970) documented this unremarkable state of affairs. The many influences described in this chapter, coupled with growth in cognitive and item-response theories, has provided an opportunity to unify item writing and item-response validation in a larger context of construct validity. The tools and understanding that are developing for more effective treatment of item responses has been characterized in this book as item-response validation. The future of item-response validation will never be realized without significant progress in developing a workable theory of item writing.

Chapter 8 discusses the topic of item-response validation, and chapter 9 presents methods to study various testing problems. An important linkage was made between item-response validation and construct validation. Three important aspects of item-response validation that should receive more attention in the future are distractor evaluation, a reconceptualization of item discrimination, and pattern analysis. Because these concepts were more comprehensively addressed in the previous chapter, the discussion will center on the relative importance of each in the future.

Distractor Evaluation

The topic of distractor evaluation has been given little attention in the past. Even the most current edition of *Educational Measurement* provides a scant three paragraphs on this topic (Millman & Greene, 1989). However, Thissen, Steinberg, and Fitzpatrick (1989) supported the study of distractors. They stated that any item analysis should consider the distractor as an important part of the item. Wainer (1989) provided additional support, claiming that the graphical quality of the trace line for each option makes the evaluation of an item response more complex but also more complete. Because trace lines are pictorial, they are less daunting to item writers who may lack the statistical background needed to deal with option discrimination indexes.

The traditional item discrimination index provides a useful and convenient numerical summary of item discrimination, but it tends to overlook the relative contributions of each distractor. Because each distractor contains a plausible incorrect answer, item analysts are not afforded enough guidance about which distractors might be revised or retired to improve the item performance. Changes in distractors should lead to improvements in item performance, which, in turn, should lead to improved test scores and more valid interpretations.

There are at least three good reasons for evaluating distractors. First, the distractor is part of the test item and should be useful. If it is not useful, it should be removed. Useless distractors have an untoward effect on item discrimination. Second, with polychotomous scoring, useful distractors contribute to more effective scoring, which has been proven to positively affect test score reliability. Third, as cognitive psychologists lead efforts to develop distractors that pinpoint misconceptions, distractor evaluation techniques will permit the empirical validation of distractor responses and by that improve our ability to provide misconception information to instructors and students.

Item Discrimination

The concept of item discrimination has evolved. An earlier discrimination index consisted of noting the difference between mean item performance of a high-scoring group and the mean item performance of a low-scoring group. Such high-group/low-group comparisons were calculationally simple. Statistical indexes like the biserial and point-biserial were theoretically more satisfactory, and routinely produced with the coming of the computer. However, these traditional item discrimination indexes have many deficiencies to recommend against their use (Henrysson, 1971). Two- and three-parameter binary-scoring item-response theories provide discrimination that is highly related to traditional discrimination. Like traditional discrimination, the differential discriminating abilities of distractors are immaterial.

In polychotomous scoring, discrimination has a different conceptualization. As discussed in chapter 8, polychotomous scoring views the differential information contained in distractors more sensitively than does binary scoring. Because discriminating distractors are infrequent, according to studies such as Haladyna and Downing (1993), MC items in the future may be necessarily leaner, containing only two or three distractors.

This reconceptualization of item discrimination compels item analysts to evaluate distractors, as well as consider the response pattern of each distractor relative to one another. Items that have distractors that have similar response patterns, unless reflecting uniquely different misconceptions, may not be very useful in item design.

Response Pattern Analysis

Complex behavior requires many mental steps. New theories propose to model cognitive behavior using statistical models that examine patterns of responses among items, as opposed to traditional item analysis that merely examines the pattern of item response in relation to total test score (Frederiksen, Mislevy, & Bejar, 1993; Mislevy, 1993b).

Some significant work is currently being done with context-dependent item sets. Wainer and Kiely (1987) conceptualized item sets as testlets. Responses to testlets involve the chaining of response, and specific patterns have more value than others. Although this pattern analysis does not fulfil the promise of cognitive psychologists regarding misconception analysis, testlet scoring takes a major first step into the field of item analysis for multistep thinking and the relative importance of each subtask in a testlet. Chapters 8 and 9 discuss item-response models and computer software that exist for studying various scoring methods. As cognitive psychologists develop constructs to the point that item writing can produce items reflecting multistep thinking, response pattern analysis will become more statistically sophisticated and useful.

CONCLUSIONS

In this chapter, we have noted several prominent influences that will likely affect how we test cognitive abilities. A unification among the diverse and all too often independent fields of cognitive learning theory and statistical test score theory is much needed. Item writing should cease to be prescriptive. In other words, the existence of a taxonomy of item writing rules developed by Haladyna and Downing (1989a) offers a stopgap until more scientific methods for item writing exist. Item writing should be part of this unified theory that involves construct definition, test development, and construct validation both at the item and test score units of analysis. Toward that end, the creative act of item writing will probably be replaced with more algorithmic methods to control item-writing biases. Creativity will be needed at an earlier stage with content specification procedures, such as inference networks, that will almost automate the item-writing process. How automated item writing will become remains to be seen.

With item-response validation, polychotomous scoring will open more opportunities to write more effective distractors and use these distractors in scoring test results. Consequently, more attention will be given to distractor response patterns that diagnose wrong thinking in a complex behavior, and the trace line will be a useful and friendly device to understand the role that each distractor plays in building a coherent item. Both item writing and item-response validation are important steps in test development and validation. As cognitive psychologists better define constructs and identify the constituent steps in complex thinking, item writing and item-response validation will evolve to meet the challenge. Both item writing and item-response validation will continue to play an important role in test development, but each must receive more scholarly attention than has been received in the past. Both will require significant study in the context of this unified theory involving both ability and achievement.

Finally, it would be remiss not to point out the increasing role of performance testing in testing cognitive abilities. The CR format has received much less attention and research than the MC format. Item writing will certainly be a unified science of observation where MC and CR assume appropriate roles for measuring aspects of knowledge, skills, and abilities. The road toward better item development and item-response validation will be quite long, as there is still much to accomplish.

References

Adams, R. (1992). Multiple-choice item writing: Art and science. *Bar Examiner, 61*(1), 5–14.

Advanced Psychometrics. (1998). *Scrutiny!* {Computer Program}. St. Paul, MN: Assessment Systems Corporation.

Albanese, M. A. (1992). Type K items. *Educational Measurement: Issues and Practices, 12*, 28–33.

Albanese, M. A. (1993). Type K and other complex multiple-choice items: An analysis of research and item properties. Evaluation and the Health Professions, *5*(2), 218–228.

Albanese, M. A., Kent, T. A., & Whitney, D. R. (1977). A comparison of the difficulty, reliability, and validity of complex multiple-choice, multiple response, and multiple true–false items. *Annual Conference on Research in Medical Education, 16*, 105–110.

Albanese, M. A., & Sabers, D. L. (1988). Multiple true–false items: A study of interitem correlations, scoring alternatives, and reliability estimation. *Journal of Educational Measurement, 25*, 111–124.

American Psychological Association, American Educational Research Association, National Council on Measurement in Education. (1985). *Standards for Educational and Psychological Testing.* Washington, DC: American Psychological Association.

Anderson, J. R. (1990). *The adaptive character of thought.* Hillsdale, NJ: Lawrence Erlbaum Associates.

Anderson, J. R., & Bower, G. H. (1972). Recognition and retrieval process in free recall. *Psychological Review, 79*, 97-132.

Anderson, R. C. (1972). How to construct achievement tests to assess comprehension. *Review of Educational Research, 42*, 145-170.

Andres, A. M., & del Castillo, J. D. (1990). Multiple-choice tests: Power, length, and optimal number of choices per item. *British Journal of Mathematical and Statistical Psychology, 45*, 57–71.

Andrich, D., Luo, G., & Sheridan, B. (1996). *RUMM: A windows program for Rasch unidimensional models for measurement* [Computer Program]. Murdoch University, Social Measurement Laboratory.

Andrich, D., Styles, I., Tognolini, J., Luo, G., & Sheridan, B. (1997, April). *Identifying information from distractors in multiple-choice items: A routine application of IRT hypotheses.* Paper presented at the annual meeting of the National Council on Measurement in Education, Chicago, IL.

Angoff, W. H. (1974). The development of statistical indices for detecting cheaters. *Journal of the American Statistical Association, 69,* 44–49.

Ansley, T. N., Spratt, K. F., & Forsyth, R. A. (1988, April). *An investigation of the effects of using calculators to reduce the computational burden on a standardized test of mathematics problem solving.* Paper presented at the annual meeting of the American Educational Research Association, New Orleans, LA.

Assessment Systems Corporation. (1992). *RASCAL (Rasch Analysis Program)* [Computer Program]. St. Paul, MN: Author.

Assessment Systems Corporation. (1989). *ASCAL (2- and 3-parameter) IRT Calibration Program. {Computer Software}.* St. Paul, MN: Author.

Badger, E. (1990, April). *Using different spectacles to look at student achievement: Implications for theory and practice.* Paper presented at the annual meeting of the American Educational Research Association, Boston, MA.

Bauer, H. (1991). Sore finger items in multiple-choice tests. *System, 19*(4), 453–458.

Becker, B. J. (1990). Coaching for Scholastic Aptitude Test: Further synthesis and appraisal. *Review of Educational Research, 60,* 373–418.

Bejar, I. (1993). A generative approach to psychological and educational measurement. In N. Frederiksen, R. J. Mislevy, & I. Bejar (Eds.). *Test theory for a new generation of tests* (pp. 297–323). Hillsdale, NJ: Lawrence Erlbaum Associates.

Bellezza, F. S., & Bellezza, S. F. (1989). Detection of cheating on multiple-choice tests by using error-similarity analysis. *Teaching of Psychology, 16,* 151–155.

Bennett, R. E. (1993). On the meaning of constructed response. In R. E. Bennett & W. C. Ward (Eds.), *Construction versus choice in cognitive measurement: Issues in constructed response, performance testing, and portfolio assessment* (pp. 1–27). Hillsdale, NJ: Lawrence Erlbaum Associates.

Bennett, R. E., Rock, D. A., & Wang, M. D. (1990). Equivalence of free-response and multiple-choice items. *Journal of Educational Measurement, 28,* 77–92.

Biggs, J. B., & Collis, K. F. (1982). *Evaluating the quality of learning: The SOLO taxonomy (structure of observed learning outcomes).* New York: Academic Press.

Bloom, B. S., Engelhart, M. D., Furst, E. J., Hill, W. H., & Krathwohl, D. R. (1956). *Taxonomy of educational objectives.* New York: Longmans Green.

Bock, R. D. (1972). Estimating item parameters and latent ability when responses are scored in two or more nominal categories. *Psychometrika, 37,* 29–51.

Bock, R. D., Gibbons, R., & Muraki, E. (1988). Full information factor analysis. *Applied Psychological Measurement, 12,* 261–280.

Bormuth, J. R. (1970). *On a theory of achievement test items.* Chicago: University of Chicago Press.

Braun, H. I. (1988). Understanding score reliability: Experience calibrating essay readers. *Journal of Educational Statistics, 13,* 1–18.

Breland, H. M., Danos, D. O., Kahn, H. D., Kubota, M. Y., & , Bonner, M. W. (1994). Performance versus objective testing and gender: An exploratory study of an advanced placement history examination. *Journal of Educational Measurement, 31*, 275–293.

Breland, H. M., & Gaynor, J. (1979). A comparison of direct and indirect assessments of writing skills. *Journal of Educational Measurement, 6*, 119–128.

Brennan, R. L. (1993, April). *The context of context effects.* Paper presented at the annual meeting of the American Educational Research Association, Atlanta, GA.

Bridgeman, B., Harvey, A., Braswell, J. (1995). Effects of calculator use on scores on a test of mathematical reasoning. *Journal of Educational Measurement, 32*(4), 323–340.

Brown, J. (1966). *Objective tests: Their construction and analysis: A practical handbook for teachers.* London: Longmans.

Bruno, J. E., & Dirkzwager, A. (1995). Determining the optimal number of alternatives to a multiple-choice test item: An information theoretical perspective. *Educational and Psychological Measurement, 55*, 959–966.

Burmester, M. A., & Olson, L. A. (1966). Comparison of item statistics for items in a multiple-choice and alternate-response form. *Science Education, 50*, 467–470.

Cannell, J. J. (1989). *How public educators cheat on standardized achievement tests.* Albuquerque, NM: Friends for Education.

Case, S. M., & Downing, S. M. (1989). *Performance of various multiple-choice item types on medical specialty examinations: Types A, B, C, K, and X.* Philadelphia: National Board of Medical Examiners.

Chase, C. I. (1979). The impact of achievement expectations and handwriting quality on scoring essay tests. *Journal of Educational Measurement, 16*, 39–42.

Chase, C. I. (1986). Essay test scoring: Interaction of relevant variables. *Journal of Educational Measurement, 23*, 33–42.

Cizek, G. J. (1991, April). *The effect of altering the position of options in a multiple-choice examination.* Paper presented at the annual meeting of the National Council on Measurement in Education, Chicago, IL.

Clauser, B. E., & Mazor, K. M. (1998). Using statistical procedures to identify differentially functioning test items. *Educational Measurement: Issues and Practices, 17*, 32–44.

Cody, R. P. (1985). Statistical analysis of examinations to detect cheating. *Journal of Medical Education, 60*, 136–137.

Coffman, W. E. (1971). Essay examinations. In R. L. Thorndike (Ed.), *Educational Measurement* (2nd ed., pp. 271–302). Washington, DC: American Council on Education.

Cohen, A. S., & Kim S. (1992). Detecting calculator effects on item performance. *Applied Measurement in Education, 5*, 303–320.

Cole, N. S. (1990). Conceptions of educational achievement. *Educational Researcher, 19*, 2–7.

Cole, N. S., & Moss, P. A. (1989). Bias in test use. In R. L. Linn (Ed.), *Educational Measurement* (3rd ed., pp. 201–220). New York: American Council on Education and Macmillan.

Cox, R. C., & Vargas, J. (1966). *A comparison of item selection techniques for norm-referenced and criterion-referenced tests.* Pittsburgh, PA: University of Pittsburgh Learning Research and Development Center.

Crocker, L., Llabre, M., & Miller, M. D. (1988). The generalizability of content validity ratings. *Journal of Educational Measurement, 25,* 287–299.

Cronbach, L. J. (1941). An experimental comparison of the multiple true–false and multiple multiple choice test. *Journal of Educational Psychology, 32,* 533–543.

Cronbach, L. J. (1970). [Review of *On the theory of achievement test items*]. *Psychometrika, 35,* 509–511.

Cronbach, L. J. (1971). Test validation. In R. L. Thorndike (Ed.), *Educational Measurement* (2nd ed., pp. 443–507). Washington, DC: American Council on Education.

Cronbach, L. J. (1988). Five perspectives of the validity argument (pp. 3–18). In H. Wainer & H. I. Braun (Eds.), *Test validity.* Hillsdale, NJ: Lawrence Erlbaum Associates.

Dawson-Saunders, B., Nungester, R. J., & Downing, S. M. (1989). *A comparison of single best answer multiple-choice items (A-type) and complex multiple-choice (K-type).* Philadelphia: National Board of Medical Examiners.

Dawson-Saunders, B., Reshetar, R., Shea, J. A., Fierman, C. D., Kangilaski, R., & Poniatowski, P. A. (1992, April). *Alterations to item text and effects on item difficulty and discrimination.* Paper presented at the annual meeting of the National Council on Measurement in Education, San Francisco, CA.

Dawson-Saunders, B., Reshetar, R., Shea, J. A., Fierman, C. D., Kangilaski, R., & Poniatowski, P. A. (1993, April). *Changes in difficulty and discrimination related to altering item text.* Paper presented at the annual meeting of the National Council on Measurement in Education, Atlanta, GA.

DeChamplain, A., & Tang, K. L. (1997). CHIDIM: A FORTRAN program for assessing the dimensionality of binary item responses based on McDonald's nonlinear factor analytic model. *Educational and Psychological Measurement, 57,* 174–178.

de Gruijter, D. N. M. (1988). Evaluating an item and option statistic using the bootstrap method. *Tijdschrift voor Onderwijsresearch, 13,* 345–352.

DeMars, C. E. (1998). Gender differences in mathematics and science on a high school proficiency exam: The role of response format. *Applied Measurement in Education, 11*(3), 279–299

Dibello, L. V., Roussos, L. A., & Stout, W. F. (1993, April). *Unified cognitive/psychometric diagnosis foundations and application.* Paper presented at the annual meeting of the American Educational Research Association, Atlanta, GA.

Dorans, N. J., & Holland, P. W. (1993). DIF detection and description: Mantel-Haenzel and standardization. In P. W. Holland & H. Wainer (Eds.), *Differential item functioning* (pp. 35–66). Hillsdale, NJ: Lawrence Erlbaum Associates.

Dorans, N. J., & Kullick, E. (1986). Demonstrating the utility of the standardization approach to assessing unexpected differential item performance on the Scholastic Aptitude Test. *Journal of Educational Measurement, 23,* 355–368.

Dorans, N. J., & Potenza, M. T. (1993, April). *Issues in equity assessment for complex response stimuli*. Paper presented at the annual meeting of the National Council on Measurement in Education, Atlanta, GA.

Downing, S. M. (1992). True–false and alternate–choice item formats: A review of research. *Educational Measurement: Issues and Practices, 11*, 27–30.

Downing, S. M., Baranowski, R. A., Grosso, L. J., & Norcini, J. J. (1995). Item type and cognitive ability measured: The validity evidence for multiple true–false items in medical specialty certification. *Applied Measurement in Education, 8*(2), 187–197.

Downing, S. M., & Haladyna, T. M. (1997). Test item development: Validity evidence from quality assurance procedures. *Applied Measurement in Education, 10*(1), 61–82.

Downing, S. M., & Norcini, J. J. (1998, April). Constructed response or multiple-choice: Does format make a difference for prediction? In T. M. Haladyna (Chair), *Construction versus choice: A research synthesis*. Symposium conducted at the annual meeting of the American Educational Research Association, San Diego, CA.

Drasgow, F. (1982). Choice of test model for appropriateness measurement. *Applied Psychological Measurement, 6*, 297–308.

Drasgow, F., & Guertler, E. (1987). A decision-theoretic approach to the use of appropriateness measurement for detecting invalid test and scale scores. *Journal of Applied Psychology, 72*, 10–18.

Drasgow, F., Levine, M. V., Tsien, S., Williams, B., & Mead, A. D. (1995). Fitting polytomous item response theory models to multiple-choice tests. *Applied Psychological Measurement, 19*(2), 143–165.

Drasgow, F., Levine, M. V., & Williams, E. A. (1985). Appropriateness measurement with polychotomous item response models and standardized indices. *British Journal of Educational Psychology, 38*, 67–86.

Drasgow, F., Levine, M. V., & Zickar, M. J. (1996). Optimal identification of mismeasured individuals. *Applied Measurement in Education, 9*(1), 47–64.

Ebel, R. L. (1951). Writing the test item. In E. F. Lindquist (Ed.), *Educational Measurement* (1st ed., pp. 185–249). Washington, DC: American Council on Education.

Ebel, R. L. (1970). The case for true-false test items. *School Review, 78*, 373–389

Ebel, R. L. (1978). The ineffectiveness of multiple true–false items. *Educational and Psychological Measurement, 38*, 37–44.

Ebel, R. L. (1981, April). *Some advantages of alternate–choice test items*. Paper presented at the annual meeting of the National Council on Measurement in Education, Los Angeles, CA.

Ebel, R. L. (1982). Proposed solutions to two problems of test construction. *Journal of Educational Measurement, 19*, 267–278.

Ebel, R. L., & Frisbie, D. A. (1991). *Essentials of educational measurement* (5th ed.). Englewood Cliffs, NJ: Prentice-Hall.

Ebel, R. L., & Williams, B. J. (1957). The effect of varying the number of alternatives per item on multiple-choice vocabulary test items. *The Fourteenth Yearbook*. Washington, DC: National Council on Measurement in Education.

Embretsen, S. (1985). Multicomponent latent trait models for test design. In S. E. Embretsen (Ed.), *Test design: Developments in psychology and psychometrics* (pp. 195–218). Orlando, FL: Academic Press.

Eurich, A. C. (1931). Four types of examination compared and evaluated. *Journal of Educational Psychology, 26*, 268–278.

FairTest Examiner. (1987), *1*, 1–16.

FairTest Examiner. (1988), *2*, 1–16.

Fajardo, L. L., & Chan, K. M. (1993). Evaluation of medical students in radiology written testing using uncued multiple-choice questions. *Investigative Radiology, 28*(10), 964–968.

Farr, R., Pritchard, R., & Smitten, B. (1990). A description of what happens when an examinee takes a multiple-choice reading comprehension test. *Journal of Educational Measurement, 27*, 209–226.

Fenderson, B. A., Damjanov, I., Robeson, M. R., Veloski, J. J., & Rubin, E. (1997). The virtues of extended matching and uncued tests as alternatives to multiple-choice questions. *Human Pathology, 28*(5), 526–532.

Fischer, G. H. (1983). Logistic latent trait models with linear constraints. *Psychometrika, 48*, 3–26.

Fiske, E. B. (1990, January 31). But is the child learning? Schools trying new tests. *The New York Times*, pp. 1, B6.

Fitzpatrick, A. R. (1981). The meaning of content validity. *Applied Psychological Measurement, 7*, 3–13.

Frary, R. B. (1993). Statistical detection of multiple-choice test answer copying: Review and commentary. *Applied Measurement in Education, 6*, 153–165.

Fraser, C. (1986). NOHARM: *An IBM PC computer program for fitting both unidimensional and multidimensional normal ogive models of latent trait theory* [Computer Program]. Armidale, Australia: The University of New England.

Frederiksen, N. (1984). The real test bias. Influences of testing on teaching and learning. *American Psychologist, 39*, 193–202.

Frederiksen, N., Mislevy, R. J., & Bejar, I. (Eds.). (1993). *Test theory for a new generation of tests*. Hillsdale, NJ: Lawrence Erlbaum Associates.

Frisbie, D. A. (1973). Multiple-choice versus true–false: A comparison of reliabilities and concurrent validities. *Journal of Educational Measurement, 10*, 297–304.

Frisbie, D. A. (1981). The relative difficulty ratio—A test and item index. *Educational and Psychological Measurement, 41*, 333–339.

Frisbie, D. A. (1992). The status of multiple true–false testing. *Educational Measurement: Issues and Practices, 5*, 21–26.

Frisbie, D. A., & Becker, D. F. (1991). An analysis of textbook advice about true–false tests. *Applied Measurement in Education, 4*, 67–83.

Frisbie, D. A., Miranda, D. U., & Baker, K. K. (1993). An evaluation of elementary textbook tests as classroom assessment tools. *Applied Measurement in Education, 6*, 21–36.

Frisbie, D. A., & Druva, C. A. (1986). Estimating the reliability of multiple-choice true–false tests. *Journal of Educational Measurement, 23*, 99–106.

Frisbie, D. A., & Sweeney, D. C. (1982). The relative merits of multiple true–false achievement tests. *Journal of Educational Measurement, 19*, 29–35.

Fuhrman, M. (1996). Developing good multiple-choice tests and test questions. *Journal of Geoscience Education, 44,* 379-384

Gagne, R. M. (1968). Learning hierarchies. *Educational Psychologist, 6,* 1-9.

Gardner, H. (1986). *The mind's new science: A history of the cognitive revolution.* New York: Basic Books.

Gardner, H., & Hatch, T. (1989). Multiple intelligences go to school. *Educational Researcher, 18,* 4-10.

Godshalk, F. I., Swineford, E., & Coffman, W. E. (1966). The measurement of writing ability. *College Board Research Monographs, No. 6.* New York: College Entrance Examination Board.

Goleman, D. (1995). *Emotional intelligence.* New York: Bantam Books

Gorsuch, R. L. (1983). *Factor analysis* (2nd ed.). Hillsdale, NJ: Lawrence Erlbaum Associates.

Green, K. E., & Smith, R. M. (1987). A comparison of two methods of decomposing item difficulties. *Journal of Educational Statistics, 12,* 369-381.

Gross, L. J. (1994). Logical versus empirical guidelines for writing test items. *Evaluation and the Health Professions, 17*(1), 123-126.

Grosse, M., & Wright, B. D. (1985). Validity and reliability of true-false tests. *Educational and Psychological Measurement, 45,* 1-13.

Guilford, J. P. (1967). *The nature of human intelligence.* New York: McGraw-Hill.

Guttman, L. (1941). The quantification of a class of attributes: A theory and method of scale construction. In P. Horst (Ed.), *Prediction of personal adjustment* (pp. 321-345). [Social Science Research Bulletin 48].

Haertel, E. (1986). The valid use of student performance measures for teacher evaluation. *Educational Evaluation and Policy Analysis, 8,* 45-60.

Haertel, E. H., & Wiley, D. E. (1993). Representations of ability structures: Implications for testing. In N. Frederiksen, R. J. Mislevy, & I. Bejar (Eds.), *Test theory for a new generation of tests* (pp. 359-384). Hillsdale, NJ: Lawrence Erlbaum Associates.

Haladyna, T. M. (1974). Effects of different samples on item and test characteristics of criterion-referenced tests. *Journal of Educational Measurement, 11,* 93-100.

Haladyna, T. M. (1982). Two approaches to criterion-referenced program assessment. *Educational Technology, 23,* 467-470.

Haladyna, T. M. (1991). Generic questioning strategies for linking teaching and testing. *Educational Technology: Research and Development, 39,* 73-81.

Haladyna, T. M. (1992a). Context-dependent item sets. *Educational Measurement: Issues and Practices, 11,* 21-25.

Haladyna, T. M. (1992b). The effectiveness of several multiple-choice formats. *Applied Measurement in Education, 5,* 73-88.

Haladyna, T. M. (1997). *Writing test items to measure higher level thinking.* Needham Heights, MA: Allyn & Bacon.

Haladyna, T. M., & Downing, S. M. (1989a). A taxonomy of multiple-choice item-writing rules. *Applied Measurement in Education, 1,* 37-50.

Haladyna, T. M., & Downing, S. M. (1989b). The validity of a taxonomy of multiple-choice item-writing rules. *Applied Measurement in Education, 1*, 51–78.

Haladyna, T. M., & Downing, S. M. (1993). How many options is enough for a multiple-choice test item. *Educational and Psychological Measurement, 53*, 999–1010.

Haladyna, T. M., Downing, S. M., & Rodriguez, M. (1999). *Multiple-choice item-writing rules*. Unpublished manuscript, Arizona State University West.

Haladyna, T. M., Haas, N. S., & Allison, J. (1998). Tensions in standadized testing. *Childhood Education, 74*, 262–273.

Haladyna, T. M., Nolen, S. B., & Haas, N. S. (1991). Raising standardized achievement test scores and the origins of test score pollution. *Educational Researcher, 20*, 2–7.

Haladyna, T. M., & Roid, G. H. (1981). The role of instructional sensitivity in the empirical review of criterion-referenced test items. *Journal of Educational Measurement, 18*, 39–53.

Haladyna, T. M., & Shindoll, R. R. (1989). Item shells: A method for writing effective multiple-choice test items. *Evaluation and the Health Professions, 12*, 97–104.

Haladyna, T. M., & Sympson, J. B. (1988, April). *Empirically based polychotomous scoring of multiple-choice test items: A review. In New Development in Polychotomous Scoring*. Symposium conducted at the annual meeting of the American Educational Research Association, New Orleans, LA.

Hambleton, R. K. (1984). Validating the test scores. In R. A. Berk (Ed.), *A guide to criterion-referenced test construction* (pp. 199–230). Baltimore: Johns Hopkins University Press.

Hambleton, R. K., & Jones, R. W. (1993). Comparison of classical test theory and item response theory and their applications to test development. *Educational Measurement: Issues and Practices, 12*, 38–46.

Hambleton, R. K., & Swaminathan, H. (1987). *Item response theory: Principles and applications*. Boston: Kluwer-Nijhoff Publishing.

Hancock, G. R. (1992, April). *Impact of item complexity on the comparability of multiple-choice and constructed-response test formats*. Paper presented at the annual meeting of the American Educational Research Association, San Francisco, CA.

Hancock, G. R., Thiede, K. W., & Sax, G. (1992, April). *Reliability of comparably written two-option multiple-choice and true-false test items*. Paper presented at the annual meeting of the National Council on Measurement in Education, Chicago, IL.

Harasym, P. H., Doran, M. L., Brant, R., & Lorscheider, F. L. (1992). Negation in stems of single-response multiple-choice items. *Evaluation and the Health Professions, 16*(3), 342–357.

Harvill, L. M., & Davis, G. III. (1997). Test-taking behaviors and their impact on performance. *Academic Medicine, 72*(10), 597–599.

Hattie, J. A. (1985). Methodological review: Assessing unidimensionality of tests and items. *Applied Psychological Measurement, 9*, 139–164.

Haynie, W. J., (1994). Effects of multiple-choice and short-answer tests on delayed retention learning. *Journal of Technology Education, 6*(1), 32–44.

Henrysson, S. (1971). Analyzing the test item. In R. L. Thorndike (Ed.), *Educational Measurement* (2nd ed., pp. 130–159) Washington, DC: American Council on Education.

Herbig, M. (1976). Item analysis by use in pre-test and post-test: A comparison of different coefficients. *PLET, 13*, 49–54.

Herrnstein, R. J., & Murray, C. (1994). *The bell curve: Intelligence and class structure in American life.* New York, NY: Free Press.

Hill, G. C., & Woods, G. T. (1974). Multiple true–false questions. *Education in Chemistry, 11*, 86–87.

Hill, K., & Wigfield, A. (1984). Test anxiety: A major educational problem and what can be done about it. *The Elementary School Journal, 85*, 105–126.

Hoffman, B. (1964). *Tyranny of testing.* New York: Collier.

Holland, P. W., & Thayer, D. T. (1988). Differential item performance and the Mantel-Haenzel procedure. In H. Wainer & H. Braun (Eds.), *Test validity* (pp. 129–145). Hillsdale, NJ: Lawrence Erlbaum Associates.

Holland, P. W., & Wainer, H. (Eds.). (1993). *Differential item functioning.* Hillsdale, NJ: Lawrence Erlbaum Associates.

House, E. R. (1991). Big policy, little policy. *Educational Researcher, 20*, 21–26.

Hsu, L. M. (1980). Dependence of the relative difficulty of true-false and grouped true–false tests on the ability levels of examinees. *Educational and Psychological Measurement, 40*, 891–894.

Hubbard, J. P. (1978). *Measuring medical education: The tests and the experience of the National Board of Medical Examiners* (2nd ed.). Philadelphia: Lea & Febiger.

Hughes, D. C., Keeling, B., & Tuck, B. F. (1983). Effects of achievement expectations and handwriting quality on scoring essays. *Journal of Educational Measurement, 20*, 65–70.

Hulin, C. L., Drasgow, F., & Parsons, C. K. (1983). *Item response theory: Application to psychological measurement.* Homewood, IL: Dow Jones–Irwin.

Hurd, A. W. (1932). Comparison of short answer and multiple-choice tests covering identical subject content. *Journal of Educational Research, 26*, 28–30.

Hutchinson, T. P. (1994). On overconfidence in multiple-choice tests. *The Psychological Record, 44*, 253–255.

Jannarone, R. J. (1988). Conjunctive measurement theory: Cognitive research prospects. *Center for Machine Intelligence* (USCMI Report No. 88-12). Columbia, SC: University of South Carolina.

Jensen, A. R. (1980). *Bias in mental testing.* New York: Free Press.

Johnson, B. R. (1991). A new scheme for multiple-choice tests in lower division mathematics. *The American Mathematical Monthly, 98*, 427–429.

Joreskog, K. G., & Sorbom, D. (1988). *PRELIS: A program for multivariate data screening and data summarization.* [Computer Program]. Chicago, IL: Scientific Software, Inc.

Joreskog, K. G., & Sorbom, D. (1993a). *LISREL8: Structural equation modeling with the SIMPLIS command language.* [Computer Program]. Chicago, IL: Scientific Software Inc.

Joreskog, K. G., & Sorbom, D. (1993b). *New features in PRELIS2.* Chicago: Scientific Software, Inc.

Kane, M. T. (1982). The validity of licensure examinations. *American Psychologist*, 7, 911–918.

Kane, M. T. (1992). An argument-based approach to validity. *Psychological Bulletin, 112*, 527–535.

Kintsch, W. (1970). Models for free recall and recognition. In D. A. Norman (Ed.), *Models of human memory* (pp. 313–373). New York: Academic Press.

Knowles, S. L., & Welch, C. A. (1992). A meta-analytic review of item discrimination and difficulty in multiple-choice items using none-of-the-above. *Educational and Psychological Measurement, 52*, 571–577.

Kolen, M. J., & Brennan, R. L. (1995). *Test equating*. New York: Springer.

LaDuca, A. (1994). Validation of a professional licensure examinations: Professions theory, test design, and construct validity. *Evaluation in the Health Professions, 17*(2), 178–197.

LaDuca, A., Downing, S. M., & Henzel, T. R. (1995). Test development: Systematic item writing and test construction. In J. C. Impara & J. C. Fortune (Eds.), *Licensure examinations: Purposes, procedures, and practices* (pp. 117–148). Lincoln, NE: Buros Institute of Mental Measurements.

LaDuca, A., Staples, W. I., Templeton, B., & Holzman, G. B. (1986). Item modelling procedure for constructing content–equivalent multiple-choice questions. *Medical Education, 20*, 53–56.

Landrum, R. E., Cashin, J. R., & Theis, K. S. (1993). More evidence in favor of three option multiple-choice tests. *Educational and Psychological Measurement, 53*, 771–778.

Levine, M. V., & Drasgow, F. (1982). Appropriateness measurement: Review, critique, and validating studies. *British Journal of Educational Psychology, 35*, 42–56.

Levine, M. V., & Drasgow, F. (1983). The relation between incorrect option choice and estimated ability. *Educational and Psychological Measurement, 43*, 675–685.

Levine, M. V., & Drasgow, F. (1988). Optimal appropriateness measurement. *Psychometrika, 53*, 161–176.

Levine, M. V., & Rubin, D. B. (1979). Measuring the appropriateness of multiple-choice test scores. *Journal of Educational Statistics, 4*, 269–289.

Lewis, J. C., & Hoover, H. D. (1981, April). *The effect of pupil performance from using hand-held calculators during standardized mathematics achievement tests.* Paper presented at the annual meeting of the National Council on Measurement in Education, Los Angeles, CA.

Lindquist, E. F. (Ed.). (1951). *Educational Measurement* (1st ed.). Washington, DC: American Council on Education.

Linn, R. L. (1983). Curricular validity: Convincing the court that it was taught without precluding the possibility of measuring it. In G. F. Madaus (Ed.), *The court, validity, and minimum competency testing* (pp. 115–132). Boston: Kluwer–Nijhoff.

Linn, R. L. (Ed.). (1989). *Educational measurement* (3rd ed.). New York: American Council on Education and Macmillan.

Linn, R. L. (1990a). Admission testing: Recommended uses, validity, differential predicting, and coaching. *Applied Measurement in Education, 3*, 297–318.

Linn, R. L. (1990b). Has item response theory increased the validity of achievement test scores? *Applied Measurement in Education, 3*, 143–166.

Linn, R. L. (1993). Educational assessment: Expanded expectations and challenges. *Educational Evaluation and Policy Analysis, 15,* 1–16.

Linn, R. L., Baker, E. L., & Dunbar, S. B. (1991). Complex, performance-based assessments: Expectations and validation criteria. *Educational Researcher, 20,* 15–21.

Linn, R. L., & Gronlund, N. E. (1995). *Educational measurement* (3rd ed.). New York, NY: American Council on Education and Macmillan.

Lohman, D. F. (1993). Teaching and testing to develop fluid abilities. *Educational Researcher, 22,* 12–23.

Lohman, D. F., & Ippel, M. J. (1993). Cognitive diagnosis: From statistically-based assessment toward theory-based assessment. In N. Frederikesen, R. J. Mislevy, & I. Bejar (Eds.), *Test theory for a new generation of tests* (pp. 41–71). Hillsdale, NJ: Lawrence Erlbaum Associates.

Lord, F. M. (1958). Some relations between Guttman's principal components of scale analysis and other psychometric theory. *Psychometrika, 23,* 291–296.

Lord, F. M. (1980). *Applications of item response theory to practical testing problems.* Hillsdale, NJ: Lawrence Erlbaum Associates.

Lord, F. M. (1977). Optimal number of choices per item—A comparison of four approaches. *Journal of Educational Measurement, 14,* 33–38.

Loyd, B. H. (1991). Mathematics test performance: The effects of item type and calculator use. *Applied Measurement in Education, 4,* 11–22.

Lukhele, R., Thissen, D., & Wainer, H. (1993). On the relative value of multiple-choice, constructed-response, and examinee-selected items on two achievement tests. *Journal of Educational Measurement, 31*(3), 234–250.

MacDonald, R. P. (1985). *Factor analysis and related methods.* Hillsdale, NJ: Lawrence Erlbaum Associates.

MacIntosh, H. G., & Morrison, R. B. (1969). *Objective testing.* London: University of London Press.

Mager, R. F. (1962). *Preparing instructional objectives.* Palo Alto, CA: Fearon.

Maihoff, N. A., & Mehrens, W. A. (1985, April). *A comparison of alternate–choice and true–false item forms used in classroom examinations.* Paper presented at the annual meeting of the National Council on Measurement in Education, Chicago, IL.

Maihoff, N. A., & Phillips, E. R. (1988, April). *A comparison of multiple-choice and alternate–choice item forms on classroom tests.* Paper presented at the annual meeting of the National Council on Measurement in Education, San Francisco, CA.

Markle, S. M., & Tiemann, P. W. (1970). *Really understanding concepts.* Champaign, IL: Stipes.

Martinez, M. E. (1990). A comparison of multiple-choice and constructed figural response items. *Journal of Educational Measurement, 28,* 131–145.

Martinez, M. E. (1993). Cognitive processing requirements of constructed figural response and multiple-choice items in architecture assessment. *Applied Measurement in Education, 6,* 167–180.

Martinez, M. E. (1998, April). Cognition and the question of test item format. In T. M. Haladyna (Chair). *Construction versus choice: A research synthesis.* Symposium conducted at the annual meeting of the American Educational Research Association, San Diego, CA.

Martinez, M. E., & Katz, I. R. (1996). Cognitive processing requirements of constructed figural response and multiple-choice items in architecture assessment. *Educational Assessment, 3*, 83–98.

Masters, G. N. (1982). A Rasch model for partial credit scoring. *Psychometrika, 47*, 149–174.

McGill-Franzen, A., & Allington, R. L. (1993). Flunk' em or get them classified—The contamination of primary grade accountability data. *Educational Researcher, 22*, 19–22.

Mehrens, W. A., & Kaminski, J. (1989). Methods for improving standardized test scores: Fruitful, fruitless, or fraudulent? *Educational Measurement: Issues and Practices, 8*, 14–22.

Meijer, R. R., Molenaar, I. W., & Sijtsma, K. (1994). Influence of person and group characteristics on nonparametric appropriateness measurement. *Applied Psychological Measurement, 8*, 111–120.

Meijer, R. R., Muijtjens, A. M. M. M., & van der Vleuten, C. P. M. (1996). Nonparametric person-fit research: Some theoretical issues and an empirical evaluation. *Applied Measurement in Education, 9*(1), 77–90.

Meijer, R. R., & Sijtsma, K. (1995). Detection of aberrant item score patterns: A review of recent developments. *Applied Measurement in Education, 8*(3), 261–272.

Messick, S. (1975). The standard problem: Meaning and values in measurement and evaluation. *American Psychologist, 30*, 955–966.

Messick, S. (1984). The psychology of educational measurement. *Journal of Educational Measurement, 21*, 215–237.

Messick, S. (1989). Validity. In R. L. Linn (Ed.), *Educational measurement* (3rd ed., pp. 13–104). New York: American Council on Education and Macmillan.

Messick, S. (1995). Validity of psychological assessment: Validation of inferences from persons' responses and performances as scientific inquiry into score meaning. *American Psychologist, 50*, 741–749.

Miller, W. G., Snowman, J., & O'Hara, T. (1979). Application of alternative statistical techniques to examine the hierarchical ordering in Bloom's taxonomy. *American Educational Research Journal, 16*, 241–248.

Millman, J., & Greene, J. (1989). The specification and development of tests of achievement and ability. In R. L. Linn (Ed.), *Educational measurement* (3rd ed., pp. 335–366). New York: American Council on Education and Macmillan.

Millman, J., & Westman, R. S. (1989). Computer-assisted writing of achievement test items: Toward a future technology. *Journal of Educational Measurement, 26*, 177–190.

Mislevy, R. J. (1993). Foundations of a new test theory. In N. Frederiksen, R. J. Mislevy, & I. Bejar (Eds.) *Test theory for a new generation of tests* (pp. 19–39). Hillsdale, NJ: Lawrence Erlbaum Associates.

Mislevy, R. J. (1996a). *Some recent developments in assessing student learning.* Princeton, NJ: Center for Performance Assessment at the Educational Testing Service.

Mislevy, R. J. (1996b). Test theory reconceived. *Journal of Educational Measurement, 33*, 379–417.

Mislevy, R. J., & Bock, R. D. (1990). *BILOG 3: Item analysis and test scoring with binary logistic models.* [Computer Program]. Chicago: Scientific Software.

Mukerjee, D. P. (1991). Testing reading comprehension: A comparative analysis of a cloze test and a multiple-choice test. *Indian Educational Review, 26*, 44–55.

Muraki, E., Mislevy, R. J., & Bock, R. D. (1992). *BIMAIN*. [Computer Software]. Chicago, IL: Scientific Software, Inc.

Muraki, E., & Bock, R. D. (1993). *PARSCALE: IRT based test scoring and item analysis for graded open-ended exercises and performance tests*. [Computer Program]. Chicago, IL: Scientific Software, Inc.

National Commission on Educational Excellence (1983). *A nation at risk*. Washington, DC: U.S. Government Printing Office.

National Council of Teachers of Mathematics (1989). *Curriculum and evaluation standards for school mathematics*. Reston, VA, Author.

Nesi, H., & Meara, P. (1991). How using dictionaries affects performance in multiple-choice ESL tests. *Reading in a Foreign Language, 8*(1), 631–643.

Nickerson, R. S. (1989). New directions in educational assessment. *Educational Researcher, 18*, 3–7.

Nishisato, S. (1980). *Analysis of categorical data: Dual scaling and its applications*. Toronto, Canada: University of Toronto.

Nitko, A. J. (1985). Review of Roid and Haladyna's "A technology for test item writing". *Journal of Educational Measurement, 21*, 201–204.

Nitko, A. J. (1989). Designing tests that are integrated with instruction. In R. L. Linn (Ed.), *Educational measurement* (3rd ed., pp. 447–474). New York: American Council on Education and Macmillan

Nnodim, J. O. (1992). Multiple-choice testing in anatomy. *Medical Education, 26*, 301–309.

Nolen, S. B., Haladyna, T. M., & Haas, N. S. (1992). Uses and abuses of achievement test scores. *Educational Measurement: Issues and Practices, 11*, 9–15.

Norris, S. P. (1990). Effects of eliciting verbal reports of thinking on critical thinking test performance. *Journal of Educational Measurement, 27*, 41–58.

Nunnally, J. C. (1967). *Psychometric theory*. New York, NY: McGraw-Hill.

O'Dell, C. W. (1928). *Traditional examinations and new type tests*. New York, NY: Century.

O'Neill, K. (1986, April). *The effect of stylistic changes on item performance*. Paper presented at the annual meeting of the American Educational Research Association, San Francisco, CA.

Oosterhof, A. C., & Glasnapp, D. R. (1974). Comparative reliabilities and difficulties of the multiple-choice and true-false formats. *The Journal of Experimental Education, 42*, 62–64.

Osterlind, S. J. (1989). *Constructing test items*. Boston, MA: Kluwer Academic Publishers.

Osterlind, S. J. (1997). *Constructing test items* (2nd edition). Boston, MA: Kluwer Academic Publishers.

Owen, D. (1985). *None of the above*. Boston: Houghton Mifflin.

Paris, S. G., Lawton, T. A., Turner, J. C., & Roth, J. L. (1991). A developmental perspective on standardized achievement testing. *Educational Researcher, 20*, 2–7.

Patterson, D. G. (1926). Do new and old type examinations measure different mental functions? *School and Society, 24*, 246–248.

Peterson, C. C., & Peterson, J. L. (1976). Linguistic determinants of the difficulty of true–false test items. *Educational and Psychological Measurement, 36*, 161–164.

Pinglia, R. S. (1994). A psychometric study of true–false, alternate–choice, and multiple-choice item formats. *Indian Psychological Review, 42(1-2)*, 21-26.

Poe, N., Johnson, S., & Barkanic, G. (1992, April). *A reassessment of the effect of calculator use in the performance of students taking a test of mathematics applications.* Paper presented at the annual meeting of the National Council on Measurement in Education, San Francisco, CA.

Pomplun, M., & Omar, H. (1997). Multiple-mark items: An alternative objective item format? *Educational and Psychological Measurement, 57*, 949–962.

Popham, W. J. (1993). Appropriate expectations for content judgments regarding teacher licensure tests. *Applied Measurement in Education, 5*, 285–301.

Popham, W. J. (1997). *Classroom assessment: What teachers need to know.* Needham Heights, MA: Allyn & Bacon.

Powers, D. E., Fowles, M., Farnum, M., & Ramsey, P. (1994). Will they think less of my handwritten essay if others word process theirs? *Journal of Educational Measurement, 31*, 220–233.

Prawat, R. S. (1993). The value of ideas: Problems versus possibilities in learning. *Educational Researcher, 22*, 5–16.

Ramsey, P. A. (1993). Sensitivity reviews: The ETS experience as a case study. In P. W. Holland & H. Wainer (Eds.), *Differential item functioning* (pp. 367–388). Hillsdale, NJ: Lawrence Erlbaum Associates.

Richardson, M., & Kuder, G. F. (1933). Making a rating scale that measures. *Personnel Journal, 12*, 36–40.

Roberts, D. M. (1993). An empirical study on the nature of trick questions. *Journal of Educational Measurement, 30*, 331–344.

Rodriguez, M. C. (1997, April). *The art and science of item writing: A meta-analysis of multiple-choice format effects.* Paper presented at the annual meeting of the American Educational Research Association, Chicago, IL.

Rodriguez, M. C. (1998, April). *Construct equivalence of multiple-choice and constructed response items: A random effects synthesis of correlation. In T. M. Haladyna (Chair), Construction versus choice: A research synthesis.* Symposium conducted at the annual meeting of the American Educational Research Association, San Diego, CA.

Roid, G. H., & Haladyna, T. M. (1982). *Toward a technology of test-item writing.* New York: Academic Press.

Rosenbaum, P. R. (1988). Item bundles. *Psychometrika, 53*, 63–75.

Rovinelli, R. J., & Hambleton, R. K. (1977). On the use of content specialists in the assessment of criterion-referenced test item validity. *Dutch Journal of Educational Research, 2*, 49–60.

Royer, J. M., Cisero, C. A., & Carlo, M. S. (1993). Techniques and procedures for assessing cognitive skills. *Review of Educational Research, 63*, 201–243.

Ruch, G. M. (1929). *The objective or new type examination.* New York, NY: Scott Foresman.

Ruch, G. M., & Charles, J. W. (1928). A comparison of five types of objective tests in elementary psychology. *Journal of Applied Psychology, 12*, 398–403.

Ruch, G. M., & Stoddard, G. D. (1925). Comparative reliabilities of objective examinations. *Journal of Educational Psychology, 12*, 89–103.

Rudner, L. M., Bracey, G., & Skaggs, G. (1996). The use of person-fit statistics with one high-quality achievement test. *Applied Measurement in Education, 9*(1), 91–109.

Ryan, J. M., & Franz, S. (1998, April). *A gender-by-format interaction perspective on the use of free-response and selected-response assessment formats.* In T. M. Haladyna (Chair), Construction versus choice: A research synthesis. Symposium conducted at the annual meeting of the American Educational Research Association, San Diego, CA.

Ryan, J. M., Franz, S., Haladyna, T. M., Hammond, D. (1997, April). *Substantive and psychometric relationships among reading, writing, and mathematics achievement with analyses of gender and format by gender differences.* Phoenix: Arizona State University West College of Education.

Samejima, F. (1979). *A new family of models for the multiple-choice item.* (Office of Naval Research Report 79-4). Knoxville, TN: University of Tennessee.

Sanders, N. M. (1966). *Classroom questions. What kinds?* New York: Harper & Row.

Sato, T. (1975). *The construction and interpretation of S–P tables.* Tokyo: Meiji Tosho.

Sato, T. (1980). *The S–P chart and the caution index. Computer and Communications Systems Research Laboratories.* Tokyo: Nippon Electronic Company Limited.

Sax, G., & Reiter, P. B. (n.d.). *Reliability and validity of two-option multiple-choice and comparably written true-false items.* Seattle, WA: University of Washington.

Schultz, K.S. (1995). Increasing alpha reliabilities of multiple-choice tests with linear polychotomous scoring. *Psychological Reports, 77*, 760-762.

Seddon, G. M. (1978). The properties of Bloom's taxonomy of educational objectives for the cognitive domain. *Review of Educational Research, 48*, 303–323.

Shahabi, S., & Yang, L. (1990, April). *A comparison between two variations of multiple-choice items and their effects on difficulty and discrimination values.* Paper presented at the annual meeting of the National Council on Measurement in Education, Boston.

Shapiro, M. M., Stutsky, M. H., & Watt, R. F. (1989). Minimizing unnecessary differences in occupational testing. *Valparaiso Law Review, 23*, 213–265.

Shea, J. A., Poniatowski, P. A., Day, S. C., Langdon, L. O., LaDuca, A., & Norcini, J. J. (1992). An adaptation of item modeling for developing test-item banks. *Teaching and Learning in Medicine, 4*, 19–24.

Shealy, R., & Stout, W. F. (1996). A model-based standardization approach that separates true bias/DIF from group differences and detects bias/DIF as well as item bias/DIF. *Psychometrika, 58*, 159–194.

Shepard, L. A. (1991). Psychometrician's beliefs about learning. *Educational Researcher, 20*, 2–9.

Shepard, L. A. (1993). The place of testing reform in educational reform--A reply to Cizek. *Educational Researcher, 22*, 10–13.

Sheridan, B., Andrich, D., & Luo, G. (1996). *User's Guide to RUMM: Rasch Unidimensional Measurement Models.* Australia: Murdoch University.

Sherman, S. W. (1976, April). *Multiple-choice test bias uncovered by the use of an "I don't know" alternative.* Paper presented at the annual meeting of the American Educational Research Association, Chicago, IL.

Sireci, S. G., Thissen, D., & Wainer, H. (1991). On the reliability of testlet-based tests. *Journal of Educational Measurement, 28,* 237–247.

Skakun, E. N., & Gartner, D. (1990, April). *The use of deadly, dangerous, and ordinary items on an emergency medical technicians-ambulance registration examination.* Paper presented at the annual meeting of the American Educational Research Association, Boston, MA.

Slogoff, S., & Hughes, F. P. (1987). Validity of scoring "dangerous answers" on a written certification examination. *Journal of Medical Education, 62,* 625–631.

Smith, M. L. (1991). Put to the test: The effects of external testing on teachers. *Educational Researcher, 20,* 8–11.

Smith, R. M. (1986, April). *Developing vocabulary items to fit a polychotomous scoring model.* Paper presented at the annual meeting of the American Educational Research Association, San Francisco, CA.

Smith, R. M. (1993). *Item and person analysis with the Rasch Model (IPARM).* [A computer program and manual]. Chicago: MESA Press.

Smith, R. M., & Kramer, G. A. (1990, April). *An investigation of components influencing the difficulty of form-development items.* Paper presented at the annual meeting of the National Council on Measurement in Education, Boston, MA.

Snow, R. E. (1989). Toward assessment of cognitive and conative structures in learning. *Educational Researcher, 18,* 8–14.

Snow, R. E. (1993). Construct validity and constructed-response tests. In R. E. Bennett & W. C. Ward (Eds.), *Construction versus choice in cognitive measurement: Issues in constructed response, performance testing, and portfolio assessment* (pp. 45–60). Hillsdale, NJ: Lawrence Erlbaum Associates.

Snow, R. E., & Lohman, D. F. (1989). Implications of cognitive psychology for educational measurement. In R. L. Linn (Ed.), *Educational measurement* (3rd ed., 263–332). New York: American Council on Education and MacMillan.

Statman, S. (1988). Ask a clear question and get a clear answer: An inquiry into the question/answer and the sentence completion formats of multiple-choice items. *System, 16,* 367–376.

Sternberg, R. J. (1977). *Intelligence, information processing, and analogical reasoning: The componential analysis of human abilities.* Hillsdale, NJ: Lawrence Erlbaum Associates.

Sternberg, R. J. (1985). *Beyond IQ: A triarchic theory of human intelligence.* New York: Cambridge University Press.

Stiggins, R. J., Griswold, M. M., & Wikelund, K. R. (1989). Measuring thinking skills through classroom assessment. *Journal of Educational Measurement, 26,* 233–246.

Stout, W., Nandakumar, R., Junker, B., Chang, H., & Steidinger, D. (1993). DIMTEST: A FORTRAN program for assessing dimensionality of binary item responses. *Applied Psychological Measurement, 16,* 236.

Stout, W., & Roussos, L. (1995). *SIBTEST manual* (2nd ed.) Unpublished manuscript. Urbana-Champaign, IL: University of Illinois.

Subhiyah, R. G., & Downing, S. M. (1993, April). *K-type and A-type items: IRT comparisons of psychometric characteristics in a certification examination.* Paper presented at the annual meeting of the National Council on Measurement in Education, Atlanta.

Sympson, J. B. (1983, August). *A new item response theory model for calibrating multiple-choice items.* Paper presented at the annual meeting of the Psychometric Society, Los Angeles.

Sympson, J. B. (1986, April). *Extracting information from wrong answers in computerized adaptive testing.* In *New Developments in Computerized Adaptive Testing.* Symposium conducted at the annual meeting of the American Psychological Association, Washington, DC.

Tate, R. (1998, April). *A comparison of selected methods for assessment of test dimensionality.* Paper presented at the annual meeting of the National Council on Measurement in Education, San Diego, CA.

Tatsuoka, K. K. (1985). Rule space: An approach for dealing with misconceptions based on item response theory. *Journal of Educational Measurement, 20,* 345-354.

Tatsuoka, K. K. (1990). Toward an integration of item response theory and cognitive error diagnosis. In N. Frederiksen, R. Glaser, A. Lesgold, & M. G. Shafto (Eds.), *Diagnostic monitoring of skill and knowledge acquisition* (pp. 453-488). Hillsdale, NJ: Lawrence Erlbaum Associates.

Tatsuoka, K. K., & Linn, R. L. (1983). Indices for detecting unusual patterns: Links between two general approaches and potential applications. *Applied Psychological Measurement, 7,* 81-96.

Technical Staff. (1933). *Manual of examination methods* (1st ed.). Illinois: University of Chicago, The Board of Examinations .

Technical Staff. (1937). *Manual of examination methods* (2nd ed.). Illinois: University of Chicago, The Board of Examinations.

Terman, L. M., & Oden, M. (1959). *The gifted group at mid-life.* Stanford, CA: Stanford University Press.

Thissen, D. M. (1976). Information in wrong responses to the Raven Progressive Matrices. *Journal of Educational Measurement, 14,* 201-214.

Thissen, D., & Steinberg, L. (1984). A response model for multiple-choice items. *Psychometrika, 49,* 501-519.

Thissen, D., & Steinberg, L. (1986). A taxonomy of item response models. *Psychometrika, 51,* 566-577.

Thissen, D., Steinberg, L., & Fitzpatrick, A. R. (1989). Multiple-choice models: The distractors are also part of the item. *Journal of Educational Measurement, 26,* 161-175.

Thissen, D., Steinberg, L., & Mooney, J. A. (1989). Trace lines for testlets: A use of multiple-categorical-response models. *Journal of Educational Measurement, 26,* 247-260.

Thissen, D., Wainer, H., & Wang, X. (1994). Are tests comprising both multiple-choice and free-response items necessarily less unidimensional than multiple-choice tests? An analysis of two tests. *Journal of Educational Measurement, 31*(2), 113-123.

Thorndike, R. L. (1967). The analysis and selection of test items. In S. Messick & D. Jackson (Eds.), *Problems in human assessment*. New York: McGraw–Hill.

Thorndike, R. L. (Ed.). (1970). *Educational measurement* (2nd ed.). Washington, DC: American Council on Education.

Thurstone, L. L. (1938). *Primary mental abilities*. Chicago: University of Chicago Press. (Reprinted in 1968 by the Psychometric Society)

Tiegs, E. W. (1931). *Tests and measurement for teachers*. New York, NY: Houghton Mifflin.

Townsend, M. A. R., Moore, D. W., Tuck, B. F., & Wilton, K. M. (1990). Heading within multiple-choice tests as facilitators of test performance. *British Journal of Educational Psychology, 60*, 153–160.

Traub, R. E. (1993). On the equivalence of traits assessed by multiple-choice and constructed-response tests. In R. E. Bennett & W. C. Ward (Eds.), *Construction versus choice in cognitive measurement: Issues in constructed response, performance testing, and portfolio assessment* (pp. 1–27). Hillsdale, NJ: Lawrence Erlbaum Associates.

Traub, R. E., & Fisher, C. W. (1977). On the equivalence of constructed response and multiple-choice tests. *Applied Psychological Measurement, 1*, 355–370.

Trevisan, M. S., Sax, G., & Michael, W. B. (1991). The effects of the number of options per item and student ability on test validity and reliability. *Educational and Psychological Measurement, 51*, 829–837.

Trevisan, M. S., Sax, G., & Michael, W. B. (1994). Estimating the optimum number of options per item using an incremental option paradigm. *Educational and Psychological Measurement, 54*, 86–91.

van den Bergh, H. (1990). On the construct validity of multiple-choice items for reading comprehension. *Applied Psychological Measurement, 14*(1), 1–12.

Van der Flier, H. (1982). Deviant response patterns and comparability of test scores. *Journal of Cross-Cultural Psychology, 13*, 267–298.

Wainer, H. (1989). The future of item analysis. *Journal of Educational Measurement, 26*, 191–208.

Wainer, H., & Kiely, G. (1987). Item clusters and computerized adaptive testing: A case for testlets. *Journal of Educational Measurement, 24*, 185–202.

Wainer, H., & Thissen, D. (1993). Combining multiple-choice and constructed response test scores: Toward a Marxist theory of test construction. *Applied Measurement in Education, 6*, 103–118.

Wainer, H., & Thissen, D. (1994). On examinee choice in educational testing. *Review of Educational Research, 64*, 1, 159-195.

Washington, W. N., & Godfrey, R. R. (1974). The effectiveness of illustrated items. *Journal of Educational Measurement, 11*, 121–124.

Webb, L. C., & Heck, W. L. (1991, April). *The effect of stylistic editing on item performance*. Paper presented at the annual meeting of the National Council on Measurement in Education, Chicago, IL.

Wesman, A. G. (1971). Writing the test item. In R. L. Thorndike (Ed.) *Educational measurement* (2nd ed., pp. 99–111). Washington, DC: American Council on Education.

What Works. (1985). Washington, DC: United States Office of Education.

Wiggins, G. (1989). Teaching to the (authentic) test. *Educational Leadership, 76*, 41–47.

Wightman, L. F. (1998). An examination of sex differences in LSAT scores from the perspective of social consequences. *Applied Measurement in Education, 11*(3), 255–278.

Williams, B. J., & Ebel, R. L. (1957). The effect of varying the number of alternatives per item on multiple-choice vocabulary test items. *The 14th Yearbook of the National Council on Measurement in Education* (pp. 63–65). Washington, DC: National Council on Measurement in Education.

Wilson, D. T., Wood, R., & Gibbons, R. (1992). *TESTFACT: Test scoring, item analysis, and full information or MINRES item factor analysis.* {Computer Program}. Chicago, IL: Scientific Software, Inc.

Wilson, M. R. (1989). Saltus: A psychometric model of discontinuity in cognitive development. *Psychological Bulletin, 105*, 276–289.

Winne, P. H. (1979). Experiments relating teachers' use of higher cognitive questions to student achievement. *Review of Educational Research, 49*, 13–50.

Wisner, J. D., & Wisner, R. J. (1997). A confidence-building multiple-choice testing procedure. *Business Education Forum, 51(4)*, 28–31.

Wolf. L. F., & Smith, J. K. (1995). The consequence of consequence: Motivation, anxiety, and test performance. *Applied Measurement in Education, 8(3)*, 227–242.

Woods, R. (1977). Multiple-choice: A state of the art report. *Evaluation in Education: International Progress, 1*, 191–280.

Wright, B. D. (1977). Solving measurement problems with the Rasch model. *Journal of Educational Measurement, 14*, 97–116.

Wright, B. D., & Linacre, J. M. (1992). *A User's Guide to BIGSTEPS-Rasch—Model Item Analysis and Scaling.* [Computer Program]. Chicago, IL: MESA Press.

Wright, B. D., & Stone, M. H. (1979). *Best test design.* Chicago, IL: MESA Press.

Yeh, J. P., Herman, J. L., & Rudner, L. M. (1981). *Teachers and testing: A survey of test use.* Center for the Study of Evaluation, University of California, Los Angeles. (ERIC Document Reproduction Service No. 218 336)

Zoref, L., & Williams, P. (1980). A look at content bias in IQ tests. *Journal of Educational Measurement, 17*, 313–322.

AUTHOR INDEX

A

Adams R., 75
Advanced Psychometrics, 188
Albanese, M.. A., 57, 59, 212
Allington, R. L., 9
Allison, J., 206
American Psychological Association, iii, 153, 184, 188
Anderson, J. R., 46, 104, 209
Anderson, R., 10, 22
Andres, A. M., 89
Andrich, D., 167, 173, 175,177, 201
Angoff, W. H., 187
Ansley, T. F., 69
Assessment Systems Corporation 167

B

Badger, E., 46
Baker, E. L., 31
Baker, K. K., 103
Baranowski, R. A.,58
Barkanic, G., 68
Bauer, H., 67
Becker, B. J., 56, 99, 189
Becker, D. F., 98
Bejar, I., 210, 211, 215, 216
Bellezza, F. S., 187
Bellezza, S. F., 187

Bennett, R. E., 26, 46
Biggs, J. B., 120
Bloom, B. S., 104
Bock, R. D., 167, 200, 210
Bonner, M. W., 36
Bormuth, J. R., ii, 75, 125
Bower, G. H., 46
Bracey, G., 195
Brant, R., 89
Braswell, J., 68
Braun, H. I., 45
Breland, H. M., 30, 36
Brennan, R. L., 44, 210
Bridgeman, B., 68
Brown, J., ii
Bruno, J. E., 89
Burmester, M. A., 53, 54

C

Cannell, J. J., 187, 206
Carlo, M. S., 104, 209
Case, S. M., 58
Cashin, J. R., 90
Chan, K. M., 45, 49
Chang, H., 198
Charles, J. W., 53
Chase, C. I., 43
Cisero, C. A., 104, 209
Cizek, G. J., 82

Clauser, B. E., 153,184, 186
Cody, R. P., 187
Coffman, W. E., 25, 42, 43
Cohen, A. S., 68
Cole, N. S., 10, 22, 153
Collis, K. F., 120
Cox, R. C., 172
Crocker, L., 150
Cronbach, L. J., i, 10, 12, 42, 59, 137, 211

D

Damjanov, I., 49
Danos, D. O., 36
Davis, G., 45
Dawson-Saunders, B., 58, 83
Day, S. C., 125
de Gruijter, D. N. M., 179
DeChamplain, A., 197
del Castillo, J. D., 89
DeMars, C. E., 34, 36
Dibello, L. V., 207
Dirkzwager, A., 89
Doran, M. L., 89
Dorans, N. J., 89, 184, 185
Downing, S. M., i, 13, 15, 27, 37, 48, 52, 53, 54, 55, 57, 58, 59, 73, 75, 76, 89, 90, 94, 102, 138, 143, 161, 175, 177, 181, 191,192, 199, 212, 216, 219
Drasgow, F., 53, 169, 175, 187, 189, 190, 199, 200
Druva, C. A., 59
Dunbar, S. B., 31

E

Ebel, R. L., ii, 43, 52, 53, 55, 56, 57
Embretsen, S., 211
Engelhart, M. D., 104
Eurich, A. C., 25

F

Fairtest Examiner, iii
Fajardo, L. L., 45, 49
Farnum, M., 25
Farr, R., 158
Fenderson, B. A., 49
Fierman, C. I., 83
Fischer, G. H., 211
Fisher, C. W., 25
Fiske, E. B., 46
Fitzpatrick, A. R., 149, 174, 179, 199, 218
Forsyth, R. A., 68
Fowles, M., 25
Franz, S., 34, 36
Frary, R. B., 187
Fraser, C., 196
Frederiksen, N., 210, 219
Frisbie, D. A., 43, 55, 56, 57, 58, 59, 98, 103, 104, 212
Fuhrman, M 93, 96
Furst, E. J., 104

G

Gagne, R. M.,104
Gardner, H., 7, 208
Gartner, D., 70
Gaynor, J., 30
Gibbons, R., 197
Glasnapp, D. R., 55
Godfrey R. R., 69
Godshalk, F. I., 25
Goleman, D., 5, 8
Gorsuch, R. L., 171
Green, K. E., 166
Greene, J., ii, 174, 215
Griswold, M. M., 103
Gronlund, N. E., 42, 43
Gross, L. J., 84
Grosse, M., 55, 58, 60
Grosso, L. J., 58
Guertler, E., 191
Guilford, J. P., 7
Guttman, L., 200

H

Haas, N. S., 9, 187, 190, 206
Haertel, E. H., 211
Haladyna, T. M., i, ii, iii, 5, 9, 12,
    13, 14, 15, 16, 17, 23, 32, 34,
    37, 42, 48, 52, 53, 54, 55, 57,
    60, 73, 75, 76, 90, 94, 101,
    102, 126, 129, 132, 133, 135,
    137, 143, 146, 147, 148, 161,
    162, 164, 169, 171, 175, 181,
    187, 190, 196, 199, 200, 205,
    206, 210, 212, 216, 219
Hambleton, R. K., 135, 149, 150,
    151, 167, 169, 174, 198, 209
Hammond, D., 34
Hancock, G. R., 53, 56
Harasym, P. H., 89
Harvey, A., 68
Harvill, L. M., 45
Hatch, T., 206
Hattie, J. A., 170, 171, 183, 195, 196
Haynie, W. J., 38
Heck, W. L., 83
Henrysson, S., ii, 179, 218
Henzel, T. R., 138
Herbig, M., 171
Herman, J. L., iii
Herrnstein, R. J., 7
Hill, G. C., ii, 59
Hill, K., 84, 188
Hill, W. H., 104
Hoffman, B., iii
Holland, P. W., 184, 185
Holzman, G. B.,138
Hoover, H. D., 68
House, E. R., 206
Hsu, L. M., 55
Hubbard, J. P., 57
Hughes, D. C., 43
Hughes, F. P., 70
Hulin, C. L., 169
Hurd, A. W., 25
Hutchinson, T. P., 189

I

Ippel, M. J., 216

J

Jannarone, R. J., 211
Jensen, A. R., 7
Johnson, B. R., 49
Johnson, S., 68
Jones, R. W., 209
Joreskog, K. G., 197
Junker, B., 198

K

Kahn, H. D., 36
Kaminski, J., 9, 187, 206
Kane, M. T., 9, 12, 149
Kangilaski, R., 83
Katz, I. R., 36
Keeling, B., 43
Kent, T. A., 59
Kiely, G., 60, 219
Kim, K., 68
Kintsch, W., 46
Knowles, S. L., 94
Kolen, M. J., 44
Kramer, G. A., 164
Krathwohl, D. R., 104
Kubota, M. Y., 36
Kuder, G. F., 200
Kullick, E., 185

L

LaDuca, A., 83, 125, 138
Landrum, R. E., 90
Langdon, L. O., 83, 125
Lawton, T. A., 10 188
Levine, M. V., 53, 175, 187, 191,
    192, 199
Lewis, J. C., 68
Linacre, J. M., 169
Lindquist, E. F., 211, 217

Linn, R. L., 31, 42, 43, 189, 190,
    193, 194, 210, 211, 217
Llabre, M., 150
Lohman, D. F., 5, 22, 104, 120, 205,
    208, 216
Lord, F. M., 53, 90, 166, 167, 200
Lorscheider, F. L., 89
Loyd, B. H., 68
Lukhele, R., 28, 45
Luo, G., 169, 175, 179, 201

M

MacDonald, R. P., 195
MacIntosh, H. G., ii
Mager, R. F., 146
Maihoff, N. A., 53, 54
Markle, S. M., 107
Martinez, M. E., 12, 26, 28, 36, 37,
    46
Masters, G. N., 200
Mazor, K. M., 153, 184, 186
McGill-Franzen, A., 9
Mead, A. D., 175
Meara, P., 69
Mehrens, W. A., 9, 53, 187, 206
Meijer, R. R.., 185, 191, 192, 194,
    195
Messick, S., 9, 12, 25, 137, 145,
    147, 149, 150, 153, 195, 211
Michael, W. B., 90
Miller, W. G., 104
Miller, M. D., 150
Millman, J., ii, 126, 133, 174, 218
Miranda, D. U., 103
Mislevy, R. J., 30, 31, 32, 38, 104,
    120, 138, 167, 207, 210, 213,
    214, 217, 219
Molenaar, I. W., 192
Mooney, J. A., 60, 133, 135, 199
Moore, D. W., 70
Morrison, R. B., ii
Moss, P. A., 153
Muijtjens, A. M., 187, 191
Mukerjee, D. P., 38
Muraki, E., 169

Murray, C., 7

N

Nandakumar, R., 198
National Commission on Educational
    Excellence, 206
National Council of Teachers of
    Mathematics, 67, 104, 118
Nesi, H., 69
Nickerson, R. S., 46, 104
Nishisato, S., 175
Nitko, A. J., ii, 42, 211
Nnodim, J. O., 94
Nolen, S. B., 9, 187, 190, 206
Norcini, J. J., 27, 58, 125
Norris, S. P., 157, 158
Nungester, R. J., 58
Nunnally, J. C., 170, 177, 195

O

O'Dell, C. W., 25
O'Hara, T., 104
O'Neill, K., 83
Oden, M., 7
Olson, L. A., 53, 54
Omar, H., 59
Oosterhof, A. C., 55
Osterlind, S. J., ii, iii
Owen, D., iii

P

Paris, S. G., 10, 188, 189
Parsons, C. K., 169
Patterson, D. G., 25
Peterson, C. C., 55
Peterson, J. L., 55
Phillips, S. E., 54
Pinglia, R. S., 55
Poe, N., 68
Pomplun, M., 59
Poniatowski, P. A., 83, 125
Popham, W. J., 42, 149

Potenza, M. T., 184
Powers, D. E., 25
Prawat, R. S., 138
Pritchard, R., 158

R

Ramsey, P. A., 25, 153, 154, 186
Reiter, P. B., 53
Reshetar, R., 83
Richardson, M., 200
Roberts, D. M., 80
Robeson, M. R., 49
Rock, D. A., 46
Rodriguez, M. C., 28, 37, 46, 73, 76,
    84, 88, 90, 94, 212, 216
Roid, G. H., ii, iii, 17, 126, 133, 137,
    171, 173, 205, 212
Rosenbaum, P. R., 61
Roth, J. L., 10, 188, 189
Roussos, L. A., 207
Rovinelli, R. J., 149, 150
Royer, J. M., 104, 209, 213
Rubin, E., 49, 192
Ruch, G. M., 25, 53
Rudner, L. M., iii, 195
Ryan, J. M., 34, 36

S

Sabers, D. L., 59
Samejima, F., 200, 210
Sanders, N. M., 104
Sato, T., 192
Sax, G., 53, 56, 90
Schultz, K. S., 175, 200
Seddon, G. M., iii, 104
Shahabi, S., 58
Shapiro, M. M., 184
Shea, J. A., 83, 125, 138
Shealy, R., 186
Shepard, L. A., iii, 138
Sheridan, B., 169, 175, 179, 201
Sherman, S., W., 94
Shindoll, L. R., 126, 129, 132
Sijtsma, K., 194, 195

Sireci, S. G., 60
Skaggs, G., 195
Skakun, E. N., 70
Slogoff, S., 70
Smith, J. K., 188
Smith, M. L., 10
Smith, R. M., 166
Smitten, B., 158
Snow, R. E., 5, 25, 26, 104, 120,
    138, 207, 208
Snowman, J., 104
Sorbom, D., 197
Spratt, K. F., 69
Staples, W. I., 138
Statman, S., 84
Steidlinger, D., 198
Steinberg, L., 60, 133, 135, 174, 177,
    185, 199, 210, 218
Sternberg, R. J., 7, 208
Stiggins, R. J., 103
Stoddard, G. D., 53
Stone, M. H., 187
Stout, W. F., 186, 198, 207
Stutsky, M. H., 184
Styles, I., 175
Subhiyah, R. G., 58
Swaminathan, H., 135, 169, 171, 174,
    209
Sweeney, D. C., 59
Swineford, E., 25
Sympson, J. B., 164, 174,175, 199,
    200, 210

T

Tang, K. L., 197
Tate, R., 170, 183, 190, 191, 195,
    196, 198, 199
Tatsuoka, K. K., 192, 193, 194, 211,
    216, 217
Technical Staff, 50, 51, 65
Templeton, B., 138
Terman, L. M., 7
Thayer, D. T., 185
Theis, K. S., 90
Thiede, K. W., 53, 56

Thissen, D., 28, 29, 31, 45, 60, 133, 135, 174, 179, 185, 199, 210, 218
Thorndike, R. L., 13, 73, 211, 217
Thurstone, L. L., 7
Tiegs, E. W., 25
Tiemann, P. W., 107
Tognolini, J., 175
Townsend, M. A. R., 70
Traub, R. E., 25, 38
Trevisan, M. S., 90
Tsien, S., 175
Tuck, B. F., 43, 70
Turner, J. C., 10, 188, 189

V

van den Bergh, H., 37
van der Vleuten, C. P. M., 187, 191
Van der Flier, H., 194
Vargas, J., 172
Veloski, J. J., 49

W

Wainer, H, i, 28, 29, 31, 45, 60, 175, 179, 184, 185, 199, 218, 219
Wang, M. D., 28, 46
Wang, X., 28
Washington, W. N., 69
Watt, R. F., 185
Webb, L. C., 83
Welch, C. A., 94
Wesman, A. G., ii, 126, 133, 174
Westman, R. S., 126
What Works, 104, 118
Whitney, D. R., 59
Wigfield, A., 84, 188
Wiggins, G., 38
Wightman, L. F., 34, 36
Wikelund, K. R., 103
Wiley, D. E., 211
Williams, B., 175
Williams, B. J., 53
Williams, E. A., 191

Williams, P., 154
Wilson, D. T., 197
Wilson, M. R., 211
Wilton, K. M., 70
Winne, P. H., 209
Wisner, J. D., 189
Wisner, R. J., 189
Wolf, L. F., 188
Wood, R., 197
Woods, G. T., ii, 59
Wright, B. D., 55, 60, 169, 187, 188

Y

Yang, L., 58
Yeh, J. P., iii

Z

Zickar, M. J., 187, 191, 192
Zoref, L., 54

SUBJECT INDEX

A

All of the above option, 77, 94
Answer justification, 157, 161
Appropriateness measurement, 153
Attacks on MC, iii–v

C

Calculators, 67–69
Construct, 4, 5, 137–138
Constructed-response (CR) item
    formats, 14–15, 16, 24
Cuing, 45, 77, 95–96

D

Developmental field test, 157
Differential item functioning, 153, 183
Dimensionality, 153, 195–199
Direct assessment, 30
Distractor evaluation, 174–182

E

Emotional intelligence, 5, 8

F

Fluid abilities, 5–9, 22

Future of item development
    barriers affecting, 208–211
    legacy of item-writing, 211–212
        factors affecting, 205–208
        new theories, 213–217
Future of item-response validation,
    217–219

G

Generic item sets
    definition, 133–135
    evaluation, 135–137, 174
Grammatical clues, 96
Guessing, 44, 174

H

Higher level thinking
    problem of definition, 103–106
    typology
        content dimension, 106–108
        behavior dimension, 109–123
Humor in items, 77, 97

I

I don't know option, 77, 94–95
Indirect assessment, 31
Instructional sensitivity, 171–174
Intelligence (scholastic aptitude,
　　mental ability), 7–8
Item bias, 183, 184–186
Item difficulty, 165–166
Item discrimination, 166–170
Item format types
　　criteria for selection, 38–39
　　high-inference, 14, 23, 26
　　low-inference, 14, 23–26
　　multiple-choice, 14
　　　　features, 41–47
　　　　taxonomy, 24
Item format validity arguments
　　cognition, 36–38
　　content equivalence, 28–29
　　gender-format interaction, 34–36
　　prediction, 27–28
　　proximity and fidelity to
　　　　criterion, 17, 30–33
Item modeling
　　definition, 137–140
　　evaluation, 141
Item shells, 18
　　definition, 126–132
　　evaluation, 133
Item weighting, 164
Item-writing guidelines, 77
　　content concerns, 76, 78–81
　　format concerns, 82
　　option construction, 89–97
　　stem construction, 84–89
　　style concerns, 9–12
Item-writing science, 42, 213–217

K

Key verification, 159–160
Knowledge (declarative knowledge),
　　8, 22

L

Learning theories, iii, 207–208
Local dependence/independence, 59,
　　61, 137

M

Multiple-choice issues
　　calculators, 68–69
　　dangerous answers, 70–71
　　dictionaries, 70
　　grouping items, 70
　　pictorial aids, 69–70
Multiple-choice item formats, 13–14,
　　16, 24, 47–50
　　alternate-choice, 52–54
　　complex multiple-choice, 57–58,
　　　　77, 82
　　context-dependent item set
　　　　(interpretive exercises, item
　　　　bundles, scenarios, super-
　　　　items, testlets, vignettes),
　　　　60–66
　　conventional, 47–49
　　matching, 50–52
　　multiple true–false, 58–60
　　true–false, 54–57, 77, 82
　　unusual, experimental, 66–68

N

Negative phrasing, 77, 88–89, 95
None of the above option, 77, 94–95

O

Operational definition, 4–5, 137–138
Option characteristic curve (see *trace line*)
Option ordering, 77, 91
Option weighting, 164, 183, 199–201

P

Person fit, 186–195
Polychotomous scoring (see *option weighting*)

R

Reliability, 45

S

Skills, 5–9, 22–23
Statistical test theories
    classical test theory, 163, 209–211
    item response theory, 163, 209–211

T

Test, 4
Test development, 10–11
Test items
    definition, 13–14
    high-inference, 14
    low-inference, 14
    multiple-choice, 14
    steps in developing, 16–18
Test score, 10
Test specifications, 17, 76, 147
Trace line (option characteristic curve), 168, 177–179
Trick items, 77, 80–81

V

Validating item responses, 18, 44, 217–219
    analyzing item responses
      characteristics of item responses
        difficulty, 165–166
        dimensionality, 195–199
        discrimination, 166–174, 218–219
        distractor evaluation, 174–181, 218
        guessing, 44, 174
        item bias (differential item functioning), 184–186
        nature of item responses, 163–165
        person fit, 186–195
        polychotomous scoring, 199–201
    procedural validity evidence 18
      content definition, 17, 146–147
      content review, 149–151
      editorial review, 83, 152–153
      item writer training, 17, 147–148
      key check (verification), 159–160
      review for cognitive behavior, 148–149
      review for violations of item-writing guidelines, 148
      security, 160–161
      sensitivity review, 153–156
      test specifications, 147
      test-taker review, 156–159
      typology, 155

Validity, 9–13
    argument, 10, 12, 27, 143
    consequential aspects of, 8, 10
    evidence, 13

W

Window dressing, 77, 87–88